02/10
39.95

ROSELLE PUBLIC LIBRARY

3 3012 00292 8253

W9-BQT-801

Roselle Public Library District
40 S. Park Street
Roselle, IL 60172

Susanna Lápossy

Life Behind the
Iron Curtain I.

English version
Susanna Lápossy: Life behind the iron curtain
Two parts in one book
Part one
From the original Hungarian book titled:
Kalandos
Életem
Története
Házasságom gyümölcseinek
Copyright©1999 Susanna Lápossy

English translation © Christina Diósy, 2005
Edited by Mollie Green and Raymond Taylor
Design by Andreas Rákai
Special thanks to the Green, Taylor and Markham families.

Order this book online at www.trafford.com/06-2282
or email orders@trafford.com

Most Trafford titles are also available at major online book retailers.

© Copyright 2006 Susanna Lápossy.
All rights reserved. No part of this publication may be reproduced, stored in a retrieval system, or
transmitted, in any form or by any means, electronic, mechanical, photocopying, recording, or
otherwise, without the written prior permission of the author.

Note for Librarians: A cataloguing record for this book is available from Library
and Archives Canada at www.collectionscanada.ca/amicus/index-e.html

Printed in Victoria, BC, Canada.

ISBN: 978-1-4251-0524-2

*We at Trafford believe that it is the responsibility of us all, as both individuals
and corporations, to make choices that are environmentally and socially sound.
You, in turn, are supporting this responsible conduct each time you purchase a
Trafford book, or make use of our publishing services. To find out how you are
helping, please visit www.trafford.com/responsiblepublishing.html*

*Our mission is to efficiently provide the world's finest, most comprehensive
book publishing service, enabling every author to experience success.
To find out how to publish your book, your way, and have it available
worldwide, visit us online at www.trafford.com/10510*

www.trafford.com

North America & international
toll-free: 1 888 232 4444 (USA & Canada)
phone: 250 383 6864 ♦ fax: 250 383 6804
email: info@trafford.com

The United Kingdom & Europe
phone: +44 (0)1865 722 113 ♦ local rate: 0845 230 9601
facsimile: +44 (0)1865 722 868 ♦ email: info.uk@trafford.com

10 9 8 7 6 5

The Authoress

Her adult age photo

Susanna Lápossy started to write her book relatively late, at a mature age. She was born in 1923. She graduated from the Collegiate School for Schoolmistress Studies in 1942. During her chequered carrier she worked as a secretary, a textile factory worker, a hygienic gymnastics teacher for lame children and later for twelve years, as teacher of first grade boys at an elementary school. She has a daughter and four sons from her two marriages.

The highly popular "searching for the roots" motivated her to write her memoir for her five wonderful children, 10 talented grandchildren and two great-grandchildren. The reason was to make the adventurous, highly exciting and happy or deeply sad stories of her life and those of her ancestors known!

The book

"Life Behind the Iron Curtain" shows the 20th century Hungarian history through the family of the authoress. . During the whole 20th century there was no democracy in the country, except for the 1990s. Rather, we can see the results of WWI, the kingship dictatorship, Nazism, WWII and communism.
The story begins at her father's birthplace VERECKE, where ancient Hungarians entered the region and founded Hungary. She spent long , happy holidays there for 18 years.
    The opinion of the first readers are as follows:
    Mollie & Fred Green
"We were all very interested indeed to read your mother-in-law's memories. I must emphasize how enjoyable we have found this book. The memories are fantastic, the descriptions so vivid I fall under its spell and just feel as if I have been transported back with her and actually "feel" the atmosphere and "see" the houses, garden etc.
I would like to meet the authoress one day. I feel she is a remarkable woman and was very fortunate to belong to such a

loving family. She seems to have "taken me right into her family"- it's incredible!

I am just reading and reading the next installment of this most interesting story. We all love it. I wish I was as gifted as she. I can't read enough about her life, so we are eagerly awaiting the next transcript.

To me it's like reading the script of one of those beloved old films we just loved to sit and watch, softly crying at times, then we would walk home, talk about 'how it was in the film' for days. I just don't want it to end.

What pleasure reading this book has brought to me! When it arrives in my post box I rush to open it. The description of her mother brought tears to my eyes- she had such overwhelming love. All through her life she's been surrounded with people who loved her and she returned this. The world would be a wonderful place if we could all have received and returned love!"

We recommend this book to all who like adventurous, readable and unforgettable books.

Preface

Dear reader!

Please sit into a comfortable armchair and take my book into your hand. When reading it you'll feel like a family member and share in the happiness, grief and adventures that the "life behind the iron curtain" allowed us to meet.

I write my memories as in a diary. With that I commemorate my dead relatives, in the first place my father and mother, my two beloved husbands, my uncle, brother, grandmother, aunts, sisters-in-law, brothers-in-law and the whole family who have already died. I got the idea from TV. It was the autumn of 1999, when one night the reporter, Peter Feledy, appeared on the screen with a widow, Mrs. Horthy whom she was interviewing. She told that at the age of 76 she received a computer from her grandchild that motivated her to write a memoir. Five years have passed since that time and her book was alo published in Hungary and that is why she visited the country again.

Well, I thought to myself, I'm 76 years old right now why couldn't I also start to write my memoir down!

Some days later I heard on the radio about a pensioned engine driver, who told about accomplishing his childhood-dream as an old man. He started going on foot from a town in the Trans-Danube region, acting "homeless" and after some months arrived to the eastern border of the country. At this time of his life and after his adventures he wrote a book. After that I asked my daughter to give me her typewriter.

On the 30th of October, the birthday of my beloved brother Géza who had already passed away I sat down at the typewriter and with ten fingers, as I learned 57 years ago, I started to type. The memories appeared to me without delay as someone would have prompted me, my fingers could hardly keep up with the typing." In this way my memoir was born in a book. I offer it to my dear, good children and grandchildren and my readers. You can discover the brightly happy and sad stories of my life and those of their ancestors as well!

(The authoress)

MY PARENTS

Part one: Pre-war peace time

1923—24

I was born on the 06.05.1923 in Budapest /capital of Hungary in central-eastern Europe/ at the Baross-street clinic at 2'30" p.m. Mother and I suffered for two and a half days, because babies also suffer at birth, but they can not tell anyone. I was the firstborn child of my mother and I weighed 4 kilos.

My mother finished the Music Academy and for years she practised daily four to six hours on the piano. She played beautifully and had artistic ambitions. (She also made oil paintings.) The doctor said- it would be a difficult childbearing, because she didn't do any exercise.

She came from the Trans-Danube region county Somogy. Her name was Irma Maria Ékes (born on the 6th of May, 1899 in Csomapuszta.) My father was a legal councillor, who studied jurisprudence in Kolozsvár. He stemmed from county Bereg, the village Alsóverecke. His name was Dr. János /John/ Géza Lápossy (born on 25.08.1886.)

I also will write about how my parents got to know each other, because it is interesting. My father was a soldier in WWI, a reserve first lieutenant. During the war he served on all three fronts- the Russian, the Rumanian and the Italian fronts.

/World War I was a global military conflict in Europe from 1914 to 1918. Over 40 million casualties resulted, including 20 million military and civilian deaths. Over 60 million European soldiers were mobilized during the war. The war was propagated by two major alliances. The Central Powers, named so because of their central location on the European continent, initially consisted of Germany and Austria-Hungary and their associated empires. The Ottoman Empire joined the Central Powers in October 1914, followed a year later by Bulgaria. The Entente Powers initially consisted of France, the United Kingdom, Russia and their dependencies. Numerous other states joined these allies, most notably Italy in April 1915, and the United States in April 1917. The Entente Powers won the conflict. Only the Netherlands, Switzerland, Spain and the Scandinavian nations remained officially neutral.-Wikipedia, the free Encyclopedia/

At last he caught the dreaded Spanish flu and became ill. He was in hospital for a long time. When he was allowed to leave, he was transferred to inland service and sent to Csallóköz to requisition grain for the military. My mother lived there with her parents and sisters. My father went to their farm to get grain and in this way they got to know each other. It was love at first sight! The age difference was quite big, 13 years. They married in 1922. My mother told me often about this very happy period. She had just finished her studies at the Academy when they got married. After nine months I was born.

I was baptized Zsuzsánna /Susanna/, Ilona /Helen/, Kornélia /Cornelia/, Katalin /Kate/. In the old days it was a custom to give girls the given names of the paternal and maternal grandmothers and of the godmother. This is why I was given so many forenames.

In the beginning I cried a lot. They called the doctor, who just said: "Oh, this child is hungry!" Mother couldn't feed me properly, so I had to eat butter-soup made first with half-milk and later with whole milk. It was very delicious and for a year I had only that. It rounded me out. At that time doctors only allowed a varied diet after the first year.

Thinking back today it was not at all a silly thing. Butter, flour and milk all contain an abundant amount of vitamin D that the body can use very well. I grew so healthy that at the age of ten months my parents decided to enter me for the competition called "Health and beauty", where I came in second place, receiving an award, a certificate and a photo.

I began to toddle quite early. I was just over one year old when on the first of July 1924 the most beautiful experience of many in my life began!

My father as always, received his annual holiday and we all traveled to his birthplace of Alsóverecke in county Bereg where 1000 years ago Árpád, the forefather of the Hungarians looked down from the crags of the Carpathian Mountain range the great plain and marked out the place of the Hungarians. In this wonderful region in the embrace of the Carpathian Mountain range the great village Alsóverecke can be found. My paternal grandfather János /John/ Lápossy lived there with his family in his fortress-like big stone house and worked as chemist in his own pharmacy. His wife Helen Borostyányi (whose father was Adalbert Borostyányi, grammar school director in Munkács) married my grandfather as a widow. Her first husband was Dezső Szabó, postmaster in Alsóverecke, who died at a very young age with tuberculosis. They had two children: Helen and Dezső. They were the stepsister and stepbrother of my father. I also got to know Aunt Helen. She worked as postmistress first in Verecke, later in Munkács. There she bought a house in the Petőfi-street. She had no family.

I didn't know my grandparents because they died before my first holiday in Verecke. When I was a bit older my father took me several times to the Verecke cemetery, where beside my grandparents in the family cemetery, enclosed with an iron fence four smaller graves could be seen. When I asked about who was buried there my father told me the tragic story of the little tombs.

When my father was 4 years old he had two sisters, 10 and 8 years old and a 6 year old brother. At that time a diphtheria epidemic broke out nationwide and within a week all of his siblings were dead. Then as a final last resort my grandfather took a piece of cloth soaked it in kerosene and wiped the infection, which could have been fatal, from my father's throat and gullet. This way my grandfather saved my father from death!

My father and
Uncle Charles

Later still another two children were born: Károly (Charles) and Katalin /Kate/. After the death of my grandfather uncle Charles inherited the family pharmacy, because he had completed his studies as a chemist in Kolozsvár. Aunt Kate became teacher in Szatmárnémeti and later on moved to Budapest, where she taught until her death. She remained unmarried.

Let's return back to 01.07.1924. After the Trianon Pact, Czechoslovakia got dominion over a part of the southern Carpathian region.

/The Treaty of Trianon is the peace treaty concluded at the end of World War I. It established the borders of Hungary and regulated its international situation. Hungary lost over two-thirds of its territory and about two-thirds of its inhabitants under the treaty. The beneficiaries of territorial adjustment were Rumania, Czechoslovakia, and the Kingdom of Serbs, Croats and Slovenes. The treaty was signed on June 4, 1920, at the Grand Trianon Palace in Versailles, France.- Wikipedia./

On the Miskolc railway line we traveled as far as Sátoraljaújhely. There was the customs checkpoint where the Czechs searched our luggage thoroughly, but only in the beginning. When they got used to the fact that every year we traveled up to Verecke they just gave us a wave of the hand when it came to us and our suitcases and we were able to cross the border without a problem. After that we took the train again and traveled to Volóc where Uncle Charles waited for us with a taxi. The car had to climb a relative high mountain, the Volóc hill and this way we reached Alsóverecke, the "family house" and the chemist's shop.

In the taxi I used to sit in the back with mother and father, my uncle in the front with the driver turning back and talking to us all the way. He had beautiful deep brown eyes. Apparently this caused me to make my first independent statement in a short sentence that as one year old lisped in child language: "You are an owl" The grown-ups, especially Uncle Charles, liked this sentence so much that even later when I got older (I clearly remember) he pulled my leg with this sentence and often repeated it.

When I was already one, Uncle Charles employed a nurse for me in the house. Ann was a 14 year old girl of Ukrainian nationality. She was with me all day; we played, swung together, and tried to catch butterflies in the vegetable garden etc., but in the evening she always returned home.

The Lápossy house in Alsóverecke with Uncle Charles

Ann was a very good hearted; a neat and quick worker. Every morning she brought us milk. We became very good friends. Uncle Charles charged her with the cleaning of the pharmacy and of the jars etc. I myself helped her regularly when I was 6-8 years old.

I enjoyed bathing the blood-suckers. At that time leeches were used as a therapy against high blood-pressure and the doctor put these small animals on the feet and hands of the patient. The animals filled themselves completely with blood and became like small little balls. I bathed these tiny animals with Ann two or three times a week and put them into a jar of fresh water.

I liked this job so much that I never missed it. It was a good game indeed to put them from the first great bottle into the other one with a great spoon.

Anca

I also learned from her the way of feeding the animals of the chicken run. At the age of three I was already brave enough to go to the poultry-run, where hen, chicken, cock, goose, duck and turkey preened themselves for me. The last one was even taller than I was. Uncle Charles took photos as I held the great bowl in my hand and threw the seeds to the poultry.

Vereckei hágó Ezredéves emlékmű Községháza

Vereckei szoros Alsóverecke Járásbíróság

Vereckei szoros

My father with my Brother Géza in the Verecke-pass

He enjoyed taking pictures very much and developed them himself in his "dark room". As small children we were never allowed to enter there until we had grown up.

The postcards about the village Alsóverecke, the Verecke-pass and those of the Carpathian Mountain were all made from his negatives and sold in the local co-op. (On the postcard of the Verecke-pass my father and little brother can be seen walking).

The entrance of the Alsóverecke cemetery

The population of Alsóverecke was mostly Jewish, with some people of Ukrainian nationality and only one Hungarian, Uncle Charles.

The bohemians came there only after WWI, as invaders due to the Trianon Pact so the officials of the army, the doctor, the scrivener and the lawyers at the county law court were partly bohemians partly Jews. My father's childhood friends were two Jewish boys who also became lawyers as my father did and also worked in the village. I knew them also because the daughter of ones my friend during the summer holidays. She was some years older than me and made wonderful embroideries which she also taught me to do.

Uncle Charles didn't have a family of his own, only us. He lived his life as a bachelor and was a great democrat. In the village everyone liked him because he helped everyone. Poor Ukrainians and Jews for example saw him and not the doctor for advice or medicine. He often gave medicines to them free of charge, but asked them to come back when they were better so that he could make an account of the effect of the medicine. Naturally, this also gave rise to many quarrels with the bohemian doctor. Uncle let him half of the great house, so the doctor lived there with his family and also held the surgery there.

The view of Alsóverecke (Postcard)

Before WWI half of the family house was a post office, directed by Uncle Charles's stepsister, Aunt Helen. When the bohemians invaded the territory, the surgery, the doctor's housing and later also the office of the bohemian scrivener moved in.

My father as a WWI soldier at the Dobozy Millennial Memorial, erected in 1896

VOLÓCZ

Hid   *Városháza*   *Vár*

Szent István-út   *Munkács*   *Kolostor*

In WWI the Russians set this house on fire together with the whole village and the church. Uncle Charles fled. When he returned, he only found burnt out walls, so he had to start building his whole life and the pharmacy from the beginnings again.

It was still the summer of 1924! I can not remember, but only from stories and photos I know those wonderful excursions that my parents and I took with Uncle Charles to the Vereckepass. On top of the Verecke-pass stood the Dobozy Millennial Memorial on which the following text could be read:

"Compatriot ! On this peak the loud beat of your heart tells
That this place is the border of your ancient dear homeland!
Prince Rákóczi the Great shed his farewell tears here!
Untie your sandals; blessed is the place where you stand!"

We have lots of photos about the memorial. We have one where father is sitting before it in his uniform, and one later when I took part in an excursion with my parents at the age of one.

Trip with my parents and Aunt Kate on the Verecke peak

With mum and dad
in Alsóverecke, at the age of 1

These happy long summers, which I spent every year at Uncle Charles place in Alsóverecke from 1924 to 1942 had decisive influence on my life.

To be trustworthy I have to note that when the Bohemians entered, they didn't demolish the memorial. It stood here until 1945. The Russians moved it and put a chalk statue of a mountain goat with a shepherd in its place. The shepherd blows his alpine horn-and very interesting that- the direction of the horn pointed towards our home, Hungary. (The photos of the statue were taken in 1971)

I feed turkeys at the age of

The Russians had so much goodwill that they erected only a mountain shepherd statue and not one of Lenin or Stalin in place of our Millennial Monument.

In the autumn of 1924 a difficult period began for my mother. Her mother, my Grandmother (Mrs. Ekes, Cornelia Henz) was brought up to Budapest. She had enormous pains. She was examined, operated but had cancer and within some months she died at the young age of 47. Mother was right in hope with my little sister and was very run-down by her mother's death.

1925

In February my little sister Edith was born, a nice brown haired grey-brown eyed baby, but she had cardiac inadequacy. The blood would flow back into her heart and therefore her body was constantly a purple-grey color. At that time her condition could not yet be healed. The doctors said: she would be lucky if she could live for half a year. In the beginning of the summer we traveled to Verecke again, where at the end of July little Edith died. She was buried in the family-graveyard. To her belongs the fourth little grave. I could not yet remember these things because I myself was only two years old. Only from what my parents told me do I know all these things. It was a very sad time for them!
But 'trouble never comes alone', says the proverb.

It was the beginning of November 1925. I was two and a half years old, so I can recall the story. At that time we lived in Budapest, in the present-day Béla Bartók Street 61. In the 1920s it was called Diagonal later Miklós Horthy-street.

/Béla Bartók 1881-1945. He was a Hungarian composer, pianist and collector of folk music. He was one of the greatest composers of the 20th century.- editor/

/Miklós Horthy 1868 – 1957 was the Regent of Hungary during the interwar years and in World War II from 1920 to October 15, 1944. He guided Hungary into an alliance with Nazi Germany, in exchange for the restoration of Hungarian territories lost after the World War I. In June 1941, Hungary entered World War II as an ally of Germany. Despite that the Nazis invaded and took control of the country in March 1944. He was forced to resign, placed under arrest and taken to Bavaria; at war's end he came under the custody of U.S. troops. He died in Portugal in 1957.-editor/

We had a two-room flat on the first floor that my father rented after his uncle died. Nowadays the flats besides and underneath are surgeries.

At that time my mother sent for a home dressmaker.
Dame Judith worked quite rapidly and nattily on the Singer sewing machine. Mum ordered it from the USA on easy terms. It's a very good machine; I still work on it and would not change it over, not even for any kind of electric sewing machine! Judith lacked only one important thing: she never basted, only pinned the different pieces of cloth together and when she began sewing she threw the needles onto the floor. I was naturally always beside her and when I received a piece of cloth for my dolls I started playing on my knees a little way away.

Mummy called us to have lunch. Juci went, but I didn't. So my mother lifted me up and made me sit on the chair. I ate the meal and wanted to stand up but could not; just fell flop and weeping showing them that my right knee hurt. On the doctor's order I was taken to the Clinic with a taxi. There the x-ray showed a good-sized needle in my knee beside the joints. Some hours later I was operated on: but the needle couldn't be found, so they stitched the wound, and fixed my leg for the night. Early in the morning I was x-rayed again and with the photo and me the doctors rushed into the operating room. On the x-ray it could be clearly seen that the needle drifted away. So using the x-ray the wound was opened again and finally the needle was found and removed. One doctor showed my mother the x-rays saying that the needle was extracted just in time, because if it had bedded itself into the joints and had to be cut out from there, then it would have made my leg stiff for my lifetime. Of all these I remember only that when I waited for the operation a nine year old boy was brought beside me, who waited for appendectomy. We had a good chat and I was first pushed into the operating room. Great was the bustle. Then I remember a kind of „smelly cloth" (ether gauze) that was put under my nose and I was asked to count slowly to five, because at that time I could count only that much.

After the operation I started feeling myself full well and also the doctors mollycoddled me, coming to my bed by turns to tell stories. I bet the stone departed from their hearts.

When I could leave the clinic my parents still brought me back for weeks for wound care. Then the doctor daubed my knee with a yellow ointment, which I named apricot jam. I remember how happy I was when I could eat apricot jamming again. Because my knee was twice cut up and stitched with cat gut, the place can still be seen, to this very day. I don't mind. I can move my legs and also dance, which I loved to do all my life. After all this, my parents loved me and seemed as if they were coddling me even more, especially Daddy, who was ready to sit beside me for hours so as to spare my leg. He told me jokes, stories, we chatted and made drawings together. When I was allowed to walk, he took me every afternoon to take the air and play hide and seek in the high grass of the nearby meadow that is now the Lágymányos tennis-court.

Our house in the Diagonal-street was the last one in the row, which was built from the Round Square to the Kelenföld railway station. After the house there was only very high grass, weed and bush, by the Soundless Lake (Feneketlen) there was a reed plot. Underneath was a kind of muskeg. This land let down to the Danube so its name became Lágymányos-that is soft land. I still can see before my eyes how the yellow-green grass and the reed hovers in the wind.

Not long afterwards the city council began to cover the territory on both sides of the Diagonal-street. They built houses up to Kelenföld and from the Lenke square, now Dezső Kosztolányi square. /*Dezsdő Kosztolányi 1885-1936. He was a Hungarian writer and poet-editor.*/ This way within ten years we could move into a new and bigger fiat on the Lenke square. By that time all the land had been reclaimed and built on.

1926

This year passed relative quietly. Mother gave piano lessons at home for teenager girls. In the evening when the students were gone I took my little chair and sat by the piano and mother played her favourites Beethoven, Bach and Chopin for me. How much did this music influence me at the age of three? Mummy told me that when she was playing the andante part of a certain Beethoven symphony I always stared to cry bitterly. Also works from Chopin, where the notes are as follows: g,c,h,c,d,e,e,d,e,f,f,e,a, g;f,e,h,c,d;e,e,d,c etc. In my long life I cried very rarely but when something touches my heart I still do weep. Mother also played Liszt, Mozart, Haydn, Schumann and Schubert works quite often. In the Music Academy the teachers who passed the room, where mother played, always thought that a boy was playing, because her playing was so spirited. She helped with the family income by doing the piano lessons, because after the death of my grandmother also Magdalene, mother's younger sister moved to us to stay with us in Budapest. She, who was my Aunt, was only 12 years older than me, and my parents paid for her studies.

My maternal grandfather Andor Ékes finished his studies in the Agricultural Academy of Keszthely and worked as agronomic leader for the Benedictine order. At that time the catholic order owned huge estates. Grandpa was ordered to work first in Zalaapáti; later sent to Csallóköz, to village Füss. He worked for the catholic order for 40 years. After WWI Hungary was cut into pieces due to the Trianon Pact! Czechoslovakia got Csallóköz and the whole northern region of the country. Together with many Hungarians my grandpa also fled. The bohemians gave him some kind of Severance pay, but not enough to buy a flat for his family, because till that time he lived in ministerial flats on catholic properties. He had a family of five. Grandpa, his wife Cornelia Henz and their three daughters: Irma, Helen, Magdalene.

After their escape from Csallóköz the Benedict priests temporarily and just „on compassion" let them live in the Home for old and sick priests in Bakonybél. At this time both my grandpa's Parkinson's disease and my grandma's cancer began. No wonder because the catholic order had not given him a penny as pension „on compassion" after 40 years of good, honest, diligent and efficient work, saying that he has already received Severance pay from the Czechs. The Severance pay quickly disappeared due to the sudden high inflation, so my grandparents stayed without a penny. Mother married in 1922, Aunt Helen did in 1924. Aunt Magdalene became a teenager half-orphan after the death of her mother, but the priests didn't want to teach her or pay for its cost! Moreover the revs became more impatient for my sick grandfather to leave his temporary flat because they needed it. So Aunt Helen had to marry the first man who was willing to marry her and would agree also to take her sick father with her.

So Aunt Helen married a steward from Csíkszereda, who had finished the Agricultural Academy in Mosonmagyaróvár. He was employed first by the Cistercian catholic order on their estate in Előszállás, in the county of Fejér. When they married he was reassigned to village Akli near town Zirc in county Veszprém. Aunt Magdalene was brought up to my parents.

My dislike of catholic priests only grew on hearing this story as a teenager. The stories of the great reformed Uncle Charles strengthened my dislike, as well.

Aunt Helen's marriage began very bitterly. Her husband loved her very much, gave her everything that she wanted. In the first year their little son Thomas was born, whom Aunt Helen couldn't feed. The doctor said to give him only tea and by the time he discovered why the baby was always crying, it was already too late. His body had dried out. Neither could it be helped in the hospital so he died as some weeks old, healthy and 3,5 kilos baby! He was buried in Akli beside my maternal grand-mother. Then Uncle Franz asked the priests to employ him in Olaszfalu /Italian-village/. He had to work at the other estate of the order, so that his wife could forget the painful and sad memories. I myself remember Italian-village well!

After our holiday in Verecke in the middle of August we traveled with mother down to Italian-village to help her sister in setting up her new flat and in forgetting. I liked being there. I remember a long house, which had lots of rooms that opened from a long glass walled veranda, where Aunt Helen arranged a winter garden. She loved flowers and what was strange to me, she even talked to them when watering and attending the plants. Her opinion was that these plants live and love good words. The different colored and sorts of flowers were very thankful for this wholehearted care and love.

Aunt Helen's second child was born, a lovely small girl, Martha. From the first day a nursing mother was employed who brought her little son as well and lived in the house. I remember she was a fat and cheerful woman. The children grew wonderfully. Within some years Martha became my playfellow. We made lots of adventures together. One of them I still remember well. Behind the house on the southern side in the vegetable garden there was a concrete cistern where luckily the water was only knee high. We sneaked there and climbed into the cistern and because it was very hot, we bathed and splashed each other with great joy. The water was muddy and green, but we didn't mind. All at once the grown ups realized we were missing! They started searching and finally my mother found us and I got the blame from her, because I as the older should have known what was good or bad.

First the green mud was washed from us and after lunch I was locked into the guest-room as punishment. I wept a little when I heard the key turning in the keyhole, but I consoled myself quickly and lay on top of the high and soft bed and in the pleasant cool temperature I quickly went to sleep. Mother became scared of the great silence and opened the door within one or two hours. Naturally I had to say sorry and promise that never again would I do such a thing and as I was the older one I had to take care of Martha. I got to know then that her parents would not let the wind blow on her because her brother had died.

1927–28

My mother became pregnant again. I didn't notice it at all. At that time children were not prepared for the birth of a small brother or sister, at any rate I was not.

My little brother Géza was born on 30.10.1927. There was more jealousy in my heart than joy. Yes, I was jealous because my parents preferred attending him and not me. Father noticed it and compensated me with daily long walks to the Gellert-hill cliff chapel and back. On the way home we always went into the sweet-shop on Gellért square, where he bought me delicious long barley-sugar, various shapes of acid drops and my favourite: sultan-bread.

Family trip to the coniferous wood of the Verecke-pass

Poor father didn't realize that it led to my early tooth-decay. Buster was born weighing four and a half kilos and from the beginning was fed cereals cooked in milk because mother couldn't feed him. Despite that he grew quickly and well and he became like a small iron man.

Mummy, Daddy, Uncle Charles, Brother Géza and me in the Verecke garden

He was a beautiful baby, whose baby buggy I pushed with great joy. Nearly every afternoon we went out walking with mother and little Buster on the „winding street", i.e. the

Ménesi-street. There we sat down on a bench in a shady place and while my brother was sleeping and I chatted with mother. And what a child is like? I loved these times so very much that the memory still lives in me and for that I could be thankful to my little brother.

This helped me my jealousy pass and we became good playmates and later very loving brethren till his death.
We took Buster to Verecke for holiday from the very beginning. Uncle Charles loved us as if we were his own children, especially Buster whom he always called nice boy, in Verecke language „schéne Bursch".
It is possible that this influenced him and later he became a very handsome man and had also good heart like Uncle Charles, whom he loved very much. „They influenced each other!"

When Buster was two and a half years old he received a small cart and a dog from Uncle Charles - a fox terrier called Maxi. It was a clever dog. Sometimes we could put Maxi in front of the cart, but mostly I was the one who pulled him.

With buster in Alsóverecke

1929

When Buster became a bit older we were able to play together without a problem. In Verecke we furnished the roofed veranda as playground for rainy days.
Uncle Charles fabricated us a big dolls house for us, which where we both could climb into, and also a grocery where there was a counter, some shelves and drawers.

These all were made of cardboard in which the medicines were brought into the pharmacy. Into the drawers we put flour, sugar, salt, beans, lentils etc.
We also had a small pair of scales and a cash register. We learned how to weigh, count, sell and buy. Buster was an expert shop keeper and supplier, he brought the goods home -into the dollhouse-on his cart, where I cooked delicious lunch and waited for the wearied shop-keeper to return home.

The 6 and 2 years old children

In case of good weather father took us to the Latorca stream to bathe. There he blocked the water with stones and made us an artificial waterfall where we all three could stand under. Uncle Charles used to come to bathe at noon when he closed the pharmacy. The Latorca was a shallow stream5-10 centimeters deep. It rises in the Beszkids, not far from the Verecke pass.

When I became older I sometimes joined Ann, when we had to wash or rinse clothes. In its perfectly pure water we found lots of nice pebbles of different size and color. In its water only the trout could live, which father and Uncle Charles angled for. They used to go for whole-day fishing and in the evening they returned with the abundant result of their day. They poured the fish from the fish-smelling leather bag on the kitchen table for Helen's – the cook- greatest joy and she made us delicious fish-dinner within a short time! I liked this fish very much, because it is nearly boneless and very delicious, even better than the Balaton fish.

The Latorca flows through the whole Alsóverecke and follows its course to the Verecke pass where between the two hillsides there is only room for the stream and the road. From there the stream flows south to Munkács and later to the west into the river Tisza. We thought it was a calm and peaceful little stream until one day of our Verecke holiday, when the following tragic thing happened.

Our house was on the main street where behind two rows of houses the stream was flowing and behind that towered the 450 ms high hill, the Magura, on the green meadows of which children used to pasture geese. From early morning the sky was cloudy. We played on the veranda with Buster when suddenly complete darkness covered the world, there was thunder and lightening and we were called into the room. There standing by the window I could see the following: the hill opposite us disappeared and a thick grey and white cloud was rolling downhill and approached us as if it were smoke. It began to rain hard, so that not even the gate could be seen. It rained continually till late afternoon.

In the evening some people came into the pharmacy and told us that in the Main square the strong timber bridge over the stream had broken and been swept away like match pieces. Within minutes the peaceful little stream became a two and a half metre high giant threatening water column. At that time we could say together with our poet Petőfi.

/Sándor Petőfi was a Hungarian National poet, lived from 1823 to 1849. He was a key figure in the Hungarian revolution of 1848- editor/

> „As a psycho having torn down his chains,
> The river was racing through the 'village'.
> Lumbering, bumping it tearing down all
> bars
> As it would swallow all that the world has."

The most tragic thing was when the body of a girl and a boy was found, who were previously pasturing their geese. In the valley a man was putting hay in his two-horse cart. The cart and the horses were found hanging among the branches of a high tree, but the owner couldn't be found, the flood must have swept him away. Some other people also disappeared in that terrible flood! Although I was only six years old at that time I can still see that thick cloud rolling down the hillside.

At the beginning of September my school began. I waited for it impatiently. Aunt Kate (father's sister) a teacher, prepared me for this event. She always had only first classes and taught them with great enthusiasm and call all her life. Her opinion was that teachers of the first classes have the most important role, because they have to lay the foundations for the further knowledge and learning of the small and uninstructed students. The pupils are like a white sheet of paper on which the teacher draws the first beauties of knowledge and character. The pupils soak up every word of the teacher like a sponge. In some cases at home the words of the teacher take precedence over that of the parents. That is why the first-class teachers have double responsibility! It is a wonderful profession! I myself experienced it, when I became teacher. Aunt Kate had the lion's share in that, as I tried to follow her worthy and uplifting work. I started with a first class as well, moreover a boys' class. (In the old days boy and girl classes were separated.) My colleagues didn't want to have boy classes, so my directors were surprised at my request, but fulfilled it with joy.

Turning back to my first steps at school. From the house where we lived also a friend of mine came to the same school. She was the daughter of the owner of the Fehérvár Street Gamma works, Esther Juhász. She had beautiful brown hair, white skin and starry brown eyes. She was just the opposite of me, because I was a blond-haired and blue-eyed girl. I often played with both of them. She had a little sister Judith, who later became the wife of the popular actor Leslie Mensáros.

The school was in the old Miklós Horthy-street 21.
At school I sat with Esther at a common desk and we competed with each other in collecting first red dots and later ones. (At that time 1 was the best and 4 the worst mark.) At the end of the school-year we both became prime-pupils.

But let's turn back in time. In November 1929 I got chicken-pox. Because also my little brother was at home, due to the old health care rules I had to go the Stephanie street children hospital into a single room, totally isolated. During this period also the scarlet fever broke out in me, so I was closed in for seven weeks. Father visited me every day after work and we were allowed to talk through a window. Fortunately neither illness was too serious so I could play with the toys father brought in and also with the nurses or doctors who came in to me. I had great time, but usually it was quite boring. With diligence I taught myself to read. When at Christmas I could get out of the hospital I was in advance to my class-mates in reading. Naturally Aunt Kate came every day happily to teach me the lessons I had missed.

Mother took Buster down to Olaszfalu to Aunt Helen and left him there for Christmas. Later they told us smiling how my two and a half year old brother fought to get his freedom back. Because the rural house was cooler than the Budapest one, especially in winter and at night, Aunt Helen decided to pull a sleeping bag on him and put him into a slatted baby cot where my brother couldn't stand up at all. He began crying and shaking the bars with all his strength and furiously shouted with angry-drawn eyebrows: I don't want this sleeping-bag! I don't want this sleeping-bag! When the sleeping-bag was changed to little Marta's pajamas his face lightened up and he walked happily around in the baby-cot, shortly later he went peacefully to sleep. His tremendous love for freedom drove him out of the country in 1956 and made him an outlaw. But I'm going to talk about it later, when I get to the year 1956. Before that time much water flows down the Danube!

During my childhood in the 1920s in the provinces - like in Verecke and also in Akli - the lights were made using kerosene lamps and candles. Later in the 1930s the „Aladdin lamp" became popular, in which a "leg of white" was glowing and diffusing the strong, wide white light. Chandeliers hanging from the ceiling were also made this way. These lamps were pumped to shine strongly.

It was summer again. I finished my first year at school successfully. For the final exam mother sewed a beautiful white dress for me and embroidered it with Kalocsa folk-motifs. I proudly recited in that dress a quite long piece of poetry that Aunt Kate taught me. I had great success and received lots of applause.

With my brother we waited for the Verecke holiday impatiently. I liked to travel on train and watch the colorful scenes passing by, which were always changing and disappearing behind the window. Our fast train left for Sátoraljaújhely from the Eastern Railway Station at 9 o'clock in the morning. At the customs we had to wait two hours and later changed for a slow train, which had to climb a high mountain. Father told us smiling to listen to what the wheels of the train moan when going upwards: „Holy Maria help me! Holy Maria, help me!" But when it reached the highest point and the wheels started to dash downwards they said happily: „If you would help me or would not, myself can I go so fast!" Needless to say that all tiredness and boredom of the day was swept away with that joke and after the delicious grilled chicken for lunch we started to chorus these words and also tapped the rhythm to it.

We were so happy and heated up that after arriving to Volóc and hanging on the neck of Uncle Charles, he could not believe that a whole day journey was behind us with tiredness and slackness. We sat into sir Burech's taxi and went slow or stopped for short, when we got amidst the returning and belling herds. In the morning we have yet been in Budapest the great city and in the evening already in another world. A real dreamland waited for us with cows staring into the car, with the happily jumping dog Maxi, the smiling Ann in the flower garden, the stocks and the Carpathian Mountain pinewood breathing out their perfume.

When the taxi stopped late in the evening, the lamp above the pharmacy lit a long louse on which there were two roofed bay verandas. After coming through the gate we went up on nine steps into the pharmacy, where complete cleanliness and the typical pharmacy smell waited for us. There stood the bright crystal glasses, the jars and huge brown drawers full of medicines. On the counter there were scales of different sizes; porcelain dishes and the cash register. In the room behind the pharmacy there was a bed, where the chemist in attendance slept, in the other part a laboratory table with some appliances and shelves were to be found. The medicine store-room opened off from here. Going further to the right from the pharmacy, we entered a huge living-room that led to Uncle Charles's room. He worked and received his guests there; it was furnished with a salon suite of furniture, a great bookcase and a nice bed. From here opened further two rooms. The first was the my parents' bedroom with the usual two beds, a sofa, two cupboards, and a small bed for children, a washstand with a basin and a mirror in front. The other one was the dining room, where twelve people could be seated at the big oval table. There was also a bed in this room, where I slept on my own. From there opened the kitchen. From the kitchen opened off the room of the actual cook and the staircase to the attic. From the kitchen we could go out to the court which only a single step led to, because the site had a slight slope towards the street. The court was bordered and separated from the hillside by silver fir woods. My father used to go up there to play the alpine horn during his bachelor life to him, as he said and the high mountain opposite sent the echo back.

In the court under the silver pine trees there was an open trelliswork constructed from battening, where fox grape, yellow nasturtium and turquoise morning-glory was climbing in to the roof. In good weather, in summer we used to have breakfast and high tea there.

When we finished exploring the rooms with buster, Helen the cook has already brought the delicious dinner, which we ate half asleep. After that we fell into fairy-sleep that encompassed us also the next day and during the whole summer.

In the morning we woke up refreshed. It was a warm July day. We ran to the trelliswork, where the first delicious breakfast waited for us. Uncle Charles brought us Ovomaltin from the pharmacy, which he mixed with the warm milk saying that the relatives from Budapest should get stronger. We had leavened village bread and put the delicious butter on top, it was made from the milk of the cows pastured on mountain meadows and as decoration the shape of the edelweiss was printed into it. Unto the butter-bread we put honey twirled by

Uncle Charles himself or strawberry from the woods made into jam. There also eggs collected from the chicken-run, and eaten soft, hard or as scrambled eggs. These wonderful tastes I keep in my mouth forever!

After breakfast we launched a discovery trip in the flower garden with my brother. As the diversity of tastes before, now a fairy range of colors waited for us.

In the middle of the huge garden there was a great flowerbed full of blood-red salvia, on the edge small white flowers and forget-me-not. In all four corners of the garden there were triangle shape flowerbeds with parti-colored rose bushes, colorful small daisies, asters and other beautiful flowers. Among the flowerbeds thick lawn carpet used to show vivid green.

In the back third part of the garden a grass terrace could be found where under the three summer-apple trees my parents relaxed in the afternoons in comfortable deckchairs. Behind the chairs by the fence there were pine trees and in front of them wonderful gladioli and stock flowers decorated the end of the garden and gave their perfume off when the afternoon or evening sunshine kissed their limbs. In the first part of the front garden by the Main street there were huge disc-like sunflowers and purple, yellow, white, purple dahlias that served also as protection from the dust of the street.

The flower garden was separated from the vegetable garden by a small stream. Here the beans went upon stakes driven into the ground and their dense green leaves hid the potato rise in the back of the garden. The bed of the small stream was always full with water in rainy days and brought the water down from the hillside and poured it into the ditch by the road. We put a board bridge over the stream. Buster loved to play there with his paper ships, but naturally only inside the garden.

The other half of the house, as I have already mentioned, was let to the bohemian doctor. Also on his side there was a roofed veranda, where the patients waited. At the other end of our garden a great wood-shed could be found and also a chicken run with a great number of poultry. In the other vegetable garden gooseberry and raspberry bushes, vegetables, carrot, tomato, paprika, celery, onion and cabbage were grown. Beside the wood-shed by the shelter of the pine trees at the fence, beehives were lined up, where Uncle Charles used to keep bees. It was interesting that bees never stung him. He told us that one must not leave any kind of odor on oneself, neither perfume nor soap, because that makes bees angry and that's why they sting.

At the end of the summer we started to prepare and pack our luggage ready and with sad heart took farewell to Uncle Charles, the garden, the house, Verecke, everything that meant freedom for us.

In autumn I started my second school year. Nothing interesting happened at school. At home father always checked my homework and sternly demanded fine and correct writing and neatness. If he had found something not in order, he tore the page out and I had to write it again. Sometimes I also got smacks on my head. With his rigid discipline he taught me the value of careful work, and I can only thank him for that. I made great use of it in my later life!

1931

At long last it was New Year and later spring again. In my childhood there were still „real" springs. We eagerly waited for the feast of unleavened bread because by that time we could put on the spring coat and thick knee high socks that we could use well until the beginning of the summer.

On the 1st of July the train took us to Alsóverecke again, towards liberty! Father and Uncle Charles were very good brothers. There were four and a half years between them. My father was spare of build, thin boned 172 centimeters tall, rigid, spare of words, a quiet, very handsome man with great blue eyes and a small moustache. Uncle Charles was a bit plump, strong boned, 167 cm tall, very good-natured and good-humored, jocose, talkative man with great brown eyes and black hair and small black moustache. In the pharmacy he was always walking in white coat that went well with his black eyes and hair. I can still see his shape as he was, when we arrived to Verecke in the evening, waiting for us in front of the lighted pharmacy door.

My father and Uncle Charles regularly played chess in the evenings. When smaller, I always watched them during their play, but this summer I asked them to teach me to play chess. I learned the steps quickly and how glad I was when I could check Uncle Charles. The chess taught me to think of my actions in advance and to be cautious.

During long and warm summer evenings we sat on the garden-bench and watched the starry sky. My father showed me the polestar, the Milky Way, the four wheeled Göncöl cart in the sky, etc. We always talked about whether life exists on the Moon or on the stars and what could it be like? It intrigued me enormously!

The most wonderful thing is that already during my lifetime the landing on the moon has happened and we have got to know that nobody lives there. This news disappointed me a little and I think it would also father, if he still lived, because in imagination we populated the moon and the stars so vividly and colorfully. These Verecke evening chats remain in my memories so clear forever, I think on them thankfully.

Another experience was that some days after we arrived to Verecke for holiday, Uncle Charles taught us how to prepare beautiful bunches of flowers. We cut some nice pine branches and put gladioluses on top in different colors or dahlias and viola flowers. We took care of that the different colors should match each other. These were so very beautiful bunches that florists would have been jealous for them. Regularly with father and Uncle Charles we took these bunches and went to the cemetery to salute our dear dead relatives.

By the entrance there was a monument, before it a stone bench, with a black iron or bronze turul eagle. /It is the *mythological falcon of the ancient Hungarians-editor./* Behind it on the hillside a path led to the family- cemetery. Here we laid the flowers the bunch there and prayed for the salvation of my grandparents, aunts and uncles and my little sister Edith. It was a family ceremony that we repeated also before we traveled home and never missed it.

Twice a week /on Tuesday and Friday/ there was market day in Verecke. Every second week on Wednesday we had a great market and animal market. This time we had lots of new things to see, as Budapest children. We saw cows running and heard them mooing, sheep and goats bleating and also donkeys and felt as if we were in a zoo. There was high traffic also in the pharmacy. People came and went, including mothers with sick children. This time we were not allowed to go near the pharmacy, we could only have a look at it from the garden and greet the people, saying „Dobre ráno!"(Good morning!), „Dobre dén" (Good afternoon!), „Dobre vecser! (Good evening!), depending on which part of the day the customers arrived.

I learned so many things in Verecke e.g. on the wall of Uncle Charles hung a weather-gauge. The day before any excursion Uncle Charles looked at the weather-gauge and told us whether good weather could be expected or not. If good weather was to come, Uncle Charles agreed with Mr. Burech that the following day, usually on Sunday at 11 o'clock he should come with his taxi to the pharmacy, because we were going on an excursion.

The excursions could lead into different directions. Once we went up to the Verecke-pass from the east. We went through the Rákóczi-housing (Pudpolóc), after that we ascended on the serpentine street to the top of the Beszkids. There was the pass where the Millennial Monument stood and also the Czech-Polish border with the officers and the wooden booths. On the hilltop it was always breezy, even in good weather. A wonderful panorama opened up before our eyes. In the east we could see as far as Lemberg /Lvov in Russian, Lviv in Ukrainian/ and the great plain around it. To the northwest we could see the church-towers of Kassa, the 1000 meter high Pikuj Mountain and the smaller Tokaj and Zemplén hills, but naturally only in clear and sunny days.

Father told and showed us how the ancient Hungarians came in the old days on horses and ox-carts under the direction of chief Árpád and getting up the Beszkids from Lemberg. When they looked at this wonderful region and thick meadows and they didn't feel anymore the like to return to Etelköz, from where they had come. The seven chiefs held a meeting and decided to descend from the mountains and give the final home for the Hungarians here in this land surrounded by the Carpathian Mountain range. We acknowledged that it was a good decision, because there is no other such a beautiful homeland in the world! (The Keszti-panorama perpetuates the entrance of the ancient Hungarians into the region. This oil painting was exhibited first in the City Park, now it can be seen in Ópusztaszer.)

After the "history lesson" we took out the blanket and the baskets with food, just like in the old days 1000 years ago- and happily started eating fried chicken, cheese with green paprika, liver paste, apple roundel and drinking refreshing Polena mineral water to it. We offered these also to the Jewish taxi driver, but he didn't eat, because our food was not kosher to him, so he only tasted the cake. After the lots of rambling and playing, when the sun turned to the west and was about to go down, we started to pack our things together, said farewell to the custom's officers and descended from the mountain in the taxi to our home in Verecke.

There was a Greek Catholic church in Alsóverecke, where on some Sundays my parents took me and my brother to. When I entered the building first I stood nearly riveted to the earth. I have never seen such an ornamented church before, not even in Budapest. It was full of gold covered pillars and on the walls there were side by side colorfully painted icons. During the service the altar in the middle of the room was circled many times by the pope dressed in a wonderful golden robe and his cortege. They incensed a lot; we nearly turned giddy from it. They said the mass-text in Ukrainian and were singing also that way, the women and men, who were dressed in beautiful Ukrainian national costumes.

My nanny Anca also had such a traditional meeting dress. Once I borrowed it from her, pulled the dress on and Uncle Charles took photos of me. The blouse was made of linen, woven by women with standing white collar, its arms and cuffs embroidered with cross stitch using colored thread. In addition to that they wore a black silk skirt and a colorful apron. I took a fancy to that dress so asked Ann, to teach me the how to do cross stitch.

As 15 years old in
Ukrainian folk-dress

It is such an enjoyable and beautiful art of embroidery that later on I made lots of work pieces using this method.

Uncle Charles supplied us every summer with the products of the Czech shoe factory Bata". Those were well made, neat and nice leather sandals with wicker uppers, for autumn and closed shoes for winter. These lasted till the next summer if our feet didn't grow before then.

Uncle Charles looked after us as if we were his children, but he also helped his only beloved brother, my father. I have never met such a benign, gold-hearted man in my childhood as he was. He didn't behave like that only towards us but also to the population of the village, who came to him as to a priest for good advice and help in their smaller or greater problems. He also helped them sometimes with money, medicines or clothes

At Uncle Charles I learned about democracy that everyone is equal and we have to help each other if we could!

There was a Ukrainian boy, who regularly used to come to our house to chop timber. He was treated as the fool of the village, but Uncle Charles told us that this poor boy was only dumb, he couldn't speak, made only strange sounds out and laughed at it. Uncle Charles could communicate with him because the boy understood everything, naturally in Ukrainian. Once it happened that we were standing on the veranda in front of the pharmacy when this boy came to us and I saw how well they could understand each other using gestures. We were standing opposite the boy when he started to show towards my neck and all at once he made a grab at my neck and in the next moment he showed laughing and moaning a horrible, great cross-spider in his hand. We were both taken aback. Uncle Charles looked at my neck and said that the spider could have been exactly beside my pulse when the dumb boy discovered and grabbed it. Uncle Charles fondled his head and complimented him and gave him money- one crown, which the boy put happily into his pocket. Although my knees were trembling, I but also thanked him very much.

This summer also ended. Before our farewell father made some beautiful bunches that we took to Budapest with us so that we could enjoy the good scent of pine and flowers a week longer, remembering Verecke.

The 1931-32 school-years began, which was my third class. After the freedom of Verecke my brother couldn't bear the confined life in Budapest with iti and the orderly, well behaved walks. An opportunity opened for my parents to rent an empty, but fenced grassy garden in the Ménesi Street, where other families with children also used to go. (They received the address from us.) This solved my brother's and my need for running and playing. We could spend the whole day outside. There was a timber hut there, where toys and deckchairs could be locked up and stored. Some good acquaintances were made among parents and also children. Older couples without children as well, who wanted to breathe good air visited that place.

Because the autumn was long and warm, we could make the best of the garden. I remember an old couple who mother was on friendly terms with. The woman was a foreigner, perhaps German or English and she did not speak the Hungarian language very well; her husband was a colonel, of course already on pension. They had a son, who worked as geologist on the island of Java and had lived there with his family for years. The parents visited them often. She told us the following story about one of their visits with funny pronunciation that I liked so very much. Her son and his family lived in a two storey house, which was not fenced. The bedrooms were upstairs. One night the full moon lit up the room and the woman could not go to sleep, so she went to the window and admired at the beauty of the garden and neighborhood in the moonlight. Once one of the bushes started to move and a tiger approached the house. She just looked perplexed and not a sound came out of her mouth. The tiger kept walking up and down on the pavement for a while and when he had already enough, left peacefully. Next morning the woman told her exciting adventure of the night tremulously, but her son told smiling that it was an everyday thing and when he worked, the tiger-hunters always escorted him.

We said goodbye to the garden. In the winter we didn't go there any more.

1932

I liked attending school. During the first two years a very kind teacher taught us who also had some children; she loved little girls very much, maternally. In the third year there was a change. We had a middle age, thin, very strict, spectacled so called „spinster" for teacher. She also behaved like that and was always wearing dark clothes and on the top of her head she had a small knot of hair that was always shaking when she shouted. So we were afraid of her in the beginning, but she had the heart of gold towards anyone who completed their tasks well. I still remember her name: Irma Kövi. She taught us also in the fourth year. It was awful and inexplicable for me when I later saw her with the „yellow star" on her breast.

I finished the third year as I had the first two, with top marks. At the end of the school year mother sewed me the exam-dress and embroidered it beautifully. Aunt Kate taught me the poem that I was to recite during the exam-festival. After that there was nothing else to do, but to travel to Verecke. This summer I can report on two memorable excursions. The first was a beautiful one, the second painful that had its

Trip to the Szkotárszka tunnel (my Brother Tom in the middle)

consequences for a lifetime. With the family-taxi we traveled up to Volóc and then further alongside the railway line to the Beszkid's tunnel Szkotárszka, where the train goes first on two pairs of rails on high iron framework viaducts above the ravine and later disappears in the tunnel.

It is a wonderful region, where after the tunnel the train turns towards Lemberg and Poland. We visited Szkotárszka nearly every summer. It is a dead region, only eagles and hawks flew above us and we went rambling. Every summer a Czech teacher spent the holidays with his family there, in a disused railway carriage. He had many children and said he couldn't afford to have a proper holiday. In the meantime Uncle Charles made friends with him and as we did with his children. It was an original camping holiday, but at least it could last for two months.

The other journey led to the Verecke-pass, but not for the first time. This summer we met some relatives there, who came from Munkács for a trip. They were the Czinkótszky family, where the wife Edith Hreuss was the first cousin of father and Uncle Charles. They also had children, two big daughters and a son Stephen, who was only a year younger than me. This boy became the husband of the cousin of my second husband. How small is the world! But at that time we didn't even guess it! After the great joy over meeting again we had tea, the adults started chatting and we children went to play and bathe in the Latorca stream and collect pebbles in the water. Then one of the girls recommended us to climb up that steep glade, where a column and a bronze eagle (turul bird) were the top. So we did! Coming downhill the two girls grabbed my hand and we began to run. I was in the middle and was running, but only for a while, because I fell and landed on my stomach with the girls still holding my hands. My previously straight nose and my face were hurt and cut so much that blood was running from my nose. Uncle Charles opened the first aid kit and gave me at once first aid. Because the bleeding did not want to stop, we decided to pack and go home. On the way home I started to feel better, but the bone of my nose was surely broken, because it turned out to be a crooked nose, an aquiline-type that after all I like, it makes my face characteristic.

On the photo of the Verecke-pass, where father and brother Géza was walking, that steep hillside where we ran down is also to be seen, which resulted in breaking my nose.

In the autumn the school-year 1932-33 began, my fourth year at school began. I could not enjoy going to school for a long time, because at the beginning of October I caught scarlet fever again. Father took brother Géza to Italian-village to Aunt Helen.

Together with mother we were completely separated from father in the bedroom of the Diagonal-street flat, so that he could go to work without problem. From the bedroom opened the bathroom where one could enter the hall. The household employee supplied us with food through the bathroom and she disinfected everything that came out from us. On the entrance door a red card was hung outside saying: „Be aware! Infectious disease!" All these things were done under the advice and supervision of the doctor.

This scarlet fever illness was very serious. My fever jumped up to 40-41 degrees Celsius. I became unconscious for about one and a half days. There was no other medicine at that time for that, just Quinine alone to ease the fever and wet cold pack that mother changed every half hour on me. Together with my parents also the doctor could only pray for me. In the end the „cold" started to come out through my nose, but it was not a common one, but thick festering. For this ordinary handkerchiefs were not enough. Mother cut sheets that were burnt after use. This bacillus-flow lasted for a week until the pus totally emptied from me. The doctor told that if the pus hadn't come out through my nose but would have gone up to my brain, I would have been past help.

I couldn't have eaten for two weeks, drank only bouillon, lemon tea and lemonade. I was so weak that I couldn't even hold my hand up. After the crisis my appetite came back so that I could have eaten the iron nail that is why the maid did her best and always cooked the most delicious meals. Father supplied me with oranges and bananas.

Mother had already had scarlet fever in her teenage years, but this awful amount of bacillus made her tonsils inflamed so she also had to stay in bed for a week and at that time the doctor visited her. We were separated from the world for six weeks, closed into the room. On the fifth week stamp like skin pieces started to come off from my palms and feet and I looked like as I was molting. The doctor warned us that this dreadful illness is infectious most at that time, so we had to burn or disinfect everything. Fortunately we had a tile stove in the room, so it could be easily done.

After six weeks employees of the old KÖJÁL (Regional Epidemic Authority) came to us and disinfected the whole flat. For Christmas father brought my brother home, so the whole family could celebrate healthy and happily together again. My brother and I were extremely when we realized that under the Christmas tree a doll-house, a grocery and a lorry with some board games waited for us. The red roofed, light green walled doll-house was as big as me with a label „Susan house" on the wall and a detachable front with a balcony on the first floor. It was wonderful! On the ground floor there was a big dining room with reality-like small, brown furniture. In the middle of the room there was a round table with four chairs. By the wall there stood a credenza, a side board and a china cabinet.

There were also table covers, carpets, curtains, lampshades, a lamp with a small light bulb operated with batteries that gave light indeed. There were small bronze lamp stands, copies of silver dishes and small pots also in the china cabinet. Beside the dining room there was the kitchen, which was also beautifully furnished with a cupboard, some stools, and a case for timber, a table, a furnace and a lamp. On the first floor there was a bedroom with a double bed, with a white cupboard, a table, two small armchairs, a mirror and in front of it a stool. From the bedroom opened the bathroom with white bath-tub, a basin, a towel rail with towels on it and a WC water tank, which could be filled with water and it worked, indeed.

Brother could admire the shop with small drawers and shelves, the counter with the pair of scales on it, the cash-register with ejecting drawers, on the shelves colorful tiny vegetables, cabbages, carrots, apples, pears and oranges made of gypsum, put into small baskets. Naturally he also received a big lorry that transported the goods to the doll-house.

This Christmas compensated me for my long, awful and nearly fatal illness. As later we got to know, father visited an unemployed acquaintance of his, an engineer in the autumn and saw what he was working with, so he ordered this dollhouse for me and kept on praying that I could still play and be happy with it.

God held me on His palm; I didn't die, which indicated that lots of things were still ahead of me to do.

1933

I started my fourth class with renewed strength in January. In my school years a label hung on the wall of every classroom, where on a black card the following text was written with golden characters:

> „I believe in one God,
> I believe in one homeland,
> I believe in God's eternal truth,
> I believe in the resurrection of Hungary. Amen."

I liked the texts of historic and geographic matters. We learned the names of the 63 counties of Great Hungary and also their capitals, which I know to the present day. The teacher told us that before the Hungarians entered the country there was a struggle for the possession of Pannonia between the Germans and Svatopluk Morva monarch, who dreamed of a great Slav empire. Neither of them could obtain it, because the Hungarians appeared. They came through the Carpathian Mountain at that time and occupied the disputed territory for themselves. The country that was occupied by our ancestors was also kept by their descendants, so that this land, which nations with the greatest power could keep only for a short time, was kept permanently by the Hungarians.

At the final exam, where I received excellent mark again, I recited the long poem of Géza Gyóni (with the help of Aunt Kate) that had the title: "Send them away only for a night". It had a great affect on the audience of the gym, which was full. So I took farewell to the elementary school, because from autumn I went to study at the St. Margaret grammar school for girls.

In the meantime, still in the spring we moved with parents from our Diagonal-street flat to Lenke square 7, into a three-room flat on the fifth-floor. At the end of May I took the holy-communion.

So many new things happened to us this year, but the greatest one was when on the 10th of June 1933 my second brother Thomas was born, whom we called "tiny", despite his 5 kilos weight. He looked like a month old child with blond hair and blue eyes. It seems he was infected in the hospital because tiny purulent pimples appeared on his skin. At that time Dr. Joseph Luke hospital child doctor began to teach mother to pluck the pimples off with wool soaked in alcohol. The pimples didn't want to disappear, but more and more appeared, so in the end they became deep boils and could be opened only with a knife. Then the doctor decided to give him blood transfusion. My blood, because it is of the type "o", was just appropriate for that operation. I gave blood to Tiny twice. He had suffered so much up to that point and his development had been held back. After the transfusions the deep boils quickly disappeared and with them all the upset and anxiety under which the whole family suffered for months.

At the beginning of the summer we didn't travel to Verecke, but Uncle Charles came to Budapest for a month. In the big flat we had enough room for him, where a corridor was leading to his room.

So as not to be always around my sick brother, my parents organized different kinds of beautiful trips for example we climbed up the John-hill lookout tower, the Disznófő pub, the Lion-stone, the Hármashatár-hill, using the tram or other means of transport and going on foot from the terminus. We four- father, Uncle Charles, my brother and I rambled through the whole Buda-hills. In hot weather we went to the Margaret-island to bathe, to the Palatinus or the Széchenyi bath beside the Zoo, to the Gellért bath or to the Csillaghegyi one. These were whole day trips, which we always finished in a pub. In the evening although tired, but with great enthusiasm we told mother everything that happened to us. She poor woman was sentenced to confinement to quarters with my sick brother.

When in the second part of August my brother became healthier after the life saving blood transfusions. So we joined Uncle Charles with father and Buster and traveled to Verecke for two weeks, so as not to miss that period of the year.

Uncle Charles made us stronger with pike liver oil and iron-wine. The oil we took heroically one spoonful every day before lunch, but the iron-wine we liked very much. It was like real red wine. He recommended us to take them in winter as well, because it enlarges strength, makes the bones stronger and we would never be anemic. We took his good advice and were not ill. As for me, after the strong scarlet fever, cardiac murmur was diagnosed so I was excused of physical education lessons. This was how I started the first year of grammar school in the years of 1933- 34.

Nearly every subject was taught by a different nun-teacher. In the beginning it was quite unusual for me, but later I took a liking to them very much. Unto the cover of our exercise books we chose our favorite saying. Mine was as follows: "Live as you should die every minute and work as you would live forever!" I still try to keep that nowadays! I received a red ribbon medal for my good behavior and diligence at the end of the school-year.

In the autumn I started taking piano lessons at a private teacher, who lived opposite to our Diagonal-street flat. Margaret Nosz was an elderly single woman. We didn't really like each other, but she could teach well. I attended her lessons for a year. At the end of the year she organized a spectacular exam lecture in the piano room of the Gellért hotel, which I also took part in with the number "Für Elise" by Beethoven. It turned out to be so successful, that the audience gave me cheers three times and I had to play it again. No need to say that mother was the proudest among all the parents!

In the next autumn my parents- at my request- registered me into the Fehérvár-street State Music School, where a very kind, but tough teacher, Irene Csák taught me further for less money, because it was a state school. She noticed my "perfect pitch" and talent and taught me according to that. With her I studied with great enjoyment. Here I also had successes at the end of the second year open exam with the Chopin number "Impromptu". Later on I met dame Irene on the street wearing "the yellow star" /discriminating sign for Jews/ and we were talking I felt deeply ashamed of the world, how such things could happen in Hungary!

Returning to our Diagonal-street flat, where some famous people lived, with whom my parents were very friendly. Such were István /Stephen/ Juhász owner of the Gamma Works and his family I have already mentioned, their two daughters. For example Imre /Emery/ Szacsvay, popular actor of the National Theatre lived there. At that time was already quite old and in my childish eyes he looked like father frost. When returning home from his daily walk he always stopped to chat with me and gave me caramel sweets from the great pocket of his coat. I was four years old at that time and I still remember his friendly face.

Imre /Emery/ Molnár pianist, composer and conductor also lived there, as well as József /Joseph/ Asbóth tennis champion. The family Ujj where the husband became a great communist in 1919, after WWI, had lots of children. They were very poor; mother helped the gentle and silent woman with children's clothes. On the ground-floor there lived an elderly couple without children, Dr. Gyula /Julian/ Kuzma and his wife. They were nice people. The man was my father's colleague at the legal department. His wife Ella, in no time started to teach mother, the inexperienced young wife how to cook, bake and make children's clothes. She treated her like a daughter and gave her good advice and loved me very much. I often spent half days at their place, just like in a nursery school, when mother went shopping or prepared lunch. Dame Ella often told me about her nieces Ella and Sarah, whom partly she brought up. At that time the girls were already in their twenties and members of the Palestrina choir. They could sing beautifully and with the choir they traveled round the whole world. I looked at the many postcards they sent home and listened to the happy and talkative dame Ella and I felt as if she was my grandmother. That's why my parents and I had to take farewell to the many kind acquaintances when we moved into a bigger flat so that the family with three children should have more place.

1934

This summer we traveled to the Lake Balaton for the advice of the doctor so that my brother Tom should recover from his long and exhausting sickness. My parents rented a part of a villa in Balatonszemes first for a month, later again for another month. Uncle Charles spent the summer with us. We also took the house-maid with us who was a great help for mother.

I remember that in the first month our lodging was behind the railway station by the pharmacy. Five minutes from there the silky sandy shore of the Balaton could be found. When first had a look at the Balaton at town Aliga through the branches of trees, I couldn't imagine that such a great and wonderful lake opens up before our eyes at town Balatonszemes.

In the mornings brother Tom played in a shady place in the warm sand, but brother Géza and I ran into the water, where we could quickly learn to swim and row the boat. In the afternoons three times a week we were registered to the tennis court, where a trainer taught us how to play tennis. There I got to know two girls of similar age, Babi and Mici, who spent their summer holidays at their grandmother in the "Cat Home" by the Szemes shore walkway. Their grandmother and mother were Hungarians, the father was a Serb. They lived in Belgrad, but spent every summer at Lake Balaton. We became very good friends and I played often at their place, especially if the weather was no good for swimming or playing tennis.

It's impossible to describe the wonderful lights, which could be seen at sunset and changed continuously and slid across the peaceful water from Badacsony, where the sun went finally down. The golden sun first started to fade and then disappeared in the soft and lukewarm evening waves.

For the second month, which was August we moved into a one-storey villa by the railway line on the shore promenade, where we had rooms on the ground floor with uncle Charles upstairs. Our neighbor was the famous Gundel-Villa, where the many nice, shapely Gundel girls spent their holidays with their parents. There was high life at their house. Lots of relatives and guests, especially young men arrived frequently.
Gundel is the legendary Hungarian restaurant founded in 1894.-editor/

In the first two weeks of August we got to know the stormy, unquiet and rainy Balaton. From Uncle Charles's balcony we got a good view of the water that showed us its angry colors. The several meters high black water columns turned into poison-, bottle- and turquoise-green, after that into white-grey combing waves so that together with the rugged wind constantly attacked the weak sandy shore. This was a new experience for us children. After two weeks the wind died out, the combing waves settled, the sun started to shine again, and the water of the lake became so peaceful and smooth again, as if it had never behaved otherwise earlier.

On the 20th of August the Gundels organized fireworks on the shore that we could admire from the balcony.

Utilizing the last beautiful days of the summer we made a trip by ship to Keszthely, Badacsony and said farewell to the Balaton with sad heart.

When Uncle Charles traveled home to Verecke, father set him on his way to the Czech border, saying that the whole summer long they had not even been able to talk to each other. This always happened when Uncle Charles spent the summer with us. If father had enough holidays, we traveled to Verecke for one or two weeks, so as not to miss this period from the summer.

After this wonderful Balaton holiday we could hardly get used to our fifth floor flat, especially because from the middle room opened a small balcony with a thin iron fence, which father called simply "disaster balcony". Our parents didn't allow us out without a grown-up. Brother Géza was a very lively child, the small Tom just started to toddle that time. Father decided to move again. At the beginning of October we had quite good weather, so the thing could be done quickly. We moved into the Magyarádi street, a house recently built by the Italian-Hungarian Bank, where on the first floor we had a three and half room and hall flat on the corner. There were balconies on the corner and in the middle room, but these had massive stone balustrades and the flat was on the first floor.

I remember we moved on Saturday-Sunday. During that time I was just reading, hidden in armchairs turned to the wall, the book was Mór Jókai "No name castle". After that time I got the like of reading so very much that still nowadays I am an enthusiastic reader.

My brother Géza started the first year at primary school in the years of 1933-34 in the same school that I had attended in the Nicholas Horthy street 21.

In the autumn of 1934 we both started our second school-year, Géza at primary and I at secondary school. I liked attending the Margaret-school. The building was a brand new one, built at the beginning of Villányi-street. The facade of the building was decorated by an imposing row of columns and wide stairs that kept the long corridor on the first floor. Above the third storey a huge dome rose up to the sky. At both ends of the building there were the two porter's lodges. The first worked in the evening, the other in the afternoon.

The classrooms opened from the wide corridors to the left and right on the ground- and on the first floor. On the second floor the resident students lived, that they used for sleeping and studying. The third floor was only for the nuns, no living creature was allowed to enter there! On the ground floor under the dome there was a great hall, the so called "small Jesus" hall. Prominent guests were received there. At this time the great wings behind the columns were opened and the guests ascended on the middle stairs covered with red carpet.

I attended the first class, when the grammar school was visited by Schluschnig and Dolfuss Austrian prime minister and chancellor. (Not long afterwards Dolfuss was murdered. In the background stood already Hitler, who began his "murderous power" just at that time.)

The big site of the Margaret-school was between the Villányi and Ménesi streets. The site behind the building was divided into three terraces. On the first terrace there was the court for physical education, where in good weather we had physical education lessons and also the 20 minute breaks we spent out there. On the second terrace the red tennis courts and in winter the white skating rinks could be found. The third terrace was at the highest place and opened directly to the Ménesi-street, where the rose garden breathed forth its perfume and under the shady trees and bushes sitting on small benches our lessons were held in the autumn and spring, when the weather allowed. These lessons were very good and we always eagerly waited to go out into nature.

The gym could be found on the ground floor of the building, under it in the cellar there was the swimming-pool. Above the gym, on the second floor the gala room for celebrations could be found with the chapel next to it. It was compulsory taking part there in celebrations of mass Sundays and feast-days. At both ends of every corridor there were round shaped marble fountains from where on pushing a button clear water came forth that we were also allowed to drink.

By the standards of those days the institution counted as an ultramodern one, for which we had to pay 25 Pengős a month.

The students wore a uniform that looked quite nice. The autumn and spring costume was a blouse of butter color with deep blue skirt, deep blue silk necktie, for everyday use we had light blue Panama shirt, deep blue skirt and a tie. In the winter for feast days instead of the shirt we had deep blue upper part made of the material of the skirt and with that we wore brown thick tights and brown shoes or boots. The uniforms could be bought in Kovacsevics Milenko's store that was first on the corner of the Ménesi and Nicholas Horthy streets that nowadays works as a commission shop. Later he built a four-storey big shop in the Louis Kossuth street (that later was nationalized and got the name "Pioneer store", while the ex - owner changed his name to the Hungarian-like Nagykovácsi Milenko.)

The winter and Christmas of 1934 arrived, that ended very sad and tragic for Aunt Helen and her family, at which all relatives were shaken. For Christmas little Martha, my cousin got a big sleigh. She used it frequently until one day she fell over and the iron sleigh hit her shinbone. Her leg had an ugly bloodshot, which was first treated at home on the advice of the doctor, but when it began to swell and when it became painful and the poor girl had even fever, she was taken to hospital in Zirc. There she was operated on, but she could not be helped. Little Martha died at the age of nine with toxemia at the end of January 1935.

Aunt Helen got to the edge of madness, so for weeks she was given sleeping pills. After that time she became pregnant again and on the advice of the doctor she stayed in bed for the 9 months of her pregnancy. In the meantime in autumn Uncle Franz (Aunt Helen's husband) bought a site in the Wind-flower

/Kökörcsin/ Street (Nr. 18.), not far from our flat and employed construction workers to build a house on it.

Into the one storey house four flats were planned, two bigger and two smaller ones and in the half cellar a flat for the caretaker. The house was quickly finished. Uncle Franz offered us the big flat on the ground floor. I remember we had a look at it. It was a three-room flat with a small half room, a living room and a small garden behind the house. It would have been ideal for us, but only 50 Pengős separated us from moving there, because they couldn't agree on the price. Uncle Franz didn't want to reduce the price; father didn't want to spend more on the rent than the lodging allowance he received from the state. Probably the future of our family would have been different if we had lived in the Wind-flower-street flat.

1935

Aunt Kate moved into our neighborhood in the autumn, into a one room bachelor flat in the Nicholas Horthy-street 86. The window of her room opened to the Magyarádi-street opposite our flat, so we could easily communicate with each other. Besides teaching at school she also had a private student, a native French girl, who was as old as me. She was called Krisztian Mantel. Her parents and two Aunts had moved from France, because her father took the job of the French teacher at the Polytechnic in Budapest. Also their flat was near the University on the Budafoki-street.

Aunt Kate taught her to write, read and count in Hungarian, so that after a year she could start in Hungarian school. Krisztian had a stiff shoulder and round back. The doctor prescribed her to do therapeutic physical exercises that were held in the Baross-street clinic. Aunt Kate recommended me to use this possibility as well; because I was excused from physical education lessons. We also went there with mother, where we met and became good friends, I with Krisztian, mother with her mum, where we met three times a week from 5 to 7 p.m. The French were very good humored and while we were doing our exercises the mothers had very good time. For the summer we departed, while Krisztian with her parents traveled back to France to the relatives. As for us, the whole family traveled to Verecke, and my brother Thomas came with us for the first time.

On the Beszkid, by the pass with my parents and brothers

Uncle Charles found a new job for me, because he thought that I was already a trustworthy big girl. When there were lots of things to do in the pharmacy, I could work as an assistant many in the laboratory behind the pharmacy; I mixed and put i.e. ointments into small wooden boxes or weighed painkiller powders and put each dose into paper bags, etc. This was a serious work for me that I had to do accurately and scrupulously, but for me it was also great joy, because I was

allowed to walk in the pharmacy in a white jacket. In the meantime I didn't forget about the blood-suckers, which we bathed regularly with Ann also this time.

Every weekend we made some kind of excursion. We went into the Verecke-pass, where in the pine wood beside the road we sat down on the small green and drank the delicious milk-coffee made of beans, and ate cocoa cakes and apple pie. When my brothers were playing hare and hounds, I went into the woods and lying on my back I looked up to the blue sky in between the 5-7 meters, or even higher tree branches, where a vociferous hawk flew by or an eagle was sailing gracefully in the air. After this everything became silent, the world seemed to be dead, only the silent whispering of the fragrant pine trees could be heard in the kiss of the breeze. In this time I soaked up so many wonders that they were enough for the whole next year.

The three Lápossy children in the Verecke garden: Susanna, Géza and Thomas

If we ascended to the Verecke-pass, I could admire the flying of the eagles even better as they were soaring above on the wings of the wind. Since also I had an aquiline nose, I felt somehow being in relationship with them and with sad heart I watched how freely they could fly wherever they wanted to. The relationship feeling I extended also to the American Indians! I read the buck-books one after the other and I was happy to get to know that their most important bird was the eagle!

In the second part of the summer we visited Aunt Helen. At that time I noticed that she was pregnant. Father came with us to look after my two brothers and take them on excursions. In the mornings we sat at Aunt Helen's bed in turns with mother. We diverted and read to her and chatted with her. We could probably turn her attention away from the gloom that the death of her daughter caused. She lay in bed the whole day long; only in the afternoon she was helped out into the garden into the fresh air. She was still wearing black clothes and her face was very sad. Not long after our holiday at their place, on the 4th of October 1935, her daughter Judith was born. She was a beautiful brown haired, brown eyed vigorous small girl, to whom I became the godmother. Little Judith became such a nice and good-natured girl, who quickly healed her mother from her gloom and Aunt Helen could laugh again!

In the school-years of 1935-36 I began the third class at grammar school. We started beside German (that I learned from first class of the grammar school) also French, which was taught by a nice young nun, Sister Geraldine. That's why the whole class studied French with pleasure. So that my pronunciation should be better, I took French lessons twice a week at the Aunt of my French friend to learn and speak the language better.

During my years at grammar school I had two very good friends: Sarah Kuncz and Martha Piacsek. They lived not far from us so we visited each other regularly; especially they came to us, because in our new flat I had a separate room where we could undisturbed and whisper amongst ourselves, just like teenagers do!

1936

In springtime Aunt Helen and the family moved to Akli again, where previously they used to live (their first son had died there). Uncle Franz as agronomist was responsible for a 10 hectare big apple garden of the Cistercian catholic order and the cold store there. Such delicious Jonathan, Starking, Golden and Goldred apples I haven't tasted since that time! I remember that little Judith didn't really eat anything else for years only apple and milk. She grew into a beautiful healthy small girl with nice skin,.

This summer we traveled to Balatonszemes again and Uncle Charles came with us. My parents rented a whole villa, which was called "the Garden Home" not far from the beach and the railway station. We took also the maid with us. In this well planned house it was comfortable for all of us. I continued my friendship with Babi and Mici from "the Cat House". We went playing tennis, swimming and boating, so we enjoyed the pleasant warm summer. Sometimes the water of the Lake was as warm as around 26-28 °C, as if it had fully warmed up.

On 25th of August we celebrated the 50th birthday of my father. I remember we went into the village flower shop and Uncle Charles had beautiful rococo bouquets made for all three children and found verses that we learned and recited for father, who was very happy to receive them. After the happy celebration in the evening, something happened which we did not understand at the time. Father showed his hand to mother and Uncle Charles as it was shaking a bit. Uncle Charles knew straight away what it was all about, but didn't say a word to him.

Some days later we traveled home and father - with Uncle Charles's help- went to a famous nerve specialist (Prof. Völgyessy), who diagnosed the beginning Parkinson disease in father, which was the consequence of his serious Spanish Flue of 1917-18. He gave him a medicine called Belladonna for the problem that retarded the complete development of this illness. For years the treatment worked well; father could go on working, so our hope was strengthened. Only mother knew how serious illness it was, because her father suffered from the same illness during the last six years of his life. I saw my grandfather, when I was 6 years old and we spent our summer holidays in Italian-village. He was just sitting in an armchair and his head, hands and feet were shaking. Aunt Helen fed him like a little child. For me it was so awful to see it at that age! Father fought heroically against this disease and looked as if he could stop it temporarily with his great willpower.

In the years 1936-37 I attended the fourth class of the grammar school and we had to decide whether I go on studying in the grammar school or begin the newly founded schoolmistress college, also housed in the same building of the Margaret order. Uncle Charles insisted on the first solution, saying that only after 8 years of grammar school I could graduate at the College of Pharmacology and so I inherit his pharmacy. The idea of the schoolmistress college was backed by Aunt Kate, who said that after graduating, within 5 years I could start working as teacher.

After these my parents decided that I should go to study in the schoolmistress college because of the illness of my father and the fact that I needed to get a job as soon as possible. Naturally they asked me, as well. I chose the schoolmistress college on emotional grounds, because from the fifth year of the grammar school a nun called Rutilla, would have been our class teacher. She taught us the subject needlework and I and many of my classmates did not really like. That's why many of us left grammar school, which we later didn't regret at all. We chose well, because our teacher was expected to be a nice middle aged nun experienced in teaching, Sister Frieda. She taught us economy and household studies. We learned how to spend the household money wisely, to cook and bake, which we could practice in the laboratory-kitchen of the institution. Later we happily ate what we cooked.

The whole class liked Sister Frieda very much. We were all cheered up by her good-mood and unending optimism, even if sometimes we were sweltering because of studying. She led our class for three years and always backed and fought for us like a lioness, even under the most troubled circumstances. After three years the director of the institution took her out of teaching in college and employed her as the hostess of the institution, who received the guests of high standing and looked after them.

In the 4th and 5th classes a silent and hard, but good-hearted woman taught us: nun Ilmenda. We soon got to like her. At the end of the school-years 1936-37 I said farewell to the first four years of the grammar school.

So did my brother Géza, who finished the first four years of the primary school. My father made him enter the Military Secondary School in Sopron. Father would have liked to be an officer when he was young, but it was not possible for family reasons, so he saw his lost dreams coming true in his son. Also the boisterous nature of my brother needed some kind of strict boarding school, because mother could not "handle" him. Finally he liked the military secondary school that he began in the autumn of 1937.

1937

We were still at the summer of 1937. The train was taking us towards Verecke and offered for us five those many wonderful summer experiences. We got off the train in Volóc, where I liked to arrive so very much.

Because it was already a family of five people we could hardly get into the taxi, which was sent for us and we had also suitcases. Uncle Charles didn't come to meet us, but at the usual place in the evening in front of the lighted pharmacy he waited for us in his white jacket. We, the three children were hanging on his neck, so that he could hardly keep on hold us up.

Uncle Charles told us the great news at supper, that he had opened another chemist's shop in Volóc. Some days later we also had a look at it. In a new house behind the railway station the pharmacy and the flat of the chemist could be found. Mr. Szász, the dispenser with whom we made friends quickly showed us the different rooms. We visited the town Volóc as well, which was surrounded by high mountains, from which timber was extracted and transported by train to the Schöhnborn estate and into the furniture plant.

Coming back from Volóc and on top of a smaller hill between Volóc and Verecke Uncle Charles made the taxi stop, we got out and Uncle Charles told us the following story.

"One winter day the whole region, the Mountains and woods dressed in snow-white clothes. I was younger and did not use a taxi, because there wasn't any in the village at all, so I traveled on a cart with the coachman to the Volóc railway station. There I collected the medicines ordered from Prague. We put the parcels on the sleigh. On the neck of the horses there were bells, the sound of which nearly rang us to sleep. The sun was about to set when we reached the top of the hill. Suddenly a bumping woke me up. Scared we saw that the horses, frightened by something, had reared up and pushed the sleigh backwards. The coachman mutely pointed towards the woods, where motionless dark shadows with what looked like sparkling eyes were sitting side by side.

These are wolves! - came to my mind, but I didn't say it aloud because of the scared coachman. Silently and calmly I asked him just take firm hold of the horses and give them the command to run. He did so and the horses started to sprint! Looking back to the shadows, they appeared every time to be more distant, and did not move. Only when we finally came down from the hill into the valley and the lights of the houses in the village lighted the snowy street before us we could speak a word. I told the coachman that our trip was successful, because we didn't have to throw the medicine parcels to the wolves!

After this story we sat back into the taxi quite scared. Because for me, Budapest children such things were unimaginable.

This summer we went to Munkács to visit Aunt Helen, who lived in a flat roofed, modern, one storey house without a family, she had only two little dogs. Aunt Kate spent the summer holidays at her.

There in Munkács Uncle Charles bought me a camera that I tried right away. After that I took lots of photos, which were developed by Uncle Charles. In the summer Géza and I learned to shoot with the Flaubert air-gun. Uncle Charles thought that Buster shouldn't go back to the military school without any shooting knowledge.

The school year of 1937-38 brought us lots of news.
Brother Géza was taken to the Military School in Sopron. I missed him very much for a long time. His absence was made only stronger with the fact that I also "lost" two of my dear friends. Sarah Kuncz went on studying in the grammar school, that's why our friendship was weakened,. Martha Piacsek moved to town Debrecen, because her father was placed there as agronomist He was entrusted with the rearing of the Hungarian grey cattle. She continued her studies in village Putnok. We said farewell to each other with sad heart and I felt myself very lonely.

With such feelings I arrived at the entrance of the Margaret Institution, few minutes before 8 o'clock. I found my room for the first class on the first floor. I always arrived at that time during the five years of my study! Reaching the classroom I met a very nice, bronze red haired, tall girl, who also was about to enter, which we did after one another. There was a free place only in the first desk of the middle row.

The red hair girl gave me a sign to sit there. We introduced ourselves, her name was Louise Hazay. From the first minute at the first sight she looked like a girl I would get on with. As I later found out, she thought the same about me. Not long later the head of the class, nun Frieda entered the room. She read the nominal roll and had a look at us and later started to decide the place where each one of us should sit. We both, Louise and I, should have sat in the last desk of the side row beside the window. We were sitting there during the five years of our study, side by side. There and at this time a strong lifelong friendship began it and still endures.

I remember that in the desk in front of us sat two girls, who every day came over from the "Orphan Home" in the Ménesi street, run by the Merciful Sisters (white hat nuns). We became quickly good friends, matched each other well. While Louise and Sarah were good-humored, happy natured and talkative girls, Gabi and I were the calm, quiet and sometimes too sober-minded ones.

As an experienced teacher sister Frieda read us the home order and afterwards she told the good news that for the girls attending College thick brown tights were not compulsory any more. They were allowed to wear also brown silk tights, because they study and prepare for "LIFE". But the other items of uniform compulsory, such as the hat made of deep blue fabric, like the rock, which was a bit military-like with the badge of the Institution and for feast days it was decorated with osprey. We from the College set our hat at an angle so as to look nicer, preparing for the above mentioned "LIFE".

Sister Frieda let us furthermore know at college there will not be any extra subjects, all would count as major subjects, such as drawing, music, physical education and also needlework. At the end of every year, when we finished studying a certain subject we took a final exam in it, that was written on our diploma. The teachers gave us a lot to read, write and draw. Only German could be studied, French no more!

She wished us to have hard strength and diligence for the awful amount of lessons to be learned. At home I told mother all these and she and I decided to give up piano and French lessons and concentrate only on studying. I finished physiotherapy, because at College I took part in normal physical education lessons. Krisztian's Aunt, my French teacher, although sorry. Not so Dame Helen, my piano teacher, who fell nearly in despair, because as she said, she would not soon have such a talented student as I was, so for a long time she tried to convince mother that I should continue. Now I regret having given up extra piano lessons. I met lots of new challenges at College.

Louise lived on the Round Square in the Nicholas Horthy-street 60, on the high ground floor with her parents and her younger brother in a one and a half room flat with a hall. Her father worked as a customs officer. He was a sober and peaceful, but good-humored man. Her mum was a very nice, happy woman with doll-like face, who could sing beautifully. They also had a piano, where Louise played the current favorite numbers and we sang them together. We both were important members of the school choir singing mezzo-soprano and such students were always in short supply.

The Gyárfás cinema was also in their building (nowadays called Béla Bartók cinema), at that time it was also called the Simplon-cinema. Louise could always get some pictures about the actual films, actors and we went to watch the films together, but strictly only with the permission of the college. We also had to ask permission later, when we went to dance, naturally only with chaperone. One student who was frequently found in public places without permission was expelled from the institution. The nuns educated us according to very strict moral values that helped us the whole life long. I think on them gratefully!

1938

We also spent this summer in Verecke. Brother Géza had lot to tell Uncle Charles and us about the military school and he happily relaxed. He received a small camera from his favorite uncle and during the excursions we raced to take photos of the beautiful landscape, the family and each other.

As a big girl, I received a cook-book from Uncle Charles, who said that it was the right time for me to learn how to cook. I supplied the family with sweets and cakes, three times a week I could choose anything I wanted to cook and received the necessary ingredients. Naturally I was a beginner in cooking, so I made sweet scrambled eggs, which the family tried to eat after lunch, laughing. But on the 14th of August, my name-day, I made a real fancy-cake. It was a rose color very delicious high punch tart for twelve persons. The edible dyes and spices I got from the pharmacy. With this masterpiece I earned the appreciation of Uncle Charles, my parents and my two brothers!

So that this summer should not be without annoyance, now I write down the thing as happened. One day after noon, when the pharmacy was closed we went to the cooperative shop on the main square with Uncle Charles, where he bought salami. Returning home we visited Rozen Moricz, his favorite merchant, where he asked something and as usual they told some jokes and after that we left the place happily. Coming out of the cool shop, the heat before storm summer hit my breast out in the dusty street. Uncle Charles talked to me, but I only heard it very faintly and in the end nothing. I fainted! I came to myself in a cool and tidy room and saw a kind face old man with long white beard and ringlet, a Jew patriarch in black caftan leaning towards me as if he came out of the Bible. In that moment I thought I was already in Jerusalem with Jesus! After that I noticed the voice of Uncle Charles and that of the doctor, who gave me an injection into the vein telling me that I should still rest for half an hour and after that I could go home. At home they told me what a shock I caused with my collapse.

When returning home on the street Uncle Charles talked to me and he felt that was talking to the wind and after turning back he saw that I was lying on the dust as if dead. Then he realized that I had fainted. He was extremely frightened and ran to me. The patriarch standing in the gate and seeing what happened offered his help and house, which I was taken into and put on the bed in the clean room while they called the doctor. Till that time I was unconscious. As I have already written, the things happened later I can already recall and also the doctor giving me injection. The level of blood-sugar fell, said the doctor. Then I had to drink something and rest for another half an hour in the cool room by the open window, which led to the garden full of beautiful flowers, the perfume of which was also let into the room. After this problem, which fortunately ended well, our summer holiday went on normally.

I found a good number of old magazines in the bottom of the book-case called "Theatre life", collected over the years. I made a great fun of cutting out the photos and biographies of my favorite actors, actresses and I made an album of them at home in Budapest. Such actresses were Greta Garbo, Diana Durbin, Shirley Temple and other famous actors of that time. My album was a real success in the class and others followed suit. My friend Louise was constantly besieged to get photos from the display window of the Simplon cinema.

In 1938 the Below Carpathian region was given back to Hungary under the 1st Vienna Decision. The joy in our family was enormous, because there wasn't a Czech border in town

Sátoraljaújhely any more so we could travel to Volóc and Verecke freely!

The school-year of 1938-39 started silently. Brother Géza and his whole school year were transferred to another town, from Sopron to town Kőszeg, where he ended his primary school years. In the second year of collegiate school we had already decided which subjects would be our favorites. My favorites were as follows: math, physics, geography, botany, psychology (we made a small final exam at the end of the year), pedagogy, history of pedagogy, drawing, music, and housekeeping-economy.

This autumn, because we approached the age of 16, what most interested us was dancing. Louise was our dance teacher; the "dance-hall" was the end of the corridor before the lavatory. All who wanted to learn to dance met there in the breaks. In front of the door we appointed a watcher who told us if danger was around. Louise learned the popular dances from her brother and gave her knowledge over to us: waltz, English waltz, foxtrot, slow-fox and tango. There were also smoking girls, - but we were not interested in it-, who sang the tunes of the actual numbers to the dances. I learned to dance here so well that I could use my knowledge later in parties and balls very well.

At the Christmas of 1938 Uncle Charles came to us, he eagerly asked what kind of present we would like to get. After short thinking I wished to get silk tights and a roll of "winter salami" saying that "teenagers are always hungry!" Christmas evening I noticed happily the salami on the tree and the wonderful smoke-color real silk tights and my last doll, Lencsi, a popular one of that time (Uncle Charles's idea). Mother gave me fabric for my first ball-dress, plum blue taffeta-silk material and also an invitation card to the New Year's Eve ball of my cousin. She was two years older than me and studied at College by the Margaret Order, was the grandchild of my mother's maternal aunt, Judith Vagács (Lulu). Her father was a furrier and had a shop in the Margaret Boulevard, which was demolished by the bombs of WW II. In addition he was a painter, whose beautiful paintings decorated the walls of our flat.

From the silk ball-dress material we had a dress made by Dame Sápi, who lived in the next building, where Aunt Kate also did. She lived and worked in the half-cellar of the house. In the next room her husband had a carpenter workshop. She was a fantastic woman who never studied sewing, and was a real talent. With the tape-measure around her neck she measured the material and cut it without using a cutting pattern. She created such beautiful and elegant dresses, costumes, coats that no one wanted to believe that it wasn't made in a city centre Váci-street, posh mode salon and didn't cost an arm and a leg. Also the long plum-blue ball-dress was a success with its only decoration, a light rose color small apple-flower bunch. In this dress I danced during my first New Year's Eve ball party. There were naturally also delicious and picturesque beautiful cold cuts, jellies and tarts, which was a gastronomic pleasure for the numerous teenagers. Of course this happened naturally under maternal supervision.

Now I write an extremely interesting case down from the end of the 1920s. As mentioned above, the parents of my niece Lulu had a fur shop where umbrellas were also made. The iron casting used for the umbrella was brought to them from the forge every week by a teenager apprentice, Johnny. He was a silent, nice and punctual boy, so my Aunt and the whole family liked him very much. They gave him double tip and sometimes clothes, because he was very poor. Some years later he became Prime Minister János Kádár. My aunt Magdalene liked his speeches, saying that also Uncle John grew up in county Somogy in Kapoly, just like the Ékes girls did!

/János Kádár was the communist leader of Hungary from 1956 to 1988. He served twice as Prime Minister after the crushing of the 1956 revolution from 1956 to 1958 and again from 1961 to 1965.-editor/

1939

In the beginning of March one evening, my mother was coming home from theatre alone because father couldn't accompany her due to the constant shaking of his body. Stepping down from the tram at the Lenke-square she was taken ill. Luckily the adult son of our neighbor who had traveled on the same tram noticed it, jumped up and helped her home.

Our doctor was quickly called who diagnosed heart failure and gave restorative injections. But mother's condition did not want. So the doctor called a heart specialist, Dr. Mózer and they talked over the case. All night long were the doctors at our place and gave mother one injection after the other.

I was praying on my knees all night, father came in frequently, just hugged me and started to cry. I had never seen him crying before, so this time I understood without words that there was a big problem!

Around dawn mother got a little better and as a result of the sedative her heart became normal. Dr. Mózer recommended mother's complete examination in the newly built Nicholas Horthy Hospital (actually Andrew Bajcsy-Zsilinszky Hospital), where he was the chief doctor of the medicine section.

In the morning mother called her good friend Mrs. Susanna Popper, our child-doctor, who after taking a glance at the empty injection carriers clapped her hands together and told her laughing: "Irma, if your heart could take all these medicines of opposite effects, it is as strong as that of an elephant. It has not got any severe problems. Don't worry, you won't die of it!" How right she was, because mother lived till the age of 95 with God's help!

Next day she went into hospital. She was examined for two weeks, but nothing could be found, all results were negative. We visited her with father; I remember our 15th of March visit. That day was holiday from school, at 9 o'clock in the morning we had a mass celebration in the institution, where we all arrived in silk blouse and skirt without cloak as it was good weather. When at 11 o'clock we left the building there was a snow storm that swept me home, where I arrived to nearly frozen and of purple color. I quickly drank hot tea and took a bath. Visiting mother in the afternoon I was already wearing winter coat, a hat and boots and I told her my previous adventure with the spring.

There used to be sudden changes in the weather also earlier, not just nowadays! This summer my parents decided that only father and my two brothers would travel to Verecke, mother and I should stay in Budapest, because she didn't dare to spend the summer holiday there because she felt ill quite frequently .

This summer was very happy and good for me. With the permission of our mothers Louise and I started to take tennis lessons on the Lágymányos tennis court beside the Bottomless Lake. In the tennis club we were students of the same teacher, although I could already play. We organized our day perfectly. In the morning mother stayed in bed on the doctor's advice, at 10 o'clock I met Louise in the club and went to play tennis on the court. After the tennis lesson we went into the club again where Louise started playing her favorite song-hits on the piano, which made the teenagers who were there, including me, start to dance. The boys started to pay court to us and we chose the nicest ones of them. First were the "old boys" as Stephen Sz. for Louise and Gabriel B. for me, who also became our tennis partners.

At noon Louise and I said farewell to each other till our afternoon meeting. On my way home I did the shopping and bought meat, cucumber and fruit. At home mother had already cooked the potato and as soon as I got home I fried the meat and laid the table. During lunch I told mother my successes, afterwards I had a little rest and at 4 p.m. I met Louise again either at their place or in the club and evaluated the boys.

After 5 o'clock when the sun was not shining so hot, we played tennis again and after some weeks we could do it quite well. After 7 p.m. we were highly engaged in playing the piano, singing and dancing. At that time we talked also to younger boys, e.g. Eugene, who became my faithful and very good dance partner.

Sometimes the mothers also came to the club to chat and have fun, or we went to the City Park, the English Park, to have dinner in the Alpine Village where we could also dance with the faithful Stephen and Eugene.

When we were without escort, we strictly had to arrive home by 9 p.m. In the evening Aunt Kate came over to us, whom I told the occurrences of the day.

When father arrived home with my brothers, they took me down to Italian-village for 3 weeks so that also I could breathe fresh village air for a while. Aunt Helen waited for us happily and showed us little Andreas, born about a year earlier. My brothers could play well with Judith, who was already around the age of 4. I could talk to Aunt Helen openly about things that bigger girls are interested in. Interestingly she was less formal than mother and I could talk to her openly about everything also later.

My favorite place in Akli was the back part of the 10 acre big apple garden where there was only high grass, the birds and me. I took a rest there when I had had enough of the children, sunbathed or read a good book or wrote into my diary. I felt as if I was at the end of world on the smooth grass bed; looking up to the blue sky and the snow-white drifts, where only the silent chirping of birds and the sunshine breaking though the tree-branches could find me.

We returned to Budapest on the last day of August where the usual city smell and noise waited for us. It was very good to be in the city again after the long period of silence.

In the school-year of 1939-40 I started my third year at college. I had much more to learn and write, but despite all these we continued to play tennis with Louise in the autumn.

For the winter the tennis court was converted into a skating rink, where the summer company met again.

This winter we started to visit one another for parties, and went also to relatives and other friends from 5 to 8-9 p.m., usually in the week-ends. There were also tea-parties at our place. We played on the piano, danced or played board games and had great fun eating delicious sandwiches, cakes and drinking tea. Every girl brought her mother and also the cavalier, who took her home in the evening.

We gave Mrs. Sápi, our dressmaker an enormous amount of work to do. She prepared nice dresses for mother and me following my designs and drawings. These were generally short dresses. I remember mother's organ blue color, light wool ensemble with a thin gold belt or my red stand-up collar Russian-type wool dress in which we felt ourselves very elegant and made a hit.

1940

Now I am going to tell you what my favorite dresses looked like, all were the creation of Mrs. Sápi. Mother and I bought the fabrics in the Kálvin-square superb textile shop (Székely and Lipsicz). We could order the quality and color of the material and always found a piece that was nice-looking and suitable for us. The service was very polite and we got always easy terms if we bought more.

For spring mother bought coffee-brown light weave fabric for a dress and a warm corn-yellow textile for jacket, which she wore with other skirts as well. I chose a light blue texture for myself and a dark blue material for a jacket to it. Laer we went to the department store of Nagykovácsi Milenko in the Louis Kossuth Street, where we bought shoes matching the colors of the fabrics. I remember mother bought herself a pair of brown, high heeled shoes, and for me a pair of dark blue, middle height shoes and a red closed sandal with flat sole and a red and white envelope-like flat handbag. These were already things for older girls!

Milenko Nagykovácsi organized his customer service very well. He offered the possibility of paying on easy terms for his customers, who traded regularly. He gave us a small booklet, where the total amount of the goods bought and the monthly sum to be paid were written down. We could buy anything in any amount and only the amount of repayment changed. It was a sure income for the merchant and was also good for the customer, because it wasn't necessary to pay the whole amount at once. New sections were always opened in the department store, such as: textile, shoe, china and toy departments. The store had quite a large turnover.

Let's return to the dresses, which I designed from the trendy dresses that I saw in the Diana Durbin films. From the light blue textile I have a dress made, the fore upper part of which had vertical capillary stitching that followed in a skirt opening from the knee made of narrow stripes. The dress had short sleeves and its only decoration was a pocket onto which my monogram was embroidered with red and dark blue thread. What I liked very much was my dark blue jacket with the red handbag, the red sandals with blue socks which were really a Diana Durbin-like, sports loving style. I combed my hair into loose waves falling onto my shoulder and parted in the middle, just like Diana had at my age, in the films Louise and I watched in the cinema.

In the springtime Louise and I studied a lot together, preparing for the small diploma at the end of the year. We both had excellent results. We said farewell to nun Frieda at that time. She stayed in the Institution, although not as a teacher but in a higher position.

My mother's health problems of became ever more frequent, so she went into hospital. Father and we children traveled to Verecke for a month. We had lots of trips, took lots of photos, bathed and also fished, because we liked the boneless trout very much. I have never eaten such delicious fish. I also learned how to prepare it and although I was quite happy to fry it I didn't like cleaning it first. After Verecke we traveled to Akli for a month, where mother joined us.

With the three children and lots of luggage she didn't want to change trains, so we traveled from the Southern Railway Station in Budapest to Kádárta, where a two-horse chaise sent for us by uncle Franz was already there waiting. The whip, Uncle Valentine in beautifully decorated pelisse and the two white, wonderful Lipicza horses took us home on the long winding track in the forest. Mother with my two brothers sat in the back, I was beside Uncle Valentine in the front. He told us exciting stories about the vast forests of the Bakony hills. He said that in the old days from there highwaymen (betyárs) had attacked the defenseless chaises, stage-coaches passing by unexpectedly quick and stuck its passengers up. It was said that they didn't harm anyone who gave up their valuables without a fight, they took "only "the money and jewels. Then left on their lightning-quick running horses. Uncle Valentine also told me that not far from Akli there was a spot, a highwayman hiding-place, that he knew and could show me; I just had to ask permission from the "boss", Uncle Franz.

It was a long way home and Uncle Valentine still had numerous exciting stories to tell. For example in snowy, cold nights it was not advisable to travel neither on chaise, nor on sleigh. In the old days horses and sometimes even people fell prey to wolves. After these stories I was eagerly waiting to arrive, because in the meantime it was already dark and in the back mother and my two brothers were sleeping.

This summer I acted as a detective, because I always came up against the mysterious past, which excited my fantasy.
I convinced Uncle Franz that the next Saturday afternoon we should have a look at the hiding-place of the highwaymen. We

four Uncle Franz, Uncle Valentine, brother Géza and me took the road to Bakonybél. We also took a telescope. After some miles the chaise stopped at the edge of the forest and Uncle Valentine stayed there with the horses and we three walked into the woods. After walking about ten minutes we discovered a huge, deep hole. On Uncle Franz's command we crawled to the brim of the hole and looking down we could see the vertical cliff on this and the on other side. Uncle Franz said that we could be in as high a place as the Gellért-hill in Budapest and asked us to have a look at the cliff wall opposite to us where at the bottom some cave-like holes could be seen. The outcasts hid and lived there in the old days, where no-one, not police or any other people dared to descend. Only the birds were flying above that ravine. This was a very exciting and interesting sight for us. On the way home we constantly asked questions from Uncle Franz and Uncle Valentine.

At home, when we told Aunt Helen our fantastic experiences she told us if we were so very much interested in such stories, she could tell us even more fantastic ones. We eagerly waited the next day when the promise should have been fulfilled. Akli heath could be found around 14 kilometers from Zirc north of the Lake Balaton, beside the road leading to Bakonybél. The site belonged to the Cistercian Order of Zirc until WWII.

On the left side of the road, on a slope stood a smaller, one-storey residence with agricultural buildings, surrounded by a tall stone fence. Behind the castle the 10 acre big apple garden could be found and a small cold store. When we were there, we could also see a beautiful flower garden. This building used to serve as a holiday house for the monks.

Aunt Helen and her family lived there, on the ground-floor of the L-shaped house, in lodging. In the smaller part of the L shape corridor could Uncle Franz's office, the kitchen, the pantry, a separate room for the maid be found. In front of it was a big hall, where in the evenings the workers of the farm were always waiting to give Uncle Franz an account of what work they had completed.

In the longer part of the L shape dark corridor, from which the rooms opened, first the living room, the dining-room, the salon, bedroom, bathroom and one for the guests. From the end of the corridor opened a small chapel, the inner entrance of which Aunt Helen had walled up afterwards. One could enter only from the courtyard. Every Sunday and feast day a priest, a monk from Zirc held a mass celebration in the morning. I had to describe this in detail, because only after all this could brother Géza and I understand the following legendary story, which Aunt Helen told us.

In the old days, around 1848 the "red monks" lived in the building, but that time it still didn't have a chapel. It was a bit further away on top of a hill. There are only fields there right now and no building, but the stones from the wall, cups and bowls that the deep plough brought to light all prove that the chapel was there. The pieces found could now be seen in the Zirc Abbey Museum. Reputedly between the distant chapel and the building there was a tunnel.

We three, Aunt Helen, brother Géza and I ascended upstairs. There empty rooms with stuccos, wonderfully ornamented tile stoves and nice tiled floors could be seen. From there we went up to the attic, where she showed us in the grounds a deep hole covered with an armful of reeds. We saw that between the ground- and the first floor there was a narrow platform, where a ladder could be put straight into the hole, which I could clearly imagine. What could be there down in the bottom, how deep would it be and where could it lead to? To answer these exciting questions I made an "investigation plan" and for the implementation I received Aunt Helen's permission on the condition, that I would neither do it on my own, nor tell Uncle Franz a word.

First I needed helpers, who didn't live in Akli and could stay silent. I had good luck. At the beginning of our holiday I got to know a nice brother and sister, who spent the summer in the other end of Akli, at the relative of an agricultural worker. The girl was the same age as me, her brother was three years older and this summer started to help count the quantity of the harvest. Their father worked in the Ganz MÁVAG Works as gang boss. I got to know Judith and Stephen through Aunt Helen's cook. I elected them to be my helpers, and they happily took part in the project. First of all we looked for a long ladder and a powerful electric torch.

**In the apple garden
of Akli, 1941**

We three started to puzzle out the mystery and we told our plans only to Aunt Helen. We helped Steve and passed him up the ladder to the attic, which put the ladder down to the platform. When he descended on the ladder, he illuminated the bottom with the torch and saw that there was an earthed floor. He threw down a burning sheet of paper so that we should know whether there was enough oxygen there or not? Fortunately the paper was burning slowly, so there was air there. After that I descended down the ladder to the platform and let first the ladder down to the bottom, on which again Steve went down first. From the bottom he reported what he saw.

The tunnel became a bit wider, but one could get in there only stooping or kneeling, because it was built very small. One of its sides was walled up with bricks and as we knocked it, it gave a hollow sound. Here could be the beginning of that tunnel in the story!

We helped Judith come down, so we three, side by side on our knees knocked the bricks. We heard the emptiness from the other side and made up frightening stories about bones and treasures! I made them swear not to tell this very exciting and interesting story to anyone in the village. Anyway some days later they traveled home. Aunt Helen and I kept on talking about the tunnel that we discovered.

-Let's open the way out! - I suggested enthusiastically.

-No way! - Aunt Helen said frightened. - Don't think that as a layman you can start to do such wrecking!? You need skilled workers and archaeologists for that!

So we agreed on that and let the matter rest.

Aunt Helen also told me why she had the door to the chapel at the end of the corridor walled up. While the entrance to the chapel was open her cooks regularly left after a short time, till one day a new girl Therese explains the mystery. She said that the people of the region were very suspicious and at night the girls heard strange voices and thought that the spirits of the red monks haunted that house. To her mind after erecting the wall the whole thing disappeared, although she said not to be suspicious.

Her younger sister, Anne also worked there with the poultry or tidying up. In the afternoons, when she had finished work, we went out into the threshing-floor with my two brothers. We climbed to the top of the haystack and were sliding down till that time when brother Géza disappeared in between the haystacks and nearly suffocated, so we had to get him out as quickly as possible. Naturally at home we didn't boast about the event.

Every Sunday morning Uncle Franz had to travel to Zirc to give account to the agricultural manager, a priest, on the state of the estate of the catholic Order. He took also us quite often. We took our cameras and while he was questioned by the priests, we were walked in the huge garden of the Abbey and taking photos. It was a real English Garden with lawn, different kinds and shapes of leafy trees, shrubs and bushes, pine trees. I saw there for the first time in my life squatter pine tree and a long vista of lime trees, where the blooming branches on both sides of the road leaned on the other one. Their perfume was so strong that nearly knocked us silly. We saw the monks, who were praying the Brevarium in the mornings and in the evenings and walking up and down.

Coming out of the Abbey, we went to the market, where Uncle Franz told the coachman to put huge watermelons into the cart. We were eagerly waiting to eat from the honey-sweet melons after the delicious Sunday lunch.

We had a very good time as usual this summer but again it passed very quickly, only the photos commemorate it.

In the years 1940-41 we got a new teacher as class-teacher, nun Ilmenda. Also our teaching practice at school began, so we had to prepare many long and detailed curriculums written in handwriting, with tiny characters. We started also new subjects beside the old ones, such as constitutional sciences, economy etc.

This year I gave up skating and sold my skates, because I was always cold on the skating-rink. Instead I asked for a warm winter coat that was made to my design by Mrs. Sápi. It was a light grey, fashionable lined with squirrel fur collar with a belt. It was as warm as a stove.

In January, February of 1941 we were invited to the Balls of the Judges and Prosecutors, of the Doctors and of the Engineers. The last two were held in the rooms of the Gellért Hotel. I went there with mother, Louise, the boys and other friends. Mrs. Sápi, my dressmaker again did her best. She sewed me a beautiful turquoise thin silk dress to my design, which had a Greek style, puckered top with a long rock that is a ball-dress with an apple flower decoration. Mother got a long black dress and a gold stapled jacket.
We were invited o the Ball of the Judges and Prosecutors through my father. Some years ago he was nominated to be the Major Hungarian Crown Lawyer.

Eugene B., who was a cadet and came with me as dance partner, looked very impressive in his white aviator uniform beside my turquoise dress. Our good dancing made every other pair stop dancing finally, so in the middle of the room only we two were dancing. Eugene was a brown haired handsome boy as tall as me. (He was reminiscent to Alain Delon in his shape and his tough personality.) The band was playing only for us and we were dancing tango, waltz and English waltz. This ball was a wonderful and memorable one for me; we received lots of applause as if we were professional dancers.

Also Louise looked very smart in her cyclamen color dress and the black jacket embroidered with Matyó motifs. We were the best both for our knowledge of dancing and our dresses. One of my cousins, Stephen B. (Pubi) always came with us to the balls. His mother was a cousin of my mother from his mother's side; she was 100 years old in 2000. At the balls we were never without a dance partner and also the mothers had a very good time. Mother, Louise and the mother of Krisztian loved to chat and watch the whirling of the young people dressed in colorful ball-dresses, sometimes till day break.

1941

Magyarádi Street, where we lived in the Nr. 40, was later named as Ulá*szló-street. The entrance of the house opened from a short dead end called Tengerszem Street, which after 1945 was called Bucharest Street. So without moving we lived in four streets.

In 1939 the engineer Miklós /Nicholas/ Balassa and his family moved into the 3 room flat on the first floor beside us. His wife Maria became a very good friend of mother. She was a nice, tall, blond woman for me, who at that time I didn't dare to call by her first name. They had a daughter Pötyi and a son Muki, who were the playmates of my brother Tom. They were the same age and became good friends and often came to us to play.

/ In the meantime World War II broke out with the German invasion of Poland in 1939. It was a global military conflict, between two opposing military alliances: the Allies and the Axis powers. Over 60 million people, the majority of them civilians, were killed, making it the deadliest conflict in human history.-Wikipedia/

The Easter of 1941 arrived.
To our greatest horror on Easter Sunday morning sounded the air-raid alarm at that time and not long afterwards the Serb planes arrived to bomb Budapest for "the first and luckily for the last time, as well". They dropped 2 or 3 bombs, but our air defense brushed them off. There was enormous panic. The air defense commander of our house and the neighborhood quickly organized the watch of the gate and closed it. The watches changed every two hours day and night. I was listed to be on duty Easter Monday from 2 to 4 pm. At that moment I understood that there was war indeed, although it had already been on for years.

I was standing behind the closed gate. It could already be around 3 p.m., when tall, good shaped, brown haired young man appeared in soldier uniform and asked me with friendly smile to let him enter. Later it was cleared that he wanted to visit the Balassa family, so I let him come in. We both had a thorough look at each other! For both of us this was the real "First great encounter!" (For which we can thank the Serbs!)

At four p.m. I gave the quarters over to the next watch.

At home I asked mother excited who that young man could have been, visiting the Balassa family. She couldn't give me a reply. In the afternoon Pötyi and Muki came over to us to play with my brother Thomas. At 7 o'clock in the evening the bell rang, I opened the door and saw the young man standing in front of me in soldier uniform. I nearly fainted when he introduced himself: Lajos /Louis/ Diósy. He was the younger brother of Maria and came for the children. In the meantime he also asked me in behalf of Maria, whether they could come over to us after dinner to chat a little? Being shocked I could hardly say a word, but in the end said "Yes, of course you are welcome!"

It was a sudden attack indeed! My Louis, whom the family called "Buster" later told me, that he caught the fancy of me so much at once, that he didn't want to hesitate, but wanted to get me know right away. At nine o'clock p.m. Maria and "He" came to us. The first meeting was so successful, that they left only at midnight.

My parents also liked Louis "Buster" very much. It turned out that he was a reserve Sergeant and from autumn he would be taking in a 6 months re-training in the Budapest Lehel Square police station. (Now his daughter Susan in employed there as meteorologist, 59 years later.) It's fantastic! Can't be accidental! (It is the providence of God!)

Buster was to live in Maria's flat and commuted to the military base from their place. During these two weeks he took part in re-training. His parents lived in Szekszárd and he received the draft call from Pécs as reserve soldier at the division for coachmen and cavalryman. He finished the Agricultural Academy at Keszthely in 1940, but afterwards he was constantly a soldier with the SAS draft. As long as he was in Budapest, every evening came to fetch the children, sometimes with Maria. In the meantime Maria persuaded me to call her by first name so as not to make her seem older. I could hardly get used to it. As it turned out for me, he had also another sister Martha, whose husband was a railway engineer. Previously he had transferred to a new workplace in Budapest-Kelenföld. They had a nice official flat in the railway station. Their son Ivan was the same age as my brother Thomas, who started the primary school in 1939. The two weeks passed quickly and Buster had to return to Pécs. I was very sad!

Strange, but very good feelings arose in my heart that I had never felt before concerning any boy I've ever met. "Could this be love?" We will see!

At the end of April I became fevered, but had no pains at all. Despite the fact that I didn't have a cough the local doctor diagnosed pneumonia. My fever increased more and more and I got worse all the time. My mother called our previous child-doctor, Dr. Joseph Lukas, who was by that time already the chief doctor of the St. Stephen Hospital. He had me to be transported into the hospital, although I was already 18. I got a separate room. He examined me and stated that I had general sepsis. He gave me a blood-transfusion on the spot with mother's blood. This was repeated twice.

I was in hospital for a month. Also the Louis' mother visited me, together with Maria. I got to know her at that time. She was a lovely woman, who told me that Louis was worried about and wished me good health. When I was allowed to go home it was nearly the end of the school-year. I realized that I lagged behind with the studying very much. For two further weeks I was convalescing from this illness and tried to make up for the subjects. Mother and I studied together; she asked me the different topics. But when at the end of the year I went back to the Institution one of our teachers, who taught geography, history, constitutional and economic sciences didn't want to give me the final mark saying that I had been absent for such a long time. Mother didn't let it happen. She went to the director and asked that in the director's presence the teacher should set a separate exam for me, because I knew the material thoroughly. This all happened!

With the permission and on the order of the director I got my grade card. The above mentioned teacher, nun Hildegard in the 5th year was down on me, because she did not get her way.

After these excitements I felt our trip to Verecke as liberation. Uncle Charles was eagerly waiting for us and tried to strengthen my weak body with the -then fashionable- Deér-pills, which made my appetite stronger.

This summer was full of new adventures as well. Uncle Charles wanted to please us, so he ordered the equipment for a tennis court for brother Géza and me- that is a net, rackets and balls- at his favorite merchant, Rozen Moritz. Furthermore he asked the director of the Verecke Agricultural School to covert the yard into a hard tennis court. The director happily did so, because in the summer from the mother country "young hopefuls" arrived to the school, which was operating as a hostel. They were 17-18 years old young boys, whose father were in the military.

Playing tennis was a good summer program. The court was perfectly equipped, the rackets and balls arrived from Prague so my brother; I and the boys played serious matches every day.

At the Verecke tennis-court with (Brother Géza and his friend in the background)

Uncle Charles rented also bicycles for us so as not to walk that much. I remember to have learned ride the bike on a grassy tennis court quite quickly. My brother already knew how to ride so he ran after me and held my bicycle.

Among the boys there was one, Mike Sz., who wanted to go on studying jurisprudence and started to seriously pay court to me, I could hardly stop him. He was a very good tennis player, who lived in town Kecskemét. In the autumn he wrote me some long letters to Budapest but didn't receive any reply, so this "romance" quickly faded.

I was already drawn to someone else! It was Louis Buster, who the whole summer long was occupied with military things. We exchanged some postcards and waited for the autumn when he was allowed to come to Budapest.

This rich Verecke holiday ended in the middle of August so my brothers and I were strengthened in soul and body, when we returned home and looked forward to the new school-year of 1941-42.

In the hospital at spring I was advised to have my teeth examined by a specialist, because that could probably be the cause of the sepsis that affected me. So at the end of August a friend of Aunt Kate- a patient of Professor Dr. Mathias in the Clinic of Stomatology, arranged an appointment for me. The professor was an old, small built, sprite-like, good-humored man who, when he saw the x-ray of my teeth, told me, despite being only 18; half of my upper denture must be extracted. As he said my teeth were "swimming in crappy" that could cause lots of problems, such as heart inflammation or arthritis among others.

He called his favorite young doctor dr. Leslie Papp right away and they spoke about the future of my teeth. They extracted 7 teeth in twos and threes. At the bottom by every root there were huge inflammations. This was the cause of my sprig time fever and illness! It took the wounds 6-8 weeks to heal and only after that could the doctor take a cast and have a fixed prosthesis be made. He sent me to his dental technician who lived in the Andrássy Street. He showed me into a huge salon; where in one corner a dentist chair could be seen. The other parts of the room were full of Persian carpets and antique furniture. I thought to myself that my new denture would surely cost a fortune!

The technician had a look at my teeth and took a sheet of paper to make a drawing of them and he started to color it using black, red, blue, yellow colored pencils. I asked frightened: My tooth is going to look like that? Laughing he replied that there's no need to be afraid, because these colors are really there in my old teeth. (My son George who became dental technician or "dental sculptor" confirmed this, saying that the material of the porcelain teeth has to be colored that way so as to seem real.)

I received seven wonderful fixed porcelain jacket crowns in time for Christmas, which looked like the original ones! Till that time I had lots of problems without my teeth. For example my Louis started the military training in Budapest in September and he came over to us every afternoon or evening. At first I always shielded my mouth, but it was a satisfaction to get to know, that despite this sorrowful fact he wasn't disappointed in me, moreover he thought it very nice that I was lisping. He also helped me doing my homework that is he read me long texts so as to be able to write them down. In the meantime we also took walks or danced at home to the music of the gramophone. He could dance very well. We decided that after Christmas, when I had already received my new teeth that we would go out dancing together.

We agreed to communicate using dots and dashes in the evenings. We were sleeping on either side of a common wall that was between the salon of the Balassa family and my room Until I got to know Louis, I couldn't imagine what happened sometimes in the salon of the Balassa family. I heard that in the silence cards were hit against the table or sudden sharp shouting followed and then again silence.

Louis (above in the middle) with his family

This all became clear to me when Maria told me that they often held bridge-parties. At Christmas I got to know the other sister of Louis, Martha. She was the complete antipode of Maria, who was nearly as tall as Louis, 178-180 centimeters (Louis was 184). Martha was a smaller built, petite, beautiful brown hair, good-natured woman just like a porcelain doll. Her husband was Géza Fokvári, an extremely good humored man, the cousin of Nicholas Balassa. There was always happiness at their place.

We often went out to Maria's favorite dance hall, the Bellevue hall, where there was music and one could dance. It could be found in the Buda side of the city at the foot of the castle near the Margaret-bridge. The cost of my teeth was 1,200 Pengős and naturally we went out, when my teeth "grew out" again. The cost of my teeth was an enormous amount of money at that time!

When Transylvania was re-attached to Hungary in the autumn of 1941, brother Géza was reassigned to continue the upper classes of his military school in Marosvásárhely. At Christmas he couldn't stop praising that nice place and the wonderful Transylvanian landscapes!

1942

As we felt that there would not be too much time for us to be together, we used every minute in January and February as long as his re-training lasted and at the weekends we went to balls to the Gellért Hotel or had dinner with Maria. We fell in love so very much that at the end of February when he had to return to Pécs and became an ensign, we started to correspond.

In the 5th year of the college we studied a lot with Louise, whom I didn't care about when Louis was there. But also she and my friend Krisztian came with us into the balls. My turquoise color ball-dress was altered by Mrs. Sápi to my design. She put wide pieces onto the upper part and a square neck so that it should look new. Louise wore an apricot color dress. Naturally our mothers always came with us. When we were about to leave for a ball, father always hauled us over the coals that at such wartime it is not right to go out dancing.

Mother tried to defend me saying that Susan can't help it that she is right now 17 or 18 years old. But yes we did have yes bad conscience! Then there was also the Lenten tide of these happy cakes and ale!

With Louise in the ball of Lawyers and Prosecutors in 1942

In the meantime the war raged on and on, but we didn't want to take any notice of it at all, although Louis wrote to me, saying that presumably he would be sent out to the Russian front.

Their flat was at the railway station as I've already mentioned. Maria was also there and we were looking forward to meeting their brother.

At one p.m. the train arrived. As always he stepped down from the wagon smiling and ran to us. I saw only him in the crowd of civilians and soldiers. He was so very young and handsome! In a short time we had to say farewell.   His sisters brought him delicious home made meals.

Later the sign for departure sounded. We promised to write to each other, if possible every day. I received his last kiss on the cheeks and then he disappeared inside the wagon. The train left the platforms of the railway station haltingly sad and slow as if it had the feeling that not. Not much later I received his sad telegram saying that on the 1st of May some wagons full of soldiers would arrive to the Budapest-Kelenföld Railway Station. Quite early, at 10 o'clock we arrived to Martha's place. Unfortunately not many of the soldiers would ever be brought back alive!

   This was the most upsetting May 1st of my life!
It was full springtime around us and we all three were crying on each other's shoulder.

   But life still carried on and also my 5th school-year! We were all preparing for taking common farewell to the school on the 10th of May for which our college year was about to perform the show. The text, music was directed by our class, naturally organized by Louise. I remember, Louise and I acted the role of "two old women" with a plastic parrot and a cat on our shoulders. It began at 12 o'clock and lasted for 2 hours.

The stage could be found in the front of the Institution, beside the columns. There was such a crowd in and outside the walls and also on the Villányi-street that not even "a nail could be thrown onto the ground". We had great success and the nuns seemed to be pleased and our play remained memorable for a long time. In the evening we held a march with torches around the St. Emery statue group on the Round Square. The crowd was as big as it used to be for the Easter time procession. Even the traffic stopped for a while. After the celebration we got one month free time out of school, when we had to prepare for the final exam that was quite difficult and detailed in every subject. We had to chose a theme and show our knowledge known on that topic.

Louise and I divided the topics between us and made a daily schedule. Early in the morning from 5 to 7 we studied at home, from 7 to 8 took a shower and had breakfast from 8 to 10 studying again, at 10 o'clock I went to their place, where on the flat roof-terrace there was also a shower and we went on studying and our sunbathing costumes. We talked the different topics over and asked each other questions on them and also had something to eat. So we discovered the importance of the "workplace breakfast". After that I returned home for two hours, we both had our lunch at home then a short siesta followed so we could go on studying with renewed strength.

At 7 p.m. we met in the tennis club and if there was nobody we could play as relaxation, chatted or tuned. I gave up dancing, saying to me that until my Louis was in the front I wouldn't dance, go to cinema, or go out, but live like a nun. This decision was also backed by Louise, who acted very understandingly and comfortingly in my very sad situation. That is why we were really good friends just because we agreed about most things.

The oral and written final exams were very successful for both of us. At the end of June 1942 we received our diploma and bade farewell to each other, the classroom and the Institution. Our future was in the shadow of the war not at all cloudless! During that time I also received the first card from my Louis from the military camp with the number of the camp stamped on it, but only a short message saying that he "is all right" and can write only cards due to censoring, but I could write more detailed letters about everything, which he eagerly waited for!

So I started the biggest correspondence of my life, first every day, later three times a week, which custom I strictly kept up while he served on the front. Later he told me, that these letters kept him alive! He knew and felt that I was waiting for him!

In the beginning of July we traveled to Verecke again, although father's shaking was getting worse, as well his left hand his head was also shaking a little, but he did want to come with us, as if he had felt, that this could be the last opportunity to see his birthplace and the house where he was born, but we didn't know that at that time. Uncle Charles organized lots of excursions for us and we visited every beloved and for us important place. Our first trip led to Szkotárszka to see the viaducts again, the railway lines and the tunnel, where also Louis left our country in May on the military train. We visited also the Verecke-pass and Volóc, wonderful places, which we were already taking farewell to in our hearts.

Uncle Charles also chose a new place to visit, which was the Szinevár Lake. In comparison to Verecke, it was a long way to go. Early in the morning we left Szolyva towards Ökörmező that was already in county Máramaros. Behind Ökörmező the taxi took us up to the top of a 1200 meter high hill. Descending from there we found the Szinevár Lake in the middle of a wonderful pine wood. The water of the lake was crystal clear, cold and deep. In the middle of it there was an island with a meadow. On one side of the lake there was a wooden hunting-box. Some people were in it, who told that last week important guests had been there, Nicholas Horthy and his escort.

Brother Géza and I took lots of photos of the wonderful landscape all around the lake. They were so successful that Uncle Charles enlarged them and made so many copies that nearly the whole lake could be "surrounded" with them.

Returning home in the afternoon we stopped at the top of a high mountain, where we stepped out of the taxi. Father showed us at the border of Máramaros County, the Lápos Mountain and told that also the Lápos River had its source there. Flowing further in the north of Szolnok- Doboka County it flows into the Szamos river. Beside the river could be seen the great villages Oláh-Lápos as far as the plain Magyar-Lápos. Father had already been there once before; because he was looking for his ancestors by the law, when every civil servant had to prove his Christian origin in Hungary. He told us that the Lápossy family derived from there and moved later to Munkács, where his grandfather became the chief doctor of the town. His father John Lápossy then moved to Verecke as a chemist. Here he had their house built.

The family used to have the additional name of Magyarlápossy Lápossy that was later left off. (On the 31st of 01. 2000 there was an enormous cyanide contamination in the waters of the rivers Lápos and Szamos Rivers in Rumania.) Father told us also the storey of his Lápossy grandfather as follows: "He worked and lived in Munkács as a follower of the reformed church. He became widow twice, also had children from his previous marriages, members of the reformed church as well. At the age of 63 he married a 23 years old nice young girl who was a catholic. To indulge her he turned to Catholicism when his son John was born. When the little boy was 6 years old, my grandfather on a cold winter day got cold and in a sudden inflammation of the lungs he died. John my father (the authoress' grandfather) was brought up without a father. Later he went to study in the pharmaceutical Collegiate School in Kolozsvár. From there my grandfather moved to Verecke to be a chemist and because he already followed the catholic religion, his children Géza, Charles and Kate also took that religion. "

Uncle Charles didn't like that at all. He considered himself to be an original Calvinist! At the end the family lost its other members of the reformed church.

On the terrace of our Ulászló-street flat

Let's stay with our ancestors. Father explained that at the end of the 1600s two brothers arrived from Switzerland to study at the Collegiate School of Nagyenyed. They both married

Hungarian girls and settled down in Transylvania. They changed their names to sound Hungarian from Lohrberer to Borostyányi.

My father's maternal grandfather Adalbert Borostyányi lived in Munkács. His daughter Helen married from there to Verecke, first to Béla Szabó the postmaster, who died young of tuberculosis. From this marriage he had two children Helen and Béla. (I myself knew Aunt Helen.) My widowed grandmother married again later, to John Lápossy chemist. So Helen Borostyányi became the mother of my father. As Aunt Kate told me, her mother was a very rigorous woman, so she as a small child always took refuge at her father's side if she had some problems. He used to be kind and benign. Father inherited hardness and self-control from his mother and I inherited them from father as well as the great necessity for justice. From Uncle Charles I got the love of freedom, from Aunt Kate my pedagogic sense.

My talent for arts I inherited from mother (for instance in drawing I always had the best marks), also the love of music and dancing. From all my ancestors I inherited my unfaltering uprightness and passed these on further also to my children! After WWII mother heard once about a beloved and popular district doctor in Mezőtúr, Dr. Lápossy. Mother wrote him a letter and he replied very kindly and let her know that he stemmed from the second marriage of Uncle Lápossy from Munkács indeed and was already quite old. He moved to Mezőtúr quite young and lived there his whole life long.

They exchanged some letters, but some years later she received the notification of his death. I know that the whole Lápossy family is up in heaven whatever their religion and praise the Lord. I get sometimes inspiration from them how to go on writing my story.

Returning to our journey, on the 20th of August we were again about to go to the Verecke pass, when the radio had a sudden break in the actual broadcast and the dawn aircraft accident of prime minister Nicholas Horthy was announced. We nearly collapsed, but despite that started to ascend the hill. In the taxi this was the only theme. The taxi driver Mr. Burech said that surely the Germans had done it and they want to make him frightened, because he acted quite liberally with the Jews. "But if something happened to the old man, what could happen than to us? "- asked he. Poor Mr. Burech, as if he had felt his fate in advance!

In 1942 after receiving my
diploma, as a serious teacher

We visited the cemetery and all felt in the silence that we took the last farewell to our dead members of the family, to the house, Ann, Verecke, the Beszkids, to the odor of the alpine fir woods and that of the flowers in the garden. Still a little of that odor was saved and transferred to Budapest with a bunch of flowers.

September of 1942 arrived. True I was a bit afraid to work at that time as a teacher and I also ran out of time. Aunt Kate had me enrolled into an after school instruction course for teachers. In this Margaret Baber helped. She worked as typist beside the chief officer of the Educational Division of the Capital. The course began on 15th of September in the Wesselényi-street Elementary School and taught us typing and shorthand writing. We had lectures three times a week in the afternoons from 3 to 7 o'clock, two hours shorthand writing, the other two hours typing. The course lasted for a year and we received also a certificate in the end. I liked attending those lessons and could later use my knowledge very well. (In my old age I still do so.)

The Christmas of 1942 Uncle Charles spent with us in Budapest. He spent a long time with father discussing the course of the war and the possible future.

1943

In the beginning of January frightening news arrived from the Russian front. In the middle of January the withdrawal of the German and Hungarian troops began. It was hell for the soldiers in the minus 30-40 degrees Celsius cold weather (about -20 Fahrenheit).

We had not received a word from Louis since long.

I remember it was Easter Holiday again. Maria and I went to seven churches and to the holy tomb and asked God with strong faith to help Louis to come home safe and sound. After Easter the second husband of Martha, Charles Massányi, who worked in the MÁVAG Factory as a bridge constructing engineer told me that one of his engineer colleges was looking for a secretary and asked if I would like to work with him? Yes, the course had already finished and I only had to take an exam- I replied. I went to the MÁVAG and applied for the job and I got it.

I started working on 17th of April 1943 with Ivan Binder, three rooms away from Charles Massányi. I was suddenly thrown into the "deep water", because besides corresponding in Hungarian, I also had to type letters in German. I later heard that there were some secretaries before me, who were not able to do the job because none of them could read the handwriting of engineer Binder. As a matter of fact he wrote his letters down at home and the next day brought them into the factory and left us with them. In the afternoon he came back to sign the letters.

At first I needed a whole day until I could decipher and find the key to his unreadable writing, but in the end I succeeded, so his usually hard look started to soften and we could work together very efficiently. In the end I also received a praise from him although not directly, but through Charles.

On 1st of Mai we received happy news from Louis saying that on the 5th the soldier train would arrive at 12 o'clock to the Kelenföld railway station.

I remember that at 10 o'clock Maria called me on the phone at my workplace telling me to ask for a little time off to and go to the railway station. I rushed quickly there and I just got there in time. The train arrived slowly and very tired and thin, but still unhurt soldiers stepped down and my Louis was among them!

The great happiness that his sisters and I felt can't be described we felt. We hugged the very thin, but healthy Louis after his one year long absence and the great trials he went through. By God's grace I received my Louis back as a present for my 20th birthday. He became a real man at the age of 23 in "the hell of the war".

Some days later he traveled to town Szekszárd to visit his parents and later came back to Maria and me, because he got a month leave. During the time he spent in Budapest he came to fetch me from the MÁVAG Factory every afternoon, so that after work we could spend every minute together. He had lots of dreadful stories to tell, which happened to him during that one year.

He began his sad and shocking stories with the time when the trains full of soldiers left Volóc at the beginning of May 1942. The soldiers in summer uniforms traveled through the viaducts and the Szkotárszka tunnel /which we used to visit/ and traveling east they arrived at an unknown town. They organized their new camp so that everyone could find his right place. There were lots of people under the direction of Louis, whose job was to support the soldiers fighting in the front line with food and other necessities.

They spent one or two weeks at the same camp (on his first card the number of the first camp could be read). They also marched forward because they followed the front line. Luckily they never were in the front line!

Every soldier asked for pullovers from home because they had only summer uniforms, not winter ones. Louis asked his mother to send him pullovers. For the icy cold he wanted some winter hats, ankle and joint warmers as well. In addition he received my detailed life saving letters four, five of them at the same time.

Once, having arrived at a place they saw the ruins of a huge building that used to serve as a Hungarian store-house, where the winter uniforms were kept. Louis with his soldiers saved as many heavy blankets and coats as they could. They took some for themselves and the rest they sent to the front together with food, as long as they had some. The most horrible thing was that the rest of the house burned down with the winter uniforms unfortunately so the Hungarian soldiers fighting on the front could never wear them. Lots of disastrous negligence happened on the Russian front concerning the weapons, so no wonder that nearly the whole 2nd Hungarian Army was destroyed! Most of the soldiers without guns in summer uniforms suffered hero's death or were frozen.

/The Don River tragedy of the Second Hungarian Army happened between the days of January 12-15 1943. From the 200.000 Hungarian soldiers 120.000 died in the icy cold Russian winter.- editor/

In the middle of August the 23 years old Louis- he was born in Pálfa on 16.08.1919- had his first great shock, when one dawn a cart was drawn into their camp full of dead German soldiers. The interpreter said: the Russian partisans killed the German soldiers at night in the woods and send the message to the Hungarians to retreat or otherwise they could end up the same way!

Louis's troop got 10-12 Russian prisoners of war, about whom it was not clear whether they were spies or partisans. Anyway Louis treated them kindly. They got the same food as the Hungarian soldiers. After a while they also helped getting food, because the re-supply stopped. Moreover once as they were ascending a hill Louis and his group, behind them German soldiers, and suddenly tra...tra...tra, machine gun fire could be heard. All the Germans were shot down, but not even one Hungarian. It couldn't be accidental!

The prisoners of war stayed with them in the retreat as far as the Hungarian border. They would have liked to come over to Hungary, but the Russian border guards didn't allow them to do and then it came to light that they were partisans. But anyway their presence was some kind of safety for Louis and his soldiers.

At the beginning of October suddenly the cold Russian winter began. The moving of the fronts stopped and was disabled due to the extraordinary cold and snowy winter of 1942-43.

In the middle of January 1943 also the official Hungarian and German retreat began, which could be worse than death.

My Louis thought back with horror on the soldiers and recalled those, who were frozen like ice and became "statues on horse". During the retreat the soldiers on horses became ice statues. So Louis and his group didn't ride, but kept on walking, because anyone who sat down to have a 5 minute rest or fell down exhausted to the ground could stand up no more because they froze to death. Enormous numbers of unburied dead could be seen on their way home, but the thought that they walked towards home gave them such a great strength that they reached Volóc alive, where they were put into quarantine for three weeks and were disinfected.

Before traveling home he visited Uncle Charles in Verecke. He couldn't recognize him at first, because he was so thin and looked very bad, but afterwards he fed him every good food and supplied him. After this he didn't wonder at all that I talked about Verecke with such great enthusiasm as my second if not first home and Uncle Charles as my second father.

Louis's leave from the army ended at the beginning of June and because he wasn't discharged, he had to return to the military base.

In the meantime in Budapest the air-raids happened ever more frequently from the Americans and the British. It meant that at any time the air-raid warning could sound. We took quickly our small bags which only had room for our documents, underclothes, some food and ran down to the air-raid shelter, which was the cellar. Many times we sat there for 2 to 3 hours, frightened and in complete silence, although some were praying aloud or to them till the warning ended. Sometimes it happened also that we could only spend a half an hour upstairs in our flat before the alarm signal sounded again and everything began from the very beginning. Healthy, young people could hardly do it, but my father couldn't at all. By that time also his right hand was strongly and constantly shaking and he needed help in pulling his clothes on and when walking.

That's why mother with father and my brother traveled to Akli at the end of June.

We agreed on that also I would also ask time off from work and travel after them. Until that time Aunt Kate came over to our place and lived there so that I would not be alone. I remember in the evenings we always had to put black papers on the window. It was regulated by decree.

Budapest looked quite frightening in the complete darkness, just like a dead city. I mentioned Charles M. the possibility of taking my holiday time, but he said that we were a war factory, holidays couldn't be taken! Neither he liked the idea of me leaving my job.

In July I experienced twice dreadful bombings from the Americans directly against the MÁVAG factory, when we were inside, which was dangerously frightening. The architects and the secretaries went on working in a very massive air-raid shelter in the deep. During that time the bombs were tearing the buildings of the factory into pieces above us, and the earth was moving beneath just like in times of earthquakes. Also my great big patience started to fade. When mother heard about the bombing of the factory on the radio, she immediately wrote an express letter to me, expressing that the state of father was getting ever worse and because of father's fears for me. She sent the doctor's letter so that I could leave the factory.

At my workplace my reason could be accepted just because I was a "worker on contract", otherwise I couldn't have left that place, because ours was a war factory. My boss, Mr. Binder regretted my leaving- because he couldn't easily find such a secretary, who could read his unreadable handwriting- but he could understand the reason. I myself regretted leaving my workplace very much, because I liked working there. I left the MÁVAG Factory on the 15th of August 1943.

Two days later when I was in Akli and I saw the American military planes flying above us; but still the Trans-Danube region was to some extent "peaceful".

During that time Louis and I were corresponding. He was in service at the military base. At the end of September we met once or twice in Budapest together with my friend Martha

Piacsek and made excursions to Margaret Island, where photos were taken. Later my son Peter made a drawing from that photo as a gift.

A dear memory from one of our dates on the Margaret Island in 1943

At the end of September we all traveled to Budapest in the car of the Zirc abbot of the Castercian order.

From 1943 father couldn't go to work any more and his state was getting worse beyond recovery, so he advised me to apply for work in the Agricultural Department, where he had good contacts. I did it and was waiting for the reply!

In the middle of August one day Louis's sister Maria popped over to us to tell that their parents invited me to visit them for the weekend! This visit turned out to be quite embarrassing and unusual, that's why I describe it in detail. We three, that is Maria, her husband Nicholas Balassa and I departed at 4 p.m. on a slow train to town Szekszárd. We had a separate compartment, because there were very few passengers on the train. Nicholas as always told us jokes and we were laughing. As it was already Autumn it quickly became dark and because of the war the train could not use lights.

So that our journey shouldn't be boring, we started to sing Hungarian national songs, also song hits, during which I breathed so much the cold air, that when we arrived at 8 o'clock to Szekszárd, where Louis was already waiting for us, instead of a loud and cheerful greeting I could only smile and whisper something, just like a mute child. Because of singing and the cold air my voice disappeared and I could only whisper. Maria and Nicolas didn't have any problems concerning their voice.

You can imagine how embarrassed I was when Louis introduced me to his father, I already knew his mother by that time. Maria explained laughing what a good journey we had, only my vocal cords couldn't do it any longer. We had a very delicious dinner. My Louis was sitting close to me and acted as an interpreter, because I whispered him the answers to the many questions that his parents asked of me. Before going to bed I got warm milk with honey in it, which did me good, because next day I could talk normally. Next morning we went into the town, popped into the church, drank a cup of delicious coffee and visited some of his acquaintances.

With Louise at the ball of Lawyers and Prosecutors in 1943

After the wonderful Sunday lunch we said farewell to his parents and traveled back, we three to Budapest, but my Louis went to town Pécs, so we traveled on the same line until Dombóvár. On the overcrowded train we couldn't do anything else, just try to stand on our feet. Despite of my great silence, our trip was well blessed, because we didn't get any air-raids.

Maria's children were taught German by Frieda Kosch, who lived in our house on the second floor with her elderly mother, whom I knew by sight.

One day in the beginning of November she rang the bell and offered us a nice round cheese to buy, saying that Maria had also bought one. Cheese was of greater value than gold at that time, because of the lack of food during the poverty stricken wartime.

In mother's absence I took the cheese and promised to take its price up to them in the evening. Later to my ringing an elderly, small-built man opened the door and introduced himself as Alfred Kosch, Frieda's brother and led me to her mother. I got to know at that time, that also he also lived there and had often seen me previously, but I had never seen him.

He said that he worked at the Győri Textile Works as a textile engineer and the factory provided the workers different kinds of food, such as cheese, geese, geese-liver etc., at wholesale price. For a long time these products had not been sold in normal commercial trade. (Cheese has been my favorite food since that time.)

In our chat I told him that I was without work. Although I had applied for a job in the Agricultural Department I have not yet received any reply. Then he offered me his help in getting a job in the Győri Textile Works, where good secretaries were needed in the billing department. He thought that I should not be unemployed until I receive a reply from the other place, because he had heard about father's bad illness. We agreed that I would ask my parents and if that was all right, I meet him in his office.

The offer seemed to be seductive for several reasons: first more money could be earned than in the MÁVAG factory, also because of the food, while everyday people couldn't get such delicacies, moreover for such a low price. The plants of production could be found in Győr and only the factory buildings were in Budapest in a side street opposite the Bazilika /*a famous downtown catholic church*-editor/. So the place was not as dangerous as the MÁVAG factory.

With the permission of my parents I applied for a job in the billing department of the Győri Textile Works, where I was employed on the 1st of December 1943.

My direct boss was nice middle aged woman, who had no husband and always did yoga exercises i.e. stood on his head in her office, while we were away to have our lunch. The bills were typed by we three young girls. In this work I had already experience, so we made a race of who is able to type immaculately the most bills during 8 hours. Naturally we were the ones who invented this race so as not to be bored by the constant bill typing. They were pleased with my work so a month later also I got textiles as present, just like the old workers and I also got food, that we naturally paid for.

Louis had two weeks leave.
He visited us with Maria and Nicolas and proposed marriage to me in the presence of my father. He replied that he was happy to say yes, but would not accept it without reservation. The engagement should be without rings and he would only allow us to be married only after the end of the war.

On the second day of Christmas we held the engagement lunch where instead of rings my Louis gave me a wonderful amber necklace, a bracelet and a brooch. Aunt Kate was also present and told me the following quite suspiciously. It didn't mean good at all to have an engagement or marriage at Christmas. It does not bring good luck. I was not suspicious at all, but this sentence could have lived in me later and unluckily happened so.

I received from him a wonderful, blood-red azalea basket for the holidays, which ornamented my room for months. For New Year's Eve Maria invited us together with Martha and a great company for a celebration. We happily and joyfully spent our time as an engaged couple. After the holidays Louis had to leave for the Pécs military base as a soldier and disappeared from my life for decades, which I could not even suspect at that time.

1944

The grey weekdays started for me, because of the work and of the more frequent air-raids. The American planes arrived mostly on Sunday mornings. I eagerly waited for Louis's comforting letters, which were very much delayed. Not even Maria had any news about him. Only the red azalea bunch made me remember of our engagement.

Maria was embarrassed by the deep silence of Louis, but his mother said that he is constantly in service and would not be discharged, could only rarely go home for some hours, but he was OK.

In the beginning of January 1944 Alfred Kosch received a military draft as a reserve lieutenant of the mechanized troops and −as we later learned- he was ordered for wood yielding in county Máramaros /actually in Rumania/. He worked there for three months and later as he already passed the age of 42- , because he was born in Szászrégen on 13.04.1902., - he was discharged.

During that time there was war not only outside, but also in our souls, especially in mine. I was in complete doubt concerning Louis. In the middle of February I received the first vital sign from him on a card, stamped in Fadd /county Tolna/

where he wrote that he was all right, ridden a lot on the horse and sent kisses. There was no address on it so I didn't know where to reply to. I showed Maria the card and also she was taken aback, that a fiancé could only write such trivial things to his beloved one after such a long silence?

The negative feelings rose in my heart and I asked myself: what kind of husband would he be like if he acted this way as a fiancé? After great struggles in my soul it troubled to me very much to write the last farewell letter and sent it to his home in Szekszárd. In it I mentioned that I had given the amber jewels to Maria. My decision hit Maria painfully. She couldn't understand as his sister, but she did as a woman.

My parents didn't want to influence me to any side and just saw my struggle. In the end they resigned themselves to the possibility that probably this way I could set my heart at rest, because everyone is the builder of their own fortune. I received no reply to my letter, just a big parcel in March with the name of his mother as sender, which I opened with doubtful feelings. All my letters sent to the front were in it with some sentences that put me in the wrong and also questioned my previous feelings. Now as I am older I can partly understand the feelings of Louis's mother of that time, who defended her only son as a mother lion, but when I was young, I could not at all do so!

This way the gate, which previously opened to the road leading towards Louis was eternally shut. At any rate I thought so at that time!

On the 18th of March at night we were roused by a dead, steady uniform lumbering. Mother and I quickly ran to the terrace door and opened it a little, but didn't dare to go out. Also father wanted to listen to the sound better, so we helped him to the door. He stated with his "war experienced ear", that this noise from the Danube could only be made by a multitude of trucks.

Next day we got to know exasperated and unhappy, that on 19th of March 1944 Hungary was invaded by the German troops! Father was right, because the German Lorries were rolling the whole night long on the wharf of the Danube.

The bombings occurred more often. Moreover the Russians also took part in it, mostly at night. It became more and more difficult to help father when walking down into the air raid shelter. We eagerly waited for the end of Brother Thomas's school-year, when they- father, mother and Tom- could travel down to Akli. About brother Géza we had only the news that the whole armor cadet school had fled westwards from Marosvásárhely.

In the meantime Kosch came home from the lower Carpathian region, was discharged and started working in the Győri Textile Works again, where he became the chief engineer of the technical department. He got to know from his sister Frieda that I had broken my engagement. After that he often waited for me often after work and we left the factory together, got on the tram Nr. 49, because we lived in the same house, he took me home. His act was not suspicious at first, because also earlier I had "elderly admirers" on the tennis court, and probably he had such a commanding presence, which I didn't want to confess neither to myself.

In January 1944 father was pensioned off. I received a reply from the Agricultural Department, that they would employ me, but when I went in, it turned out that they would pay much less, than the Győri Textile and there was no possibility of getting food, so I stayed at my present work. This way the job in the Agricultural Department was superseded. My salary was good supplement to father's pension!

In the middle of June my parents and Brother Thomas traveled down to Akli, I stayed in Budapest and went on working in the Győri Textile Works, which was not so dangerous. Aunt Kate came over to live at our place again; sometimes we used to run down on the stairs into the air-raid shelter at nights, when the American planes arrived to bomb us. There Aunt Kate got to know the family Kosch and invited Alfred to visit us. That's why I had quarrels with her, because Louis still lived in the depth of my heart and I was waiting for his words, explaining his long silence. But no more letters I have received!

The connections were completely broken with Maria and Martha's fleeing westwards and that of their husbands' workplace and colleagues from before the approaching Russian troops.

Kosch paid a visit one evening at our place, bringing a wonderful bunch of flowers. Aunt Kate liked Alfred very much, they could chat well. After that time Alfred popped in quite often. The afternoon walks home was longer every time, interposing long walks on the old Elisabeth Bridge. From his side the paying court to me had already begun! The void in my heart he could slowly fill with his great attention, interesting and gripping stories, and life experiences.

He told me later, that they had been the first to move into the house in 1928. We moved there in 1934- when I was 11 years old- grew up before his eyes and when I had become bigger he liked me very much. Aunt Kate's constant digging, "what a good partner" Alfred would be for me and his unceasing making court had its effect, because at the end of August we both traveled down to Akli for the proposal and engagement.

The proposal happened as follows. Father didn't let Alfred come before him, alluding to his severe disease. I knew that it was the sign that he didn't want me to marry an elderly man. Mother mediated between father and Alfred. At the end he sent the message that if I really wanted to be Alfred's wife, then it could be. He wouldn't stand in our way.

This scene was very upsetting for all of us, especially for Aunt Helen and Uncle Franz. Despite everything the next day we held the engagement lunch, where Aunt Helen did her best and put wonderful courses on the table.

The three Ékes sisters in the 1970s (from the right) mother, Magdalene and Aunt Helen

I received a gold ring with a diamond in it for the engagement. (I had to exchange it after the war with Russian soldiers for flour and peas, etc.)

At home Aunt Kate, Alfred's mother and his sisters were very happy of our engagement. After this the events moved quickly. Alfred had a very big family, so we were constantly on the way to visit someone.

His eldest sister was Helen (60 years old). She had her third husband, Eugene Schmitter architect. They lived with their son Eugene (University student) in their Attila-street flat. Helen's first two husbands died. From her first marriage she had a daughter Gertrud, from the second had a son Sigismund. His elder brother, Görgényi (Kosch) Arthur (56) was the chief chemist of the Chinoin Pharmaceutical Works. He lived in the Szondy-street with his wife Vera, son Astrid (25) and daughter Angel (22). His sister Mrs. Emőkey, Clotilda (55) was a widow and lived in the Géza-street with her son Franz lieutenant. His sister Elsa (53) married John Urai mill-owner, brother of Theodore Urai actor. With their son John (15) and daughter Erika (12) lived in the Harmath-street. His brother Ernest (50) was a chemist. His sister Frieda (45) was an unmarried German teacher who lived with her mother Regina Wagner (widow, 80 years old) and Alfred in the Admiral-street. His sister Hildegard (37) lived with her husband Leslie Oláh major in the Irinyi-street by the Round-square.

In age she was the nearest to me, her husband was a distant relative of mother, so a good relation with them formed out quickly. They became also the witnesses at our wedding.

Alfred liked his brothers and sisters very much and they liked him. That's why I was also accepted fondly among them. I felt as if I was their child or grandchild. Alfred looked quite young despite his 42 years of age, did exercises, regularly went to swim, didn't smoke, nor drank alcohol. He had only just started to go bald and was one centimeter smaller than me. He always wore nice clothes; his appearance was always perfect! Above all he loved me very much, encompassed me with his care and attention. He was also liked because of his good nature in the Győri Textile Works.

After work we had long walks, which ended up with a good dinner in a restaurant. He found a flat near to my parents in the Fadrusz-street 12. The two rooms and hall flat were mostly furnished by Alfred, in very good taste. The furniture of my childhood-room also found its place there. During the whole September and October we were occupied with furnishing our flat. It became a nice and warm nest and in the end was equipped with subdued lights that Alfred had attached to the walls.

In September my parents returned from Akli.
At the end of September Uncle Charles fled from Alsóverecke to Akli with his valuable medicines from Switzerland and his clothes. Aunt Helen could write us only this thing, but after that all news were stopped and the post did not work from the Trans-Danube region.

We chose 18th of November 1944, 12,30 o'clock for our wedding to take place in the Villányi-street catholic Church. Before that we had the civil marriage. All these took place on Saturday.

After the church wedding we planned to have the wedding meal in the Gellért-square Gundel restaurant. We placed the order there. But the war horned in on it, because the previous day Gundel's restaurant got an air attack and was bombed down nearly completely. The front part of the building became a mere ruin. In myself I acknowledged it to be a bad omen, but thanked God that the bomb did not explode at the time, when we took our meal in there with the celebrating guests.

So on 17th of November in the afternoon mother and our maid went to try to get meat and materials needed for the wedding dish, so as we could give a wedding party for 12 people. We were at the morning of 18th of November and preparing for the wedding. The war prevented me from wearing a long white wedding-dress.

I had a hazel short woolen-dress with long arms, an afternoon dress for special occasions, to which friend Louise lent her nice squirrel fur-coat, because it was the end of November. Alfred got a bunch of wonderful yellow roses for the wedding, my favorite. It looked very nice with my dress. (Previously I hadn't thought I would wear such a dress on my wedding!)
We met the wedding witnesses at the Round Square Wedding Registry. My witnesses were Helen Turi, mother's youngest cousin and her husband Dr. Gerdai district doctor. Alfred had his sister Hilda and her husband. Numerous relatives and friends took part in the church ceremony.

Louise's mother was singing the song Gounod: Ave Maria and made the moment nice and fascinating with her beautiful voice. The text of the oath I said solemnly and with deep feelings not suspecting, that in some months I have to keep it. (I mean staying at my husband's side for better or for worse.)

To my greatest sorrow father was not able to be present at the wedding ceremony because of his illness, but at the wedding lunch he was already there and we ate the delicious food, which was even better than at the Gundels. Also the mood was very good, the couples of the same age could understand one another very well. Also father's humor became better, seeing our happiness.

This day passed luckily because we didn't have any bomb attacks! In the evening we went up into our own home and my cloudless girlhood was over and LIFE- written in capitals- began.

Here I would like to bid farewell to my girlhood and the first chapter of my book, as I commemorate my mother, who took me under her heart for nine months and whom I can thank for my life, and also my good father! My mother was a tall (172 centimeters high), slim shaped blond, light-brown eye beautiful woman. She was noble-poised, and always "made an appearance" wherever she went.

The color of her hair was like flowing gold. First she wore it in bun, later she had it cut, when the shingle used to be in fashion. She made a twist of hair from her previous hair and sometimes put it up as a bun. She put it down and I saw it, it was wonderful.

From my early years the love of music steeped me, because mother always delighted me with her piano playing. We sang a lot together, and I could sing everything after her thanks to my absolute hearing, so she called me "Miss Nü-nü-nü". Mother tirelessly nursed us when we were sick, which happened quite often and nursed also my father till his death.

In the balls, when she came with me I was very proud of her, because her distinct personality marked out from the others in her tasteful clothes.

She told me, that when she was a child and teenage, she was a joyful and happy girl, who liked playing the piano to the nuns and often made them laugh. Sometimes the nuns asked her: "Ékes, play something good for us!" and she sat happily to the piano and sang the favorite hits of that time and played the piano to them. Mother often didn't understand the words of the songs, but the nuns did! At school she also played serious theatre roles.

I don't know why, but mother became quite serious at father's side. Could the great age difference of 13 years be the cause of it?

Last, but not at least I can thank her that she made father's heart accept my marriage.

Well, in my marriage the age difference was 21 years!

Appendix

Map of Hungary before WWI and the 1920 Trianon-pact

Places mentioned in the first part, which are now not to be found in the actual territory of Hungary:

1. Füss in Csallóköz /Slovakia/
2. Kolozsvár / Rumania/
3. Alsóverecke / Ucraine/
4. Munkács /Ucraine/
5. Szászrégen /Rumania/

My first marriage with Alfred

Baptism of Fire

1944

We had just moved into our beautifully furnished small flat, which was even more comfortable than a hotel room. Unfortunately the Allied bombing campaign of the city had begun, but heaven was gracious to us and spared us from the bombs. It was as if the bombers knew that we were on our honeymoon.

On Sunday my mother sent us food with the maid. It was just enough for two days. Later we went out shopping and then I happily started to cook at home.

Our flat was well designed. The main corridor led into the first room, which was partially furnished with the familiar furniture of my childhood. I had brought along a collapsible couch, three armchairs, a table and a low dresser with four drawers. We placed my dresser next to the kitchen, and converted the first room into a valet room with a dressing table, a mirror and the chairs, because our bathroom was quite small. Next to the hall there was a big anteroom and a coat rack, a mirror, an umbrella stand and the shoe cupboard.

From the first room there was the small bathroom which then led out to the main room where we could look out the window and see Fadrusz Street. It was in this room that we placed Alfred's furniture. Alfred had brought a large three door cupboard that he placed near the kitchen wall. He also brought a collapsible couch, two armchairs, a table, and bookshelves along the wall, a flower stand and then a second smaller cupboard. Next to the living room was our bedroom that had a balcony which opened out to the tennis court. In the bedroom we had our double bed, a beautiful baroque desk with a comfortable armchair, a low and long bookshelf, two footrests, a plant stand and a tiled heater to keep us warm during the cold winter months.

In the kitchen there was a window that overlooked Eszék Street. It was here at the window, where there was a folding table made in the town of Zirc along with two chairs. There we could comfortably eat our meals. To cook the meals I had a fine gas oven and the heat was supplied by a central heating system.

On December fist 1944, Alfred asked me to give up my job because he earned quite enough and he wanted me to stay at home. I obliged to his request and this proved to be beneficial for all. We only lived about a minute's walk from my parent's house and since I was not working I was able to visit them frequently. My father was also quite ill so I was able to care for him all the while trying to convince him that I was happy as a wife.

Around the 15th of December Alfred came home with the news that the offices of the Győr Textile Works would be moved to the village of Nyúl next to Győr in the western portion of the nation. The company requested that we move with them as they were trying to escape from the approaching Red Army. Naturally we were both upset, because neither of us wanted to leave our old and sick parents alone. So we tried to postpone the move to the east. Every time the truck driver arrived to take us away we always told him "tomorrow". A week later he came to us and told that the Russians had finally surrounded Budapest, so our flight to the west was impossible. It was more comforting for us to be surrounded by the Soviet Army than to leave our ill parents behind.

Alfred and I stayed at home on the second day of Christmas and when looking through the window we saw a sight that disturbed us greatly. Scattered along the Fadrusz Street were several dead German soldiers. We could hear shots being fired and we then looked out towards the tennis courts where we saw German soldiers kneeling and shooting towards Keleföld to the west.

We had seen enough and immediately Alfred and I moved down to the air-raid-shelter. When our building had been constructed it had been designed with two large shelters. By the time we moved down there the rooms were filled with bunk beds in the centre and other beds along the walls. The whole place was crowded with the displaced families. In one of the corners we made a place to sleep. Alfred and I laid out our mattress on benches and our kitchen stools. From this we made a little 'bed home'. For seven weeks during the siege of

Budapest Alfred and I managed to make the place into "our home".

Earlier in the year Angel, the daughter of my brother-in-law Arthur had moved in with us in late October. She had married Zoltan Kalmár, a biologist a year previously. Both had worked in the Agricultural Ministry and lived in Budafok in their family house on top of a hill with Zoltan's mother. As the war dragged on, traveling from Budafok to Budpaest became exceedingly more difficult, so they moved into the main room that opened to Fadrusz Street.

Zoltan was a famous mushroom specialist, who had published several books on the topic. While he lived with us, he gave us many kinds of dried mushrooms. In addition to the dried mushrooms, he also was able to give us a large jar of dried vegetables. Both the vegetables and the dried mushrooms proved to be very good food during the seven weeks spent in the air raid shelter.

Six days before we had moved into the air raid shelter Angel and Zoltan traveled home to spend the Christmas holidays at home. Because of the siege they were unable to return to our home. After the siege they told us that the train they had left on traveled only to the Kamaraerdő stop. At Kamaraerdő they then traveled a short distance on foot to their mother's house in Budafok. As they were walking up the hillside to the house they could see the Soviet tanks and the looting soldiers approaching the capital. Fortunately they arrived home safely and were able to spend the time of the siege at their mother's place.

One of our neighbors was a young couple who had escaped from Csíkszereda (in Rumania). The wife Gabi was 19, her husband, an engineer was 35 yeas old. There was another young couple B. Füri who was 26, his wife and their 3 years old son. Also living in their flat was the husband's kind grandmother.

There was also a Jewish family that was hiding in our building. They had escaped from Trans-Sylvania in Rumania and we only learned of their existence after the siege of the capital had ended. Their true identity was never discovered during the war. Somehow all of their documents were in order and never attracted the attention of the Nazis or the Arrow Cross (Hungarian Nazi Party) during the frequent identity checks. As the siege wore on, the Germans and the Arrow Cross made more frequent identity checks in our shelter. Their appearance was always disturbing when they demanded identity cards from everyone. Then the men would look deeply into your eyes for a long time as they asked several questions and had a thorough look at all of us. We could never know who would be taken away or for what reason!

/ *The Arrow Cross was a regularly banned extreme right party. In the evening of 15.Oktober 1944 after the deposition and arrest of Prime Minister Miklós Horthy the Arrow Cross Party seized power. During its 170 days long reign deportations were restarted under the direction of SS Gestapo leader Adolf Eichmann.-editor/*

For a whole year prior to the siege a pastor of the reformed church and his Greek wife with their 8 months old daughter had also lived in our building. During one night in November the Arrow Cross entered our air-raid shelter and took the pastor. He was apparently charged with being part of an underground rebellion. Later we learned that he had been taken to the Sopronkõhida jail for political prisoners. The wife was a petite and beautiful Greek woman, who could not speak Hungarian well. Because of the fate of her husband she was constantly upset. When she and her daughter came down to the shelter, the air-raid commander assigned them to the store-room for cleaning the utensils. It didn't have doors, but it was somehow separated from the rest of us. Later on the small girl became blind for a short time because of the constant darkness. Luckily for the rest of us, the authorities never took anyone else away.

1945

All the residents of the house were together for a long week and despite of the fear we celebrated New Years Eve. None of us could have suspected what kind of horrors awaited for us with the arrival of the New Year.

Our small community in the air-raid shelter held together. The house commander organized our lives. We had a kitchen where the women cooked in turns, while the men were assigned the heavier and more dangerous tasks. The men were required to bring firewood from the cellars or water from an empty plot in the Eszék-street where a well had been dug. Naturally these tasks could only be done when we were not under attack. Towards the end of siege it was mostly the Soviet planes appeared in the air to drop bombs on us. The Soviets also appeared on the ground. The first Russian that we encountered was a dead one whose body lay about a hundred meters at the end of Fadrusz Street. Unseen Russian snipers were also lurking by the other side of the railway bank. They made no distinction between civilians and solders as they fired anything that dared to move.

During the siege we also didn't have water, electricity or gas. We illuminated the shelter with the light of candles. Every day, early in the morning, in the grey and silent time of dawn everyone went up to his own flat to wash himself with the water that we had saved in out bath tubs. We could never linger long while bathing as after 10 a.m. the bombings usually began and the only safe place was the shelter. It was a terrible experience as whenever bombs exploded nearby the walls and the floor of the shelter reverberated.

Despite the terror, we never gave up! During the most horrible dreadful attacks, the women prepared delicious meals from potatoes, beans, lenses and rice. I often used the dried mushrooms and vegetables. (I constantly blessed Zoltan's name because he had given us the dried food.) We took the meals on trays into our "bed homes". We also baked bread. Everyone could eat a warm meal once a day and in the mornings and evenings we had tea, bread with jam, bacon fat or simply a plain slice of bread.

It was not long before the stored up food began to run out. Later the house commander made the decision to open up the homes and the pantries of the residents who had previously fled to the west. The gather of food from empty flats was done in the presence of two other witnesses so that no valuables left behind were taken by greedy hands. The food was collected and then divided among the neediest. Once a week everybody could get food according to their needs, free of charge of course. We also got some, mainly potatoes, alimentary pastes, beans, peas, and marmalades, all what we wanted. Later on we also encountered a special addition to our diets. While one of the men was out fetching water he stumbled upon a dead horse lying in the street. The men went and butchered the animal and brought back the meat for us to cook. We took the meat and made a stew for everyone. Many of us had never experienced horse meat before. All of us found the meat to be sweeter than beef or pork, but we were so hungry for meat that none of us complained. Despite our lack of food, the constant searches by the authorities and the fear of the air-raids we still managed to pass the time by occasionally playing cards.

All the while Alfred and I were highly desired about seeing our parents. We made the decision to go and try to visit them. The shelter community naturally warned against this trip, but they helped us to form a route in which to go. Even with their assistance, they warned that all of this would be was God's extreme testing. We could sense this as well, but we were convinced that we had to go. Because we wanted to be able to keep our hands free we stuffed Alfred's pockets with all the goods that we that he could carry for our starving parents.

Before our departure Alfred drilled me in advance on what we would do. Alfred was to go in front of me and on his command "to the ground!" we would fall at once to the ground. Later he would shout "up!" and we would then stand up and run as quickly as we could. It was the middle of January when we departed in the afternoon. A peaceful white snow had recently fallen. I asked God's help in myself!

We left our building through the door that led to Eszék Street. This was the same street which the men who brought us water used. We could not leave by the big entrance door that led to Fadrusz Street as it was constantly under continuous fire. Alfred first ran through the Fadrusz Street to the wall of the house on the opposite side. There wasn't any firing, so he gave me the sign to run, and I followed. There was silence again. Sticking to the wall we turned on the corner to the Miklós Horthy Street, opposite of the tennis courts. No one could be seen on the road. We went along the walls of the houses to the corner of the Lenke square 12. (Today it is Dezsõ Kosztolányi square). Up to that point we had always been in the shadows of the houses from the Russian snipers, who were still behind the railway bank.

It was now the time for bravery and Alfred asked me if I could go through the perils of an open street. I though of my father, who had served on the fronts of WWI for four years in similar events and because I was my "father's daughter" I asked myself: Why could I not do it, if I wanted to meet him? Alfred pointed out the exact direction we should run, through the Miklós Horthy Street (today Béla Bartók Street) to the Bottomless Lake. /*Béla Bartók 1881-1945. He was a Hungarian composer, pianist and collector of folk music. He was one of the greatest composers of the 20th century.- editor*/

From there we were to run parallel to the lake till we reached the house opposite of the lake on the Lenke Street (today Bocskai Street). We were familiar with the house on the corner as there was a pharmacy, which Uncle Charles used to visit regularly, so that he could chat with his chemist acquaintance. Alfred said that once we reached the pharmacy we would be in the shadows of the houses from the Russians, but the most dangerous part would be running along the lakeside. He warned me that we would have run very quickly and I had to be alert for all his commands!

The snow along the lakeside was fresh, white and untouched. Nobody dared to walk there, so there were no prints in it. As we set off I began to pray to myself. Alfred went first and I followed closely behind. We reached the lakeside and there was still silence. Moments later Alfred started running and then fell unto the ground, flat on his stomach. I did exactly the same. We were at the midpoint of the lake, when the sound of a submachine-gun could be heard. It was the same moment that we fell to the ground. I don't know how long we stayed there, but to me it seemed to be the eternity. The long moments passed until suddenly I saw Alfred jump up and at the same moment heard him shout "Up!" Gathering all my strength, I jumped up and ran after him. The machinegun sounded again. Tra-ta-ta, tra-ta-ta, tra-ta-ta! We fell to the ground again. I looked up slightly to notice that the bullets were entering into the snow ahead of us and behind us.

We became motionless again for a short time. Alfred looked back at me and told me this would be the last run, after that he assured me we would be in the shadows of the houses. I listened to Alfred, who took a few more moments before he jumped up and began running again. I did the same. When we reached the corner of the pharmacy, the machine- gun sounded again for the third time. We watched as the bullets made prints in the snow just a little further from us. On the corner we took a little rest. Alfred reassured me that the most difficult part was already behind us. The most frightening part of the experience was that we hadn't seen anyone. There were no German soldiers, nor any dead bodies.

Alfred reminded me of the route again. After moving along with the protection of the houses, we reached Lenke Square #7 (today Dezsõ Kosztolányi Square), where we used to live. Then we crossed the Miklós Horthy Street to the house # 86, where Aunt Kate lived. In the entrance of the house there was a German soldier. As Alfred spoke German, he explained to the soldier from where and how we came and where we wanted to go to. The German soldier could hardly believe that we had survived running so freely in front of the eyes of the Russian snipers. The soldier reasoned the Russians must have seen us through their telescopes, but didn't want to kill us. We were young and they probably thought we were drunk or they just wanted to frighten the "father and his daughter".

They let us into the house and into the room of our previous dressmaker Mrs. Sápi. Sitting in the half-cellar there where some German soldiers. When they got to know how brave we had been on our journey to get there they couldn't believe it. They told us that they had only dared to go through the square in the front-line trenches. They assured us that they would not have been brave enough even as soldiers to do what we did. They then helped us by showing us the way back home using the front-line trenches. Then they were kind enough to escort us to our parents house as well.

When we were reunited all hugged one another and we cried with mother, father, my brother Thomas. We were all so happy that we got through the square safe and sound and that everyone was still alive. My poor father had lost so much weight. He was only skin and bones by that time and he was constantly shaking. Alfred hugged his mother "for the last time." We gave them all of the food that we brought. It was not much and Alfred promised to come again using the front-line trench and bring more.

This trip was my baptism of fire and I thanked God for the blessing that our very dangerous trip had ended so fortunately.

On our way back we used the trenches and by leaning a bit forward we easily get home.

Once at our building everyone in the shelter hugged us with joy and asked for a detailed report on our dangerous trip. Some of them honestly acknowledged that they sincerely didn't believe they would see us again!

Four days later Alfred went out again and used the security of the trench line. He carried a bag full of food to his mother and my parents but he returned very sad. My mother had told him that after our visit Alfred's mother kept on saying, that "this was the last time, when she could see her son", and "now she could die in peace". Two days after our visit the frail old woman started to feel cold and began shaking, but she did not say a word. My mother put a blanket on her and held her in her arms. Then the old woman sighed one and then died in my mother's arms.

Alfred made arrangements to bury his mother. So he went there again, dug a hole in the front garden and buried his mother in a box. During the siege it was the only way we could care for the dead. After the siege those who had been buried around the houses were exhumed and taken to the great cemeteries. But we are still far away from that time!

The bombings, the landmines and the fire fights became so frequent that the men couldn't go out any more. The men didn't dare to go and fetch water because it simply became impossible. When we could no longer go out to get water the men decided to dig a well in the wood-store. They managed to find water, but no one had expected that the water of the shallow wells was always bad "sour water". We all boiled it, filtered and made tea from it, but even those who were healthy experienced relaxed bowels. This became even more of a problem in our living space. As the bombings became more frequent only a few dared to go up to their flats to relive themselves. Eventually we created a latrine in the earthen cellar but we could not keep any of the necessary rules of hygiene.

Alfred visited my parents once more carrying food, but the German soldiers nervously asked him not to do that again, because the Russian soldiers had apparently discovered the trenches and they were keeping it under constant fire.

The 30th of January 1945 arrived. It was a horrible, forever memorable date for me! I remember it was Saturday, a silent grey-like day. After lunch many of us went up into our flats to wash ourselves with the ice cold water we had kept in our bathtubs. We have just finished bathing, when the house commander woman, who lived on the 6th floor announced to us and the others, that she was about to distribute food downstairs, next to the main entrance door, in the flat of the caretaker. She called to us that if we needed something, we should go there.

Around fifteen of us were standing there in the small flat. As the house commander was distributing the potatoes out, there was suddenly the sound of a loud explosion. Seconds later another explosion sounded which shook the house itself. The explosion and the blasts were so big, that we all fell upon each other. We checked ourselves and fortunately nobody was seriously hurt, only the glass of the doors and windows were broken.

We were waiting there for a long time as the frightening deep silence followed the explosions. The men then dared to go out and check the damage. They reported that the big entrance door had been torn down; the stairs and the elevator could not be seen because of the thick dust. We all reasoned that the stairs were torn down, probably in all six floors. We all ran back to the air-raid-shelter, all the while it was getting darker and nothing could be done. We could only guess what had been destroyed and how we could go on?

In the air- raid shelter they had only heard the loud noise of the explosion and felt the walls shaking. The reason of the explosion was two Russian bombs fixed to each other known as "chained-bombs". They had fallen into the attic above the corner rooms and exploded on the first floor. They had destroyed all of the flats along the Fadrusz Street corner.

Up to that point no one had been injured but our flats had become nothing more than a mere ruin! The house commander asked everyone that when we go up into our flats, we all should be very cautious. She advised only men should do it and even then never alone!

Later Alfred described detailed the state of our flat. "The entrance door was torn down by the explosion, but we still have it. In the fore hall the mirror is intact, but the furniture in the hall is all under ruin. The bathroom and half of the corner room disappeared and in its place there is only a great hole. From there one can look up only to the sky or down to the ruins of the first floor flat. The small corridor opening from the hall was unharmed together with the kitchen and the small room, and the dishes, glasses remained intact in the cupboard."

So during the siege a second miracle had happened to me. Alfred and I were still alive, because half an hour before the bomb attack we were still washing ourselves in the bathroom or doing something in the room beside it. Fortunately we went down for food distribution. Hadn't we descended, we certainly wouldn't have needed food any more!

We waited impatiently for the siege to end, because the nerves of the people in the cellar were reaching their end. We did not starve, but we only had a small amount of monotonous food. Except for the horse we didn't have meat, so even the healthy people lost weight. Tragically the sick ones lost even more. I weighed only 42 kilograms at the end of the siege. Naturally as people lived in such conditions there were also the clashes of personal views which happened more frequently as time drew on. This was just added onto our misery by the lack of food, the unsanitary conditions and the fact of our ruined homes.

On the 13th of February 1945 at noon the first Russian soldiers appeared along Fadrusz Street. We learned from him that the headquarters of the Germans in Buda Castle had fallen the previous day. Everyone sighed!

Those who had lived in the corner flats were welcomed in by the owners of the undamaged flats. A young woman, Maria T. gave us a room in her flat looking out to the Eszék Street on the second floor. She gave us this room which she managed to nearly clear out of her own stuff. Maria lived there with her 4 year old daughter, as her husband had been taken away before the siege to the Sopronkõhida jail by the Arrow Cross. My friend from the shelter Füri B. and her family lived right next door, so the children could visit each other and play together without any problems.

The house commander ordered that every young woman should disfigure her face by putting on soot from the lamps. We were told to wear black head scarves, dark unobtrusive dresses and go up to the attic or the highest floor, where the Russians did not dare to go to. In the daytime we tried to arrange things and clean the house of the ruins.

13th of February 1945
Russian soldier writes "Budapest" on a traffic sign in Russian

As the victors, the Russian soldiers began to enter and look around in the houses. They also looked into ours, as well. Two women in a first floor flat "voluntarily" welcomed the Russian soldiers in for "afternoon tea". Because of their "sacrifices", the others in the house escaped more horrible atrocities.

In our old and destroyed flat Alfred and I began to tidy up and extract the furniture from out of the ruins. The work this time was slower and more difficult that it had been when we first moved in.

My state of mind was quite interesting at that time. The things that had held great importance in my life, my values all of these had changed in an instant. I did not panic or cry and I didn't even feel bad over all of the destroyed property that I had collected during my childhood. There was only one thing that remained important. We had stayed alive!

I was continuously cleaning up and helping Alfred with the necessary tasks. When we had removed the rubble from the armchairs in the hall we pulled them into the hall and later to the flat on the second floor where we were temporally residing. After emptying the hallway we saw that the flooring along with the corner room was drastically slanting down.

The room that had once looked out to the Fadrusz Street had completely fallen down. Even the common wall with the hall was torn down and had fallen onto the furniture. Amazingly, Alfred's big three-door cupboard was still standing in place, leaning precariously towards the edge of the broken floor. The wall that it had rested against was gone and it now hung perilously in the air with only two small marble statues holding books besides it. He had placed them there intuitively on the floor next to the cupboard just before we sought refuge in the shelter. The sculptures were now jammed under the cupboard and were holding it in place from falling five stories to the ground. Eerily the cupboard was standing between the sky and the earth full of clothes with only the back facing towards the stable flooring and the hallway where we were working.

Alfred decided to retrieve his cupboard and rescue it from falling down. I could not convince him not to attempt the dangerous adventure and only later did he tell me the real reason. He planned the whole action first and then asked the help of two other men. He managed to find a long and very strong rope. One end was tied around his waist, the other was held by the men standing in the hall, where the flooring was more solid. Alfred knew precisely how his cupboard was constructed as he himself had crafted it and screwed it together piece by piece. To begin he took it apart from the back very cautiously. After removing the back he gave me the clothes and other things that were stored in it. Alfred did this while the two men held on to the rope. When the cupboard was empty he turned it unto its back slowly keeping it steady with his hands. Later it was pulled into the hall. Just moments after retrieving the cupboard from the edge, the flooring where he had been working suddenly fell down with a tremendous noise. The crash caused the flooring beneath our feet to shake, but it was still structurally sound and did not fall down. Then Alfred, who still had the rope around his waist, pulled the skeleton of the cupboard further into the hallway. Then he thanked everyone for their assistance and all of us were happy that we could have fulfilled his plan.

When we were alone, Alfred unscrewed the intact sides. It was there that I learned that the cupboard had a double bottom where he had hidden his military uniform, without the rank tabs and his sword. That is why the things in that cupboard had to be saved from falling down! He wrapped these things and took them up to the attic and hid them there. He was not the only one who was trying to do away with military uniforms at that time. I think when the house was reconstructed, probably the workers found it, but by that time we had already moved away.

The cooking continued in the cellar of the house, because only a few of the inhabitants possessed a small iron stove. These were the only type that could be used in the flat for cooking with the stovepipe extruding through the window. Those of us who had the tile ovens could only use them to heat our bodies.

It was not advisable to walk on the streets not even in the daytime. There were so many Russian soldiers milling around, just like ants. If someone had better clothing or a fur coat on, it was stolen right from him. Once as I was looking through the kitchen window we saw how a fur coat was ripped from a man in plain daylight. The situation called for a curfew between 5 p.m. and the morning light. But our house gave us plenty of work to do with tidying up the ruins.

Unfortunately the Russians continued to visit the "women" on the first floor. It happened once that I was at B. Füri's place when a middle aged Russian soldier knocked at the door. We were so frightened, but when he showed us some sweets in his hand for the children, we let him come in. He liked Füri's son especially, and he put him on his lap. Then the kind Russian showed us a photo were we could see his wife and his two sons. He obviously missed them very much. Later the same Russian came and visited Füri's place many times until he was sent to another place. It proved to us that kind of Russians could be found among the scoundrels!

It was at the end of February or at the beginning of March when in the morning a man entered our house dressed in a black leather coat and high boots accompanied by two Russian soldiers. The man in the "leather coat" spoke clear Hungarian and claimed to be a "political officer". He declared that he had come to collect the men who were of soldiering age. There were seven of them: Alfred and our neighbors: the attorney, the engineer, a 22 years old Jewish boy and still another three men. We had just learned about the boy at that time from his family that he was hiding at our place.

The "leather coat" man ordered these seven men to follow him for interrogation at the Nicholas Horthy-street 61 (where we had once lived.) The women and wives were very upset over the turn of events. Half an hour later we all went to the street in front of the Nicholas Horthy street 61 "for the first time". At the entrance a Russian soldier stood with a machine gun in his hands and did not let us go any further. Some time later the same "political officer" appeared on the scene and after our "persuasion" he advised us to bring daily food and underwear for our husbands. We were not able to find out anything else from him. He emphasized that he had already told us too much!

We ran home, prepared the parcels. When we returned there were 150 men standing in rows of fours or fives, escorted by Russian soldiers holding machine guns. They were then marched towards Gellért Square. Miraculously we caught sight of our husbands at the end of the line who managed to recognize us for just a moment. We followed the column along from a distance. Our pursuit was difficult as the entire street all along the road was filled with ruins and debris. The houses looked very ugly as they bore the signs of gun battles and bombing attacks. It was a horrible scene!

We wondered what was going to happen by the Danube as the memories of the Hungarian Nazi terror still lived vividly in all of us! The mother of the Jewish boy silently whispered: "The Hungarian Nazis took the Jews in the same way out of the ghetto and to the bank of the Danube. There they shot them into the river!" We were all praying to ourselves that "it should not to happen again!"

When we reaching Gellért Square we were all flabbergasted at the sight of the destroyed Franz Joseph Bridge (today reconstructed as the Liberty Bridge). Before reaching the bridge the marching column stopped and the Russians ordered us to put our parcels onto the curb. After we had deposited the parcels the Russian allowed our husbands to fetch them, but no way were we able to properly say good-bye. After they retrieved their parcels we saw the groups going down to the quay, but we weren't allowed to go to them. We could only watch them from afar.

Photo: The Franz Joseph Bridge ruined by the retreating German troops

The Danube was grey and unkind, broken ice, driftwood, branches and dead bodies were constantly drifted along the surface. On the shore five boats were swaying along the dock. In each boat three men were ordered to sit under the supervision of two Russians. The Russians were then busied with pulling the boat by turns and pushing the drifting garbage away from the hull of the boat.

When they reached the buildings on the other side, the three men were given over to other Russians and the soldiers returned with empty boats to take another group to the opposite side. We waited till our husbands had gotten across the river without incident and then watched them as they disappeared among the dark buildings. It was at that time when we realized that they were taken as captives. None of us knew for how long or where they were being taken to.

We wives promised to help one another. In the case that any of us got any news about our husbands, we would then tell the others at once. Later we learned that even our own husbands also promised not to leave one another. It was a miracle in how well they managed to do this!

In the middle of March the mother of the Jewish boy received the news that the group had been taken to Gödöllő where there was a big prisoner-of-war camp. Somehow she managed to go there and fortunately we didn't. It happened that three days later she returned very sad without any results. She told us that the prisoners were crowded into the building of the Gödöllő High School, which was then surrounded by a barbed wire fence and there was no end of Russian soldiers. Poor women could not even go near the camp, because the Russians started to fire in the air if someone dared to go near. She had wanted to bribe the solders with her jewels, but this attempt was unsuccessful.

We were not the only ones to suffer. Some days after Alfred had been taken, my 12 year old brother, Thomas visited me with an old neighbor of theirs. He reported to us how the "liberation" at their place happened. Two drunken Russian soldiers had entered their cellar and started to beat everyone, men and women alike. Thomas jumped in front of our ailing father to protect him, so he received the great blow. Our poor father was also assaulted and my mother as well!

In addition he told me that their house had been shot at, but fortunately the rooms had "only" splinters. Not a single window remained intact. The three of them were now living in the kitchen, where they could keep warm while cooking on the old cooker. Father was now in bed and could only drink.

I told him what happened to Alfred and showed him the big hole in place of our flat. While saying farewell we agreed that he would come to us rather than I would go to them, because for young women like me, it was much too dangerous to walk on the streets alone.

On the 30th of March my brother Tom came in the morning with the news that the Russians had opened a pontoon bridge in place of the destroyed Horthy Bridge (now Petőfi Bridge). The Soviets were allowing the Buda citizens to cross over to Pest to work and to go shopping. My brother asked me to go with him to pick up supplies. Not wasting any time I quickly made myself ready and off we went.

After leaving the Round Square at the beginning of the Verpeléti Street (now Frigyes /Frederick/ Karinthy Street) we stood among a huge crowd that was slowly drifting towards the

The floating pontoon bridge made by the Russians

pontoon bridge. /*Frigyes Karinthy 1887-1938. Hungarian author, playwright, poet, journalist and editor.*/

After meandering for two and a half hours we reached the bridge that had been constructed by the Red Army. The bridge had only been designed for pedestrian traffic and the weight of the people crossing caused the waters of the Danube to lick at our feet.

The Russians ordered us to form into rows as they led only a certain number of emaciated and starving Buda citizens over to Pest at a time. Once we reached the other side of the Danube, we were amazed to discover that there was much less rubble and destruction. The roads were clear and we easily arrived at King Street. Although the shops didn't have any display windows, the volume of products made it all look like the wealth of Eldorado for the Buda citizens.

It was such a wonder of the rich food supply that we could hardly believe such items could have been bought for money! We purchased all that we could; meat, bacon, vegetables, onions, bacon for grease, pickled cabbage, apples, and lots of bread. We were so hungry that we ate the food on our journey home. Still fearing the worst from the liberators, we hurried to return home before complete darkness. Nearly all of the food we had purchased was taken home by my brother, because I still had things to cook. I told him to cook father a delicious bouillon from beef with vegetables and try to feed him with that so his health could return.

Two days later my brother Thomas appeared again, weeping and telling us that father died on 31st of March. I quickly visited my mother, who told me the following, crying: "On the morning of 31st of March I prepared a breakfast of French coffee. When I took it to your father, he was already dead. She heard only a sigh from afar and then he slipped into eternal life!"

For father it must have been a release, because he had endured such enormous pains! I comforted mother with this sentence. Mother was very gaunt from the lack of food, but despite this she was healthy. The doctor who arrived to officially pronounce my fathers death gave my mother the "good" news that father would be one of the first ones to be buried in the Farkasrét cemetery. The cemetery was to be reopened on April 1st.

I said the final farewell to my father, who was laid peacefully on a bed in one of the undamaged rooms. His face was so peaceful and nice; he looked as if he was only sleeping and this was the way that I saw him for the last time!

A photo taken of the original building of the Admiral-street 3 built in 1926, reconstructed in 1958

The spring of 1945 had quickly arrived as I remember that I wore a short sleeve black blouse and a black skirt at the funeral. My father's funeral was held on the 6th of April. Because the roads were still clogged with rubble we went there on foot.

After the funeral we all felt very tired and I slept at my mother's place. In the evening we discussed the future and how we would all survive. My mother suggested that I should move back in with them, because I had neither an intact flat, nor my husband at the moment. I agreed with the proposal as it was the best way in which we could help each other.

During the whole month of April my brother Thomas and I were engaged in carrying the smaller household items back to my mother's home. Later the larger furniture was taken home with the help of a neighbor using a horse drawn carriage. As we lacked a horse for the carriage, my brother and I pulled it and managed to retrieve all of the large items from our damaged flat with only 3 or 4 return trips. At my mother's house the windows of all rooms were still covered with heavy darkening papers. Only later was the damaged glass replaced.

After all of my items had been moved I said my farewells to my friends living in the Fadrusz Street house. I promised that I would visit them frequently to enquire about our husbands. But at that time there was no new news of what was happening. In spite of all the hardships, it was good to be in a secure place beside my mother again!

By that time the villagers had started to come up to the capital bringing butter, curd cheese, bacon and ham. We appreciated these delicious things at a time when such things were luxuries in Buda. The rural people didn't want to be paid with money as they wished only to barter for clothing. As everything was destroyed and the previously beautiful capital city was devastated, barter became a means of life and survival for all.

None of us had any money to spend anymore, so my friend Füri had the idea to knit children's socks. She had plenty of yarn in order to make them. We worked together as I made the legs and she knitted the soles. I truly enjoyed the work as I liked knitting and Füri was an expert at selling them. Such work and the salary made my life comfortably content. When the stocks of yarn began to run low Füri was able to get yarn from the bombed out Goldberger Textile Works on Budafok Street.

We made scores of socks, because both of us had a great desire to stay alive. Out of this desire came a certain creativity and strength as well. Great money could be earned!

In the meantime I also found a workplace for my mother when I visited my friend Louise. We happily hugged each other on our first meeting and we rejoiced that she and her family had remained unhurt through the siege. She also told me of another possibility of earning money. Her three cousins had tidied up a ruined shop on the Round Square and opened the "Chit-Chat" confectionery. Louise's mother and several other women had started to bake delicious cakes for the famished 11th district citizens.

"It's an enormous amount of money that they earn, and they can hardly keep on baking enough." she said. "Can I ask your mother as well, whether she would like to join the business?" she added.

When I returned home my mother was so excited with the possibility of working and making a living that she accepted the offer at once. She wasted not time in lighting up our old stove with the stocks of wood that she had on hand. My mother and I invented three kinds of pastries: jam bags, chestnut crescent roll and sponge tart slices with vanilla or chocolate cream filling. As eggs were exceedingly rare we used raspy carrots in their place. Because of this the pastries had a beautiful orange color and a unique taste as well. We had large amounts of jam at home to supplement the pastries as well. The chestnut crescent rolls were also made without eggs from a butter pastry. Beans replaced the chestnuts and rum was used to spice it. The sponge was made from a simple corn flour. (Later the villagers began to bring us eggs, as well.)

My job was that of delivery and every day I took the ready warm sweets in cardboard boxes to the shop. Our cakes were an instant success, so we arranged with the "boss" to be specialized on these three cakes. Instead of consignment she paid at once on delivery. Of course all of it was mother's money. Some days later the "dear customers" were waiting for me outside the shop. They were so famished for our pastries that they nearly snatched them from my hands. In such a short time our three cakes had became famous! This was the way we started to get about and begin our whole life again! In all of this I began to act as the head of the family. I felt confident, because I felt that mother listened to me and frequently accepted my ideas. Such responsibility gave me strength and self-confidence, which I would needed later on.

My aunt Kate had survived the siege and we told each other the horrible things happened to us. Her flat had remained unhurt, "only" the windows had been broken. She was very happy that I moved back home into the room looking to the Ulászló Street, just opposite of her flat. This way we could look out the windows and communicate with each other. We hadn't heard any news about my Uncle Charles and my Aunt Helen. All that we knew was that there ha been heavy fighting in the Trans-Danube Region after the liberation of Budapest.

My first bit of happiness occurred, when at the beginning of May Alfred appeared, seemingly unhurt. Amazingly he was quite fat and had lost his previously thin shape. He had already been to our Fadrusz Street flat, because all of the seven men who survived the Russian camp by a miraculous fate had returned home. He was told there that I had moved back to my mother's place. Understanding the situation he had ran to see me.

After our grand reunion, Alfred told me about the awful and inhuman treatment within the Gödöllő camp. He had spent nearly six weeks under the most cruel and unimaginable circumstances.

He had seen us from the boat as it crossed the Danube. Later they were forced to walk down on foot to the town of Gödöllő. Around 16 thousand men were packed into the Gödöllő High School. They were sitting on the floors of the corridors and within the classrooms they were so close to the other inmates that it was almost impossible to lie down and sleep. They received something to eat once a day and always at night. Because of the darkness of the night the pea soup that was served from large petrol barrels was almost always spilled while the men carried it.

Because of serving food from petrol barrels the pea soup relaxed the bowels of the whole prisoners-of-war camp. They constantly had to go to the toilet. Proper toilets were not in place, so they had to dig holes on the court and put wood planks atop. Anyone losing his balance fell into the human waste. When this happened the Russian guards held the man under the human waste with poles until they drowned in excrement.

Alfred told me that the seven men from our house took care of each other as good brothers and were always going side by side and were always helping the other one.

Later the Russians were forced to put an end to the inhuman camp due to international (American and British) pressure. Alfred's group noticed once that the camp stirred up and the Russians called anyone to come forward who wanted to serve in the newly founded Hungarian army. The new Hungarian Red Army was still under organization but they were looking for men who were ready to go west and fight against Nazi Germany. The army was directed by the new Hungarian Provisional Government that had been formed late in 1944 at the town of Debrecen. All seven of the men from our building volunteered to take part as anywhere else was better than the Hell of Gödöllő! About 3,000 men also made the brave decision! The other men who were just as starving as themselves laughed at them, saying how silly they were to believe this fairy-tale told by the Russians. Alfred's tormentors asked: had not you noticed the railway wagons prepared for you? You would surely be the first to be taken away to Siberia. Regardless of the taunting, the seven men didn't change their minds and it was to their luck, as the Russians had not been deceiving.

After answering the call, the 3,000 men were ordered to stand up in marching columns and were then escorted by the Russian soldiers to the town of Jászberény. There they were given over to Hungarian officers. Those who had remained in Gödöllő were then stuffed into railway cars and deported through the Rumanian town of Focsányi to Russian gulags. There they served as prisoners of war for the next 6 to 10 years.

Alfred then broke down in tears as he told of when the Hungarian army officers looked at all of the weight the men had lost and the thousands of men at the brink of collapsing. The officers then decided to send the men to families living in the Jászság region. They wanted to feed them to become stronger. Alfred was sent to a family in village Jászfényszaru.

Later he remembered them and spoke about them often with the deepest gratefulness and appreciation.

When he arrived at Jászfényszaru the family asked him:

"What would you like to eat?"

"A bowl of pasta with poppy-seed" he replied.

They prepared it, on which honey also was dipped and he started to eat and eat and eat...In the end he didn't dare to move for two days, while his stomach nearly split. With such an abundance of food his bones took on more fat and he nearly became chubby.

Of the seven men from our building, the army discharged two of them as they were over 42. The other five men from our building were then sent out to fight, but before they entered any action freedom "broke out" on the 9th of May 1945.

We were very happy for his safe return and we then continued our plans of how our flat would be put in order and how we would get employment. But such dreams died fast in those days. Less than a week after his return of May 1945, men came calling for Alfred one evening. They took him away and the old retired lieutenant-general of German nationality living in the flat above us. Alfred also was of German nationality so naturally as "K und K" ex-lieutenant- general. They both were taken to the police station on Zsombolyai Street for interrogation.

Why were they taken away? Surely his German nationality was the reason. Previously his family had escaped from the town of Szászrégen in Rumania. They lived in rail cars along the Hungarian border, until one day they were allowed to enter Hungary. From the border they settled down in Budapest. Later they bought a house on the corner of the Ilka- and Thököly streets. At that time Alfred was 13 years old. In 1928 his father unfortunately died. Alfred's widowed mother with her two daughters moved into a house on the Magyarádi Street, where we later moved to. At home his family spoke German, just like that of the lieutenant-general. During the siege Alfred and the general had spoken in German in the air-raid-shelter. Such language skills under the German occupation offered more benefits to those who could communicate with the solders during the difficult months. It became all too clear that someone had informed against them and the police took the two men away. Fortunately for us those who remained behind after they were taken away were unhurt.

Some days later both men were transferred to the Charles Police Station, as internees. From there they had to go to the Farkasrét cemetery to sweep for mines and unexploded ordinance every day. I went there with the wife of the general to give them lunch. Naturally we had to walk there on foot, because the trams had not yet been in service at the time.

The kind Hungarian guards allowed us to give our husbands food and we were allowed to visit with them until they finished eating. I remember how tragically comic it had been that we enjoyed the beautiful warm May days and into the beginning of June with the birds singing in the silent cemetery. Without any reason a month later the men were allowed to return home.

During the internment, the ex-director of the Fehérvár-street Standard Works also put to working in the cemetery with them. The three of them could understand one another quite well in German. The director had a pretty and very talkative young girlfriend, Maria M., whom I got to know when bringing lunch to Alfred. Later on she would prove to be my benefactor. God bless her for that, even now!

Maria lived in the Mohai Street by the railway embankment and took her director friend there to feed him. While in prison the director's health rapidly deteriorated. Alfred's advantage at the time was that he had extra fat from which he could lose weight, so when he returned home from his second internment he was at his normal size.

In the meantime, there wasn't need for mother's cakes in the sweet-shop anymore, because "the old confectioners appeared" and baked their sweets anew for the "chit-chat" confectionery. So Alfred and I had to look for another possibility of earning money.

We found a small weaving mill at the beginning of the Master Street, where they were looking for skilled labor. Alfred and I both applied for a job and we were employed. He was employed as the weaving master and I worked in cotton reeling. It was a very easy job to learn, as Alfred taught me the skills within just a few minutes.

Alfred was a head weaving master, because he had finished the Textile College in Germany and learned all ins and outs of the textile industry. On top of his knowledge, he was also a diligent and reliable worker. We were well satisfied with the money that we earned while working at the mill. We worked from 8 a.m. to 4 pm. and the job was interesting for me. The labor was not taxing for me either as I was mainly sitting while working. This was beneficial for me as the route to work was a long way to walk. Every day we had to cross over the pontoon bridge over the Danube River, but I was young and we were happy just to be alive and together again.

In July we received another gift as one day my Uncle Charles turned up at our place "with only the clothes on his back". He told us of his rough and tumble, exciting and hazardous past and the miracle of his survival.

He began his tale of adventure with the previous year during the summer of 1944. The Jews of Alsóverecke were collected by the Germans and like cattle to the slaughter they were packed into rail cars at Volóc, so that later they could be transported to Auschwitz.

After the trains had left my uncle Charles decided that he didn't want to stay there any longer. After making the decision he packed his valuable medicines that he had received from Switzerland. The medicines were packed together with his clothes and he put them on a simple horse drawn carriage and took refuge. He traveled with some other people for weeks until they reached Komárom, the Hungarian border town. At Komárom they managed to slip into the Trans Danube region, where he asked to be taken to my Aunt Helen's family in Akli. My Aunt Helen and Uncle Franz had already started to hide their valuables and the sacks of flour into the sink that I had discovered during my childhood. It was a good dry place and there was lots of room for other packages and sacks.

After my Uncle Charles arrived his valuables were stored there as well. They decided to survive the war at home in village Akli. They thought that if they did that way, all of their possessions could survive the war in that sink which no one knew about. But it happened another way! During October relatives from Rumania arrived with a group of refugees. They were apparently from my Uncle Franz's "home" in Csíkszereda. The relatives persuaded Franz and Helen to flee to the west with them. At that time my Uncle Franz started to panic and he removed all of their belongings from the security of the pit. My Uncle Charles' belongings were among them as well and the entire lot was placed on a carriage drawn by two horses. To provide meat, the men slaughtered two pigs and then began the journey to the west with the whole family mixed in among the caravan of refugees.

Disaster quickly fell upon them as they had hardly reached town Ajka, when they were suddenly attacked by Soviet bombers. The only shelter that they were able to find was under the horse drawn carriages.

After the bombing attack the Germans then arrived and took away all their horses. As they were without the power to move the carts, they had to ask for shelter from nearby homes in order to escape the bombing attacks. They were able to find a room with a local acquaintance who was a farmer and his family. A few days later they returned to the scene only to find the carriages stripped bare of their contents. It was in this manner that three adults, my Aunt Helen, my Uncles Franz and Charles and the two small children, Judith 9 years old and Andreas 6 years old stayed there completely robbed.

Unluckily the wife of the farmer had persuaded Franz and Charles to hide their money and jewels from the advancing Russians. They had put their valuables into a small box and dug a hole in the forest. The woman's belongings were also put there. When the battle front had already passed them and there were no Russians around, they went back to the forest that was now in ruins to retrieve the box. Franz, Charles and the woman were searching for the box, but it had disappeared! The woman then put on an exaggerated act of depression and crying!

Such became the terrible fate of my Uncles Franz and Charles. During the time after loosing the box of valuables my Uncle Franz became simply mad and ran into the forest crying. Later he was found in torn and ragged clothes completely exhausted. He had wounds on his face, hands and legs caused by running in the forest. Later one of his fingers had to be amputated because of a septic-infection.

After loosing all that they owned they returned to Akli. In their absence the population of the village had already occupied their home. Out of pity the squatters gave them one room because of my Aunt Helen and the children. Charles and Franz fell into a deep depression and Helen became the main source of strength by supporting them. All of this happened in the spring of 1945. When my uncle Charles came to himself he visited us in Budapest. He informed us that my Aunt Helen and her family would come up within 1 or 2 months and live in their Kökörcsin Street flat. We gave Charles a small separate room for a while, till his sister Aunt Kate took him in.

My Uncle Charles was lucky that he had escaped from Verecke, because it provided his only means of survival. A long time after the war he learned of the bad news about his chemist friend and his father in Munkács. They had been qualified as being a part of the "bourgeois" and as such were executed by Soviet soldiers in front of their pharmacy. Such was the fate of so many others who were executed by the advancing Red Army. (Not long ago a mass grave was found in Szolyva during building the foundations of the bus station. 300 men were buried there.)

Charles fell into depression once again at our place. He lay in bed all day with his face turned to the wall. Alfred and I came home from work in the evening. My mother, Kate and my Brother Tom tried to comfort him and turn his attention away from his great distress but to little avail.

At the beginning of September my brother Géza at long last returned home from American captivity. He was very thin. He had been Uncle Charles's favorite and Géza was able to turn him back from his depressed state of mind. During Géza's captivity he had been infected with tuberculoses. Immediately the doctors sent him to convalescent hospital. The unfortunate events for Géza set Uncle Charles quickly "on his feet again" as Charles became Géza's most diligent visitor. Uncle Charles's life suddenly had meaning again.

Géza's treatment consisted of pressing his leaky lungs with air. It was quite painful, but there was no other treatment or medicine for Tuberculosis at that time. Between the ribs in his chest a large and hollow needle was pierced through the skin, muscles and the breast membrane until finally reaching the lungs. Then air was pumped into the needle and filling his lungs. This all happened three times a week; he had to stay in bed and was well fed. Between the painful treatments Géza prepared for his final exam at High School. At the cadet school it had been impossible to take the exam as he had fled to the west and then fell into American captivity. After the exam he was planning to go on and study at the University of Veterinary Sciences. It was for this reason that Géza had been studying the Latin language for more than half a year. Géza spent about 5 months in the convalescent hospital and in the end he was pronounced healthy. In June of 1946 he took the exam and successfully passed for entrance into the University.

But our story should not be filled with such hopes as it was then the beginning of August, 1945. It is a horrible date for me that I can never forget! For it was worse than the siege! It was the darkest point in our life, especially of Alfred and because of him, it changed me as well! That day in August was just like the atomic bomb was for Japan!
Many families in Hungary at that time had the feeling of powerlessness. August 11th was my name-day. Early in the morning as we were about to leave for work, someone rang the bell. We opened the door and there stood two men in leather coats and high Bilgerli-type boots. They informed us that they had come to take Alfred away for "interrogation". They didn't tell us where he would be taken or for what reason.

After the men had taken Alfred away, a woman from our building came to me; she was my mother's friend. She said that she had just come out of the entrance door, when a black car stopped in front of our building. The men in the black leather coats stepped out of it. She had walked a little further and watched from a distance what would happen. She had not waited long before she saw Alfred being pushed into the car! As far as she had known, people arriving in big black cars took their victims to the Andrássy Street 60. (*It was the interrogation and torturing offices of the Arrow Cross government and later the headquarters for the Communist run State Security Forces. Presently it is the location of the House of Terror Museum.-editor*)

My mother had an acquaintance, the wife of an ex-colonel. She knew that her husband had been taken there a week ago. We quickly went to her and she readily offered her help in showing us how parcels could be delivered to the people who had been taken there for 'interrogation'.

The same day I went to the weaving mill at Master Street with my Brother Tom and informed the director that I had to leave my job. The director was very sorry, but he completely understood my decision. He wrote the first entry into my official work-book indicating the dates that I had worked there and that I had been employed there as a skilled laborer. Later on I was able to benefit greatly from the generous entry! The following day I met the ex-colonel's wife and we took a small parcel with some underclothes and dry meal for Alfred.

We crossed the Danube on the pontoon bridge and traveled on the recently working trams. The disparity between the Pest side and the Buda side was great as most of the transportation system had been restored on the Pest side of the capital. We traveled to Andrássy Street and turned into the Eötvös Street, where parcels could be given down. I was a "new" relative there and a "more or less kind" officer of the National Security Service checked and wrote my data down. He then mentioned to me that only after two weeks could I bring the next parcel. Fortunately for me he accepted mine this time. It was during those two weeks that I spent looking for a distant relative, Franz K.. I asked him to get information as to why Alfred had been taken away and what charges were being brought against him? To my greatest sorrow he had only bad news. He, as a Christian (not Jewish) barrister was not allowed to get into the neighborhood around Andrássy Street 60. He had no chance to get any information. In his frustration he met with one of his old Jewish compeers, who had free entrance to the building of "hell on earth". Franz recommended him and he gave me his address.

Instead of going directly to the Jewish barrister, I waited for the next day when I could deliver a parcel. I met the somewhat likeable man from the National Security Service, who shows some kindness and interest in me. I asked him if he could find out what the charges were against Alfred and to my amazement he promised me that he would! Three days later, we met at 3 o'clock p.m. on the corner of the Andrássy street and the Great Boulevard. It was a "risky" meeting, but he came in time and shared with me: "There are many accusations against Alfred and some are extremely grave, so it would only benefit me to get a good barrister. A week later Alfred will be taken to the jail for military and political accused on Nádor Street 9. It can be found on the corner of the Nádor and Zrínyi streets, this is where the barrister can see and talk to him, as well."

Even such grave news was great news in the middle of such darkness! After speaking with the security officer he emphatically requested that he accompany me to my sister-in-law's house on Géza Street. I had a thorough look at him. He was quite handsome with a Hungarian-like face and a big moustache. I didn't understand how such a handsome man could work for the State Security Service? As we walked we chatted about everything until we reached the Géza Street. There I entered another building because I didn't want him to know where my sister-in-law lived. I thanked him for the news at the gate and he gave me his telephone number. When saying farewell to the officer, we agreed that I would call him. He probably still waits for the call till this very day!

After a half an hour I went over to my sister-in-law's house, who didn't want to believe the things happened and the news concerning Alfred. Then I became exceedingly frightened at what I had done and how I had dared to do it. Clotilda and I nearly fainted when we took Alfred's dirty clothes out of the bag. His underclothes were covered in blood! Clotilda took them and refused to allow me to take them home. I told her that I had the address of a good barrister, whom I was about to visit and that later I would return.

The "Manci"-bridge

I crossed the Danube over to the Buda side on the Manci-bridge, which was constructed next to the destroyed Margaret-bridge. Later I traveled to my mother's house on ram Nr.9, which was running up to the Kelenföld railway station. When I arrived home I didn't say a word about the security officer, because I did not want to frighten my mother.

Some days later I visited the barrister Eugene M., who lived at the beginning of the Saint Stephen Boulevard. At first sight I liked him very much; he was so old that he could have been my father. I told him where my husband had been taken to. I didn't mention the security officer; I was simply curious as to what he could find out about Alfred's case. He wrote dwon my data and when writing my maiden name, he lifted his head up and asked whether Dr. Géza Lápossy, who had worked in the Ministry of Justice, had been one of my relatives?

"Yes!" I replied." He was my father and worked there as the director of Public Prosecutions, but on the 31st of March 1945 he unfortunately died."

Hearing this he offered his condolences and began to exalt my father. The barrister had appreciated and respected my father and known him quite well. He recalled the tale of how my father had stood as a guarantor for two Jewish barristers to protect them from being disbarred.

"Yes!" I replied "I knew about it. Those two barristers were my father's childhood friends in Alsóverecke. My father was born there and the local chemist was my grandfather."

"How small the world is!" cried the barrister aloud and added that he now had a double reason to undertake my case.

It was fantastic feeling to know as if my father had been between us, setting me at ease to put Alfred's defense into good hands. We agreed that a week later I should come in for news. When he has already spoken to my husband and had more info about the charges against him, he would tell me.

I told mother at home the things happened and she replied: "See, what an emission your father had, even from above!"

Following the interview with the barrister, Maria M., the girlfriend of the internee factory director, visited me. When she heard about Alfred's story, she offered to get me a job in the Goldberger Textile Works as a skilled weaver. She now worked there and according to my official workbook I myself was a trained shuttle-winder. I happily agreed, because I knew that there would be quite a good salary to be earned there. Although mother had a pension and we had some money, the prices of goods were climbing higher at every moment.

Inflation was rising rapidly and an extra salary was certainly needed. My teenage brothers were sick or were attending school so they were unable to help. We made arrangements with Maria that she would hold my job in the factory, until I was available. I had to manage Alfred's case in the meantime which I expected would be within two or three weeks.

A week later I went back to the barrister who asked me to look for witnesses. The barrister told me that "Alfred was transposed to the department of prisoners accused for military and political causes. As a barrister, he was allowed to enter there freely, but the accusations against him were extremely heavy." So the state security man hadn't told me a lie! He accepted the case and promised that he would do his best to gain the innocence of my husband. His fee would only be paid at the time of Alfred's last hearing. In the mean time I had to find witnesses, talk to them and send them to his office to discuss the details of the legal action. Alfred had given him two addresses, which he passed on to me. These two individuals were Alfred's "star witnesses", whom I had to find.

At that time life had clearly dropped me into deep water, the deepest that I had ever been in. No one could help me, not even my family, as I had been previously accustomed to. My most important purpose was to save Alfred's life from the horrible accusations that were clearly based on fantasy delusions. I could only ask for God's help. He took me by the hand and He led me to such good and upright people, who were able to help me. I found the captain and the mess sergeant first. They agreed to become witness in favor of Alfred and they both later visited the barrister to discuss their depositions. Later the barrister comforted me by saying that he had all details of the charge. I should be at ease, because he would surely win the legal action! By that time only one pursuer of Alfred remained, because the other one had migrated to America.

At the department of prisoners accused for military and political causes, parcels and underclothes could be delivered once a week. Every Sunday we could deliver the packages and receive the prisoner's soiled linen. When I unpacked Alfred's underclothes at home, I suddenly noticed something rustling in one of the socks! I opened it and found a letter from Alfred! The text was written on toilet paper with dense rows of his tiny and beautiful characters. This was the first sign of life since he had been taken away! In this letter he told me everything about the witnesses and he gave me the name and address of a third soldier. He asked me to write a letter to him and in the next parcel and put my letter into one of the socks. He also said he needed a small pencil and some glossy sheets of toilet paper as well. He wrote the good news that he had been allowed to go for work. Every morning four prisoners had to go between 11 and 12 o'clock to the bakery on Zrínyi Street with huge baskets guarded by a soldier with weapon. It was at the bakery that they brought bread for the prisoners. He suggested that I could go there and perhaps we could meet. I decided to give it a try!

The next morning I was there at 11 o'clock. I walked around the bakery, which was right directly opposite the jail for the military and political prisoners. Once the side door of the jail opened the captives with huge baskets appeared. Alfred was among them and they approached with a soldier who held a submachine-gun. They entered the shop with me and I behaved as if I was an ordinary customer. The guard remained in the outer room and was talking to one of the bakers. The prisoners went into the store-room in the back of the house to pack up the bread. Alfred clandestinely waved a bit and I went over to him slowly. We silently looked at each other and he gave me a piece of paper that had been folded up numerous times. He appeared to be very thin, but he was alive! We didn't dare to talk, but it was such a great meeting after so long a time!

The bakery was quite close to the Géza-street, so I dropped in to visit Clotilda. I told her about our meeting and the opinion of the barrister about the case against Alfred. Afterwards we read Alfred's letter. He wrote that he had applied for the job to get more bread, to pass the time, to move a little and for the probably that he could at least see me. He asked me not to go there every day, but only once a week on Saturday, so as not to attract the attention of the guards. On Saturdays Alfred reported that the guard was lax and that I should ask the owner of the bakery to let me into that store-room before the prisoners entered to get the bread. This way there was the possibility to talk, because the guard never entered the store-room.

I told Clotilda that the following Saturday I would try on my own. I told Clotilda that she should not come, but that later I would tell her of all that happened.

The following Saturday meeting was a complete success. The baker allowed me to go into the back store-room. When the prisoners arrived for collecting the bread, I was already there hiding in a corner. Alfred hugged me with complete joy and we were even able to talk briefly. The other three prisoners were kind enough and put the bread into the baskets without Alfred's help.

I told Alfred that Maria M. had found a job for me. Beginning the next Monday I would work as a skilled shuttle-winder worker in the Goldberger Works. Alfred was extremely happy for me. He added that some days later a writer by the name of Andrew V. was to be released from the jail and he was planning on visiting me one evening. He would bring a letter from Alfred with him. In return I should give him a pair of shoes, some shirts and a suit as well if the size matched. During the siege a bomb had hit their home and he had lost everything. In the prison they had become friends and Alfred promised to assist him in any way that he could. I told Alfred that Andrew could only come at 8 o'clock p.m., as I had to work from 7 a.m. till 7 p.m. That afternoon I went to see Maria, and we agreed to meet at a quarter past six on the corner of Mohai and Fehérvári Streets. From there we would go into the factory together and apply for the job.

The Goldberger Works had suffered from several bombing attacks. Three quarters of the buildings had been completely ruined. Only one or two rooms and their machinery had remained unhurt. In spite of the damage production had started there at once and the workers were constantly busy. The rubble was cleaned up by the men while the women worked in the production division. Shifts lasted for 12 hours in the beginning, from 7 a.m. to 7 p.m., and from 7 p.m. to 7 a.m.

Fortunately for me in the spring, I had worked with Alfred in the weaving mill. So this time I wasn't employed as an unskilled labor of the Goldberger Textile Works, but instead as a skilled laborer from 10.09.1945. After securing my employment from the director I looked for Maria. She showed me a great shuttle-winder machine next to her workstation on which I was to work. Within an hour she showed me how to use the "winding-claw" and it seemed to be a very interesting job.

There were 30 small winders at upper midsection of the machine. Under them were placed the spindles with wool on them. Then again 30 click reels were put above these, where to the cotton yam ran up. We had to set them together making a weaver's knot using the winding-claw, which was constantly attached to our right hands. Our task was to always pay attention to the 30 winders and when the cotton yam was torn the machine would stop working. Then we ran to the place where the yam had broken and made a knot. When a spindle became empty, we took it off and replaced it with another one. The full click reels were then pulled off the machine. Another machine rolled cotton yam from the large click reels to a weaving roll. These were then placed into a galley, where the weaving women were busy with their jobs by weaving the rolls into different fabrics. This was the process of cotton textiles, but the weaving part was not our job.

In the beginning Maria willingly helped me a lot. She also stated that I learned quickly. A week later I was already doing the job completely alone and she complimented me on my achievements. At that time I wouldn't have changed her kind words for any money, it touched me so deeply! It was such a fantastic feeling to get into a big factory, working among the men and women of the working class. In the smaller Master Street weaving mill there were only 5 of us who were employed. At the Goldberger's Weaving Mill, 35-40 women or even more worked in the same room. Most women were middle aged or older and their faces showed the decades of hard work by the machines. Maria asked the women working next to us to put a silencer on their speech, when they were about to use their foul language. It happened unfortunately nearly every minute. Comically I told them not to bother or to pay attention to me; the machines make such a noise anyway that I could not hear a thing. If I heard something by chance, I myself would simply stuff my fingers into my ears. The women liked my attitude enough, that an older woman working on the machine opposite to me convivially covered her mouth every time she said such nasty things.

I had to get used to so many different things. Above all the big noise made by the weaving-machines and the 12 hours of standing in front of them. Sometimes near the end of the shift, if the cotton yam was of good quality, we could sit down on wood-boxes and take a short break. At weekends we worked by turns, one week during the day shift, the next week only at night. For the night shifts we were paid more of course.

Pay day was always Saturday. Because the inflation was rapidly increasing, the factory was forced to begin paying our salaries with goods and commodities. Every time we had to take home more and more goods on Saturdays. This was of course highly welcomed at home. My mother was happy, because under such an agreement she did not have to do barter so much with rural citizens. Later on we received other commodities from the "International Red Cross" due to my sick brothers. We received packages of milk, cocoa powder, sugar, tea, and margarine.

In the meantime the writer Andrew V. visited me one evening. He was taken to the Andrássy-street 60 just like Alfred and was put into the military and political division. He told me many tales of the horrible things which they had undergone. I learned that my poor Alfred had been beaten and while he was hung out from the third floor window until he signed and confessed to the charges against him. After his confession he was not tortured any more. The writer gave me Alfred's letter, saying that he smuggled it out of the prison within the sole of his shoe. He was quite nervous that the sole would have fallen off and been left behind in the jail. His size and build were just like those of Alfred, so I gave him a suit, some shirts, a pair of shoes and some socks. He received them gratefully. It felt so good to help him!

At the end of September Andrea K. visited us. She was one of my cousins from my mother's side. Her father, a colonel, had died on the front and her husband who was a police officer, was taken away by the Russians into a prisoner-of-war camp. She had no information about where he could be. I mentioned the place, where I worked and she asked me to show her the way how she could be employed as a weaver. She was employed by the factory but only as an unskilled labor. Her training lasted for 6 weeks, where she worked without salary. Later, after getting the qualification as a "skilled worker", she received two weaver machines and salary after production.

Andrea worked in the room next to ours and we discovered together during the night shift a peaceful staircase. At the bottom of the staircase we would sit down for an hour and slept on each other's shoulder. Such nightly disappearances were done by nearly everybody, so that many could have the much needed rest. Though not officially tolerated, we were none the less "allowed" to do so!

Such coincidences happened in the factory! One day during the daytime shift we received a new shift-leader George. He was a tall red haired and freckled man. When noticing me he came to me and asked whether I recognized him? After thinking back I managed to recall the following:

"Aren't you the one, who studied at the Cistercian High school and every day we were running in the opposite direction right before 8 o'clock and you greeted me?"

"Oh yes" he said smiling, "I was a great admirer of yours and knew a lot about you, but I could never get closer to you then, but you see the chance has led our ways closer again!"

"So sorry, but you are too late, because I have already been married!" I tried to cool him down, which he acknowledged with a bit of disappointment, but he remained well-mannered and considerate. George was the one in the factory who determined which worker would get which kind of material to be processed from the spindles. He always sent me and Maria the best quality material so naturally the amount of our production rose. This way we didn't have to pass our time by making so many knots, as in the case of inferior quality cotton.

Later, Maria told me laughing: "I made a good deal with you! In the end our names would be written on the notice board as Sztahanovistas!" (*Sztahanovista was the title given to workers who normally attained a 300% increase in production. The title was given after the fabled Ukrainian coal miner Aleksei Grigorievich Stakhanov who increased his own quota 14 times over. Later to 'be like Stakhanov' was used as a propaganda tool to increase production-editor*). Some time later we were able to read our names on the production board. We could indeed hold our heads a little higher among the names of older workers.

Maria was a clever, ambitious and benevolent girl with whom I used to talk a lot when going to and coming back from the factory. Over time I learned the story of her life. She had become an orphan at quite a young age and lived alone in the flat of her parents. She could not continue studying after elementary school and instead went to work in the Standard

Works at Fehérvár Street to provide for herself. There she met the director, who later became her boy-friend. I got to know him as an internee when they were in the same place with Alfred. After the director was released, he was not able to go back and work for the Standard Works and as a result was not able to find any work at all. Maria left the factory and went to work in the Goldberger Works and cared for her boyfriend in those times fraught with danger. I didn't tell anyone a thing about Alfred, only Maria knew where he had been taken to and what had happened to him. These were our little "secrets".

Maria wondered how easily and quickly I had adapted myself to the life of a factory worker and how diligently I worked. Sometimes even she could hardly keep up the pace with me.

"You see" I told her "I learned all this diligence from my parents and I learned that whenever the maximum was required of me I should give my all with results that can be trusted. We have to reconstruct our country from the ruins and our work is a part of that reconstruction. Your job is important and mine and those of the citizens living here, as well."

"You speak like a speaker" she said laughing.

"Not completely" I told her "I speak like a teacher!"

Later both of us entered the Social Democratic Party, because we both had similar views.

At the end of September 1945 on a Sunday afternoon my mother, my Uncle Charles and my Brother Tom went to visit my brother Géza in the convalescent hospital. At that time I had been working in the factory for about two weeks and my legs were very sore and in need of rest, so I decided to stay at home and relax. The golden sunshine illuminated our flat and I opened both parts of our entrance door and in the hall I sun-bathed my ailing legs. It was such a beautiful end to September, so the lines of our national poet Petőfi Sándor came to my mind:

> The flowers in the valley are still at bloom,
> The aspen is verdant by the casement
> But take a look at the winter time there
> Snow had covered the top of the crags.
> In my heart still lives the fiery summer,

With the whole spring garnishing from it,
But see the autumn in among my dark
hair,
The white-frost of winter occupied my
head."

I had hardly finished whispering half aloud the first verses of this beautiful poem, when the shadow of a tall man blotted out the bright sunshine. I couldn't see his face and I only heard his voice as my heart started to pound in my chest.

"Louis Diósy, are you here?" I rejoiced. My legs were shaking because of emotion that I could hardly stand up, but I forced patience upon myself. We shook hands and I offered him a seat and he told me the purpose of his visit.

He came to have a look at his sister Maria's flat and to speak to the family currently living there. They had been caring for it since Maria had fled to the west. He had not yet heard anything about his sister, but they were expected to return home soon. Every time more and more refugees were returning home from the west.

He added that in 1944 he wasn't able to write me more frequently because of the military situation and that I had misunderstood him. Still he did not tell of the events in any detail. He asked how I was doing, because he heard about my marriage to Alfred. I briefly told him about the siege, the death of my father and Alfred's situation. When I told him about Alfred in prison, Louis suddenly asked me to divorce Alfred and to marry him instead. He threatened that if I did not, he would never marry anyone else. This seemed so unbelievable and hollow to me that I told him the following: "Look Louis, time has already passed over us. My husband, as I already mentioned, is in jail at the moment, his life depends on my love, my perseverance and my lawyer. When I married him I took an oath to stay next to him not only in good, but in bad times, as well. The latter time has come now!" I continued telling him: "Probably the day would come, when you Louis would accuse me, if I now would push everything aside by abandoning it and go with you. I have to consider the fact, that mainly I am the head of the family now. I started working in a factory not long ago for quite a good salary. Please understand that I can't take another decision!"

I saw on his face that my words had hit him bad, but I felt in myself that I had to be able to think responsibly and to act as an accountable grown up who was able to take decisions. At that time I felt myself older than my real age was. Later we talked about some banal things and he said a saddened farewell to walk away into the fading light.

Again the words of Petőfi sounded within me:

> "But see the autumn in among my dark
> hair,
> The white-frost of winter occupied my

For many long years I did not hear from Louis again, but let's turn back to those days!"

I searched for the third witness, who had served under Alfred in the army. I found him living in the 7th district of the capital. He also completely sided with Alfred. Our barrister was completely satisfied with the witnesses that I had found.

In October my Aunt Helen with her family along with her sister Magdalene moved into their Kökörcsin street building. They came to live in their 3-room flat on the first floor, which remained abandoned after a woman living there had taken refuge in the USA.

Because of the severe housing shortage, the local Council determined housing for two families into the larger private flats. Because of this, Aunt Helen's flat was displaced with an additional family of four. They were placed into the grand room with an additional half room, which had a separate entrance. In the end only two big rooms and the hall remained under the supervision of my Aunt Helen. My Aunt Magdalene then moved in with us and found a job in the Master Street post office, because before the war she had worked as postmistress in the Trans-Danube region.

My Uncle Charles also moved in with his sister Kate. He tried to find a job and sometimes he went to work for various chemists in the neighboring pharmacies. He diligently read the advertisements in the magazine "Chemist" looking for more permanent employment. By that time he had recovered his previous mentality more or less. He usually spent his lunch times at our place, because my Aunt Kate gave extra lessons at school after the morning classes. She provided day care in the afternoons too to get more money. She also helped her brother Charles financially, in buying him clothes, because my father's clothes and shoes didn't fit him at all.

In the meantime our lawyer had informed me in advance that Alfred would be taken from the army and political division to the Markó Street jail, because his physical condition had deteriorated. The lawyer had persuaded the prison doctor to allow me to bring in a lunch every day for him. The lawyer asked me whether I wanted to do that.

"Yes, of course!" I happily replied. I was able to exchange my daytime sift for the night at the factory so that during the daytime I could take food to the Markó jail for Alfred.

As it happened, Alfred steadily improved under the more humane conditions. I organized to take him lunch every day. Maria also converted her shift to the night time so that she was with me during those long 12 hours. Because we took on the night shift our salaries also increased, a blessing that we both needed at the time.

When I returned home from the factory in the morning, I slept until 11 o'clock. During that time my mother prepared lunch. We put it into a lunchbox and I took it to the Markó jail by traveling on the tram Nr.9. to the Manci Bridge and later by foot. I put the lunchbox into a big bag and wrapped tightly. When Alfred finally received the package, sometime between 12 and 2 p.m. it was still warm. We used two lunchboxes and two vacuum sealed bottles. In one of the bottles I took him coffee with milk or hot chocolate. I returned home by half past two in the afternoon, ate my lunch and slept until 6 p.m. Later I would go to the factory. I did this routine for the five months that Alfred spent in jail.

One time when I was caring for Alfred's soiled clothes, I found another letter. This one was hidden in the toe of a sock. Alfred had written to thank me and my mother for the very delicious meals. He also wrote to tell me that he had hid his letters in the inner part of the thermos bottle. He suggested that I also put them in there and not into the socks. I had another new idea of putting the letters wrapped in a small section of wax paper under the quark filled pancakes.

Sometimes I hid my letters in one of the pancakes right besides the raisin-quark filling.

After a while the guards became aware of the letters hidden within the vacuum sealed bottles. Fortunately for Alfred he had taken my letter out immediately after he got the bottle so when the guards came to search they did not find anything. Many of the other prisoners were also using the bottles to hide letters and eventually the use of vacuum sealed bottles was forbidden.

Alfred conceived of another plan for transporting the letters between each other. He asked me to sew up two identical bags with zippers along the upper seam. So that I did not misunderstand he even made a drawing of it. The two corners underneath were to be introverted and sewn with big stitches similar to those of a sewing machine. The hole made from that design served us well as post box for our letters. Needles and thread were one of the items that could be given them in order that the prisoners could be able to repair their own clothes. They also had blades for their razors.

I prepared the two bags as Alfred had described. They were made of a strong and deep red material. Because of these bags a constant stream of correspondence ensued between us. When I gave him his new underclothes I was able to send a letter and when he gave me his old dirty ones he was able to reply. We did this postal system the entire time that Alfred was in prison without being discovered. Alfred being a "precise German" wrote long letters to me using his beautiful and tiny characters. He placed the letters into the bottom of the bag and expertly sewed it back up. Naturally he used the same color thread that I had used and his stitching was similar to that of a sewing machine. It was no wonder that he was a textile professional! These "secret" letters helped him survive the one and half year prison with interesting and colorful times.

The period of waiting for Alfred to be released dragged on for an abnormal amount of time. The only remaining plaintiff never arrived to testify at all of the three hearing dates. Alfred was brought before the court on November of 1945, April and August of 1946. The judge put the hearing off letting the "blackguard" prisoner suffer even more and longer! Alfred's luck was unfortunate in that he was put in among very good company as a political prisoner. He spent his time with the "members of the old genteel, the middle and upper classes" during his imprisonment.

In the meantime our lawyer and I kept the hope alive in him. But sometimes, when his poor fellow prisoners were taken away to be hanged, he fell into a deep apathy. Reading his letters also influenced moments of despair in me as well. I never said a thing to anyone about that, only to Maria. She always comforted and helped me with her everlasting optimism and gave me strength to go on with the fight.
God's grace helped me and I always felt that he was with me.

Christmas of 1945 arrived and the workers in the factory were given a time for vacation until the New Year. Because of the time off, I could go to jail every day and take Alfred the allowed amount of food improved by the addition of cakes from the Holidays. I remember it was spring like warm weather as many were wearing opened coats and going about without a hat. We all hoped for good results from the coming New Year. My greatest hope was that Alfred's case would end with his acquittal, my brother Géza to get better and for my Uncle Charles to find a permanent job

1946

The beginning of March was quite cold and snowy just as winter had returned. I had already prepared the unsuspicious lunch for Alfred and I still had enough time to spare so I dropped into Clotilda's house to warm his lunch at her place. She welcomed me and asked me immediately whether I had heard that on that very morning *Szálasi (leader of the Hungarian Nazis and ex-prime minister)*, Beregfi, the ex-Minister of Defense and two other officers were hanged on the courtyard of the jail. She offered to escort me, so that I would not be there alone. We arrived at the Markó jail at half past twelve p.m. It was there where we were met by a dreadful scene waited for us. A huge crowd was shouting and raving with fury in front of and around the building. They wanted to break the gates in. There were scores of policemen about. They fired their weapons up into the air in an attempt to subdue the crowd but with little success.

Clotilda and I managed to get into one of the corridors of the building. It was unbelievable as many people stood there, even sitting on each other's shoulder. They were looking down to the prison courtyard and screaming fiercely. We tried to get out from that place and eventually we were caught by a jailer. We asked him if it was possible to deliver a lunch today. He replied that it was possible, but we had to wait another half an hour. On that particular day it was only possible between two and three o'clock p.m. He led us to a door which was opened and then we were allowed to go. Some women have already stood there with lunchboxes in their hands. We all waited flabbergasted and silent and could not imagine what we had got involved into and what would seen. Clotilda and I stood there hooking at each other and trembling with anxiety.

Once the door opened up and we were allowed to enter in pairs. The guards lead us through the prison court yard to the windows where we could deliver the food. There we were confronted with a sight that struck terror in our hearts. At the other end of the court, only a few meters away from us were four of the gallows. Hanging on the gallows was the Arrow Cross leader Szálasi and his company with sacks on their heads. Their legs were just wobbling in the air as a shallow drift of snow hung over the prison yard.

How could we have gotten out from there? I do not know, because the crowd was pressing in and raging even in the side-streets. Later I went to Clotilda's place and tried to clam my nerves. I drank a little water. I was not able to eat and I hurried to get home, where my family could not imagine where I had been for such a long time. I could not even sleep in the afternoon; the impact of the sight of the executed people had left such an impression on my mind.

In the evening I talked over the events with Maria on the way to the factory. We agreed that the men had certainly deserved their fate for great sins were certainly burdening their souls. Regardless I should not have seen their end!

That night I buried myself into my work. It did me good for my disturbing thoughts and at least it turned my attention away from the horrors I had seen in the daytime.

On April of 1946 Alfred was moved to a relocation jail after his second unsuccessful hearing. The new jail was at the end station of the Nr.28 tram, opposite to the public cemetery. In the relocation jail I could bring him new clothes and food once a week on Sundays. To make my joy even more complete we were allowed a time for visitation once a month.

Szálasi before the execution on the jail-court

Due to the new circumstances I stopped working during the night shift, which had already been a big burden for me. In the meantime Alfred's condition improved considerably. We continued our secret correspondence undisturbed from the probes of the guards. Alfred wrote to be in the same cell as the Jesuit clerk Dr. Zoltán Nyisztor. At the time he had been a famous orator before the war. At that time he made a promise to the clerk as well as himself that he would convert to be a devout Catholic when he was released from prison. He promised that he would also teach his children the Catholic faith as well. Previously, Alfred had been baptized into the Evangelistic faith.

As I mentioned my brother Géza returned from the convalescent hospital quite fat, healed, content and full of energy. In July he passed his final exam for his upper education and proceeded to pass the entrance exam for the University of Veterinary Sciences. Later we received another devastating blow from the communist regime! My brother Géza was thrown out of the Veterinary University and could not continue his studies for a second year. The reason given was that our parents had been white collar workers. But my brother could not be disheartened or beat down by the Party leader Rákosi or by his communist regime! During the months of July and August Géza came to work in the Goldberger Works as a substitute office worker for those who were off on their summer vacations. So for a short time he received a salary, but at the ear of a "million Pengős", money lost its value every minute.

Inflation after the war was rampant and the government enacted a new form of money, the "Forint" from 1st of August 1946. After the introduction of the new money, we were always happy to do the shopping as more and more stores opened to sell their wares. I can remember when we could buy a bag full of products for a mere ten Forints.

/This was done after the Hungarians were able to secure gold deposits that the Germans had confiscated in 1944 and were later captured by the American forces. The reserves were promised to the Hungarians after a delegation was sent to the USA in the spring of 1946-editor./

At the end of August there was another hearing for Alfred in the Markó jail, but the accuser again failed to appear. Seeing the disregard of the plaintiff, the judge made and edict that the man was to be brought by the police to the next hearing, and then he would close the case. My lawyer tried to "set me at ease" and he reminded me that the cases were all progressing rather slowly at that time. Above all else we simply had to wait for the end, for which he certainly wanted to prove Alfred's innocence.

The time passed very slowly for Alfred and me, but we never gave up hope!

During this time the factory changed to three shifts during the day, because more and more departments were opening and demand was growing. From the ruins the old halls we rebuilt and were once again filled with workers. Maria and I worked the first from 6 a.m. till 2 p.m. and next week from 10 p.m. to 6 a.m. The afternoon shifts were always better, because this way we could manage our time better and the salary remained the same. During the national holiday of Saint Steven's Day, the 20th of August, the workers of the factory received textiles with minor defects in them. Those workers with larger families received more, while those who were single received less. For my gift I received some calico and cotton textile that was enough to make one or two dresses. I was very happy, because at this time mother had learned to tailor women's dresses from a friend of hers. Before the war my mother's friend operated a woman's dress salon. Mother sewed the dresses together, one for herself and the other for me. I could not thank her enough for the skills of her hands! Later she always made our dresses. She also began to earn money for her tailoring skills as her friends gave employed her talents as well. After the introduction of the "strong Forint" we were no longer pain in food which we had to carry from the factory. We were "simply" paid in money.

My Sunday mornings became occupied with taking a "hike" to the relocation jail. I took the clean clothes and brought home the dirty ones in that the special deep-red bag. Later I entered by the way of the cemetery when it was nice weather, because Alfred had written me to do so. His cell was on the third floor and from there he had a view of the cemetery. He asked me to go to a certain point in the cemetery from where I could see the high windows of the cells on the third floor. He told me to take a big white cloth and start waving to him. In return I should pay attention as he would wave as well. After doing this a white cloth appeared waving from behind a window. I knew that it was Alfred at once!

We were not the only ones who were observing each other, but the guards as well. When they noticed the white cloth flashing behind the window they fired into the air. I heard the guns report. It was at that time when I dashed out of the cemetery as soon as I could. At noon there was no one around there, but if there had been they would have surely thought me to be a fool! Alfred wrote me in one of his long letters that the guards had not noticed his waiving as he never received any punished for that. He told me how good it was to see my white cloth and to feel that we were together as one spirit! He thanked me so many times that I cared for him!

My brother Géza began his studies at the University in September of 1946, my brother Tom entered the 3rd year of school year in the Cistercian High School. My Uncle Charles was still working for sporadic periods. Magdalene moved back in with my Aunt Helen so that she could assist her more. During this time my Uncle Franz was also arrested and detained in prison. Helen had to go on working and making sure their small children attended school.

Franz was arrested by the testimony of an anonymous informant. They were certain that it had been the woman living under their flat who was responsible for informing on him to the police. It was against the law at that time to perform "unauthorized trade". When they moved up to Budapest from the county, they brought what was left of their own possession; the two sacks of flour. It was these that they had forgotten about in the pit. They brought them up to the city and placed them in the attic of the house. The neighbor caught sight of the sacks and immediately informed the police of their activity. At that time anyone, who had any surplus or reserve of any kind of food also had envious and hostile people around him. These individuals could easily find themselves in an internee camp. Their charges were always put under the title of "unauthorized trade".

Finally the eagerly awaited day arrived, when Alfred's fourth hearing took place on the 18th of December 1946. The trial took place in the Markó jail's building. We went there with Clotilda and some other relatives before the trial began. As we waited our lawyer also arrived and began to set our fears at rest. When the proceedings began we witnessed the most absurd sight. From one end of the corridor Alfred entered accompanied by a guard. From the other end the "plaintiff" arrived with a policeman. There was nothing on Alfred's hands, but the accuser was in handcuffs, so that he could not escape. It was only after the plaintiff entered the room was he released from his bonds. Alfred's three witnesses also arrived and they also witnessed the ridiculousness of the scene.

When I entered the room, I asked God to help me!

The room was already full of strangers, because it used to be a favorite pastime to visit the law courts as "diversion". It was a place where one could hear some "gripping" stories! The judge ordered for silence and then proceeded with the details of the trial. I wrote them here briefly so as to make the story understandable.

"At the beginning of January 1944 Alfred received a draft from the army as a reserve quartermaster lieutenant. He was ordered to harvest wood from Rahó in Máramaros County in Rumania. Twelve men were ordered from the forced labor service that was attached to their corps. These men were who worked alongside the other soldiers.

One night, when the sergeant-major went out to the court yard some of the men in the labor service hid in the darkness. They threw a blanket on the Sergeants head and then beat him repeatedly. A soldier passing by saw this event and then rescued the sergeant-major from his assailants.

The following day Alfred learned of the event. He called the whole corps together and he told the people on forced labor that the event counted as "rioting". If he informed about the incident to the upper military authorities then a court-martial process would certainly begin. As the event occurred during war-time, capitol punishment could have easily been pressed upon all of the 12 men from the forced labor unit. If the beating of the sergeant had been performed by regular soldiers, there would be no option!

Instead Alfred asked the 12 people to choose between being reported to the military authorities or to arrange collective punishment amongst them. Those who had planned the attack were to step forward and confess. The sergeant-major would then lash each one 25 times on their backs. Alfred had hoped that the incident and the punishment would serve as an example for the others!

Later two men stepped forward and chose the second possibility."

After 1945 these same two men posted an advertisement in a newspaper. They wanted to find the others who had been in the forced labor unit. The ad did not produce any results, so it was only these two individuals who then went and denounced Alfred to the courts. In the meantime one of the accusers migrated to America and the second one refused to appear at the previous court-hearings. Because of this he was forced by the police to appear at court on the fourth hearing.

After delineating the case the judge called to listen to the testimony of the "plaintiff". Alfred then was able to produce his own witnesses. The first was the captain, then the sergeant-major and finally a solder who had been there. All three bore witness in favor of Alfred.

Clotilda sat next to me and I squeezed her hand when our lawyer started to speak. He spoke just like a wise old rabbi. He did not only speak to the judge, but to the audience as well since most of them were Jews. During his half an hour long plea he highlighted the most important parts. He finished his speech by saying why the plaintiff and the other 11 people who were in the labor service survived the war. If Alfred had not been wise and humanitarian by making this decision, their fate would have certainly been different. During the oral plea a silence descended over the court and many started weeping.

After the judge pronounced the final verdict, our lawyer came to me and said: "Please go to the side door of the Markó jail. Within a half and hour you can hug your husband again for which you deserve very much! Thank you for your help!" I would have liked to hug him with such happiness! But we simply said farewell with a well-mannered handshake. He asked me to visit him in some days' time in his office. Later I ran to the side gate and in half an hour Alfred and I were reunited once again!

In the factory textile were once again given as a present and bonus before Christmas. This time I received quite a lot. Later Alfred and I visited our lawyer and thanked him for his successful work. I gave him the fee and some textile that was enough for two clothes. Textile at that time was counted as and extreme luxury. Our lawyer happily accepted them.

When saying farewell to us he said: "Now be happy and you, Mr. Kosch appreciate your wife, because she did a great thing!"

The Christmas of 1946 was as beautiful for us as those that are written in fairytales! The Holiday was celebrated with our family and with my Uncle Charles and my Aunt Kate. It was a happy and peaceful time!

1947

After the trial I undertook daytime shifts in the factory. In the afternoons we visited Alfred's relatives and he told them the tales of his past one and half years. They listened intently and they requested that they wanted to help him. The most reasonable proposition was his sister Elza's husband's idea. He owned a Board Producing Company and he suggested to Alfred to make a weaving loom in his plant. He planned to produce textile from the very hard wood that he used for boards. At that time he still possessed his own plant even before nationalization of factories! Alfred just had to give him the drawings and the technical descriptions. Later he collected so much money for the endeavor that he could have started a small mill on his own. They agreed to the project and made a deal that summer. Alfred rented a small place on the corner of Verpeléti (now Karinthy Frigyes Street) and Vak Bottyán

Street. The weaving machine and the shuttle-winder were taken down into the half-cellar and Alfred then started working in his own small weaving mill. The weaving was made by Alfred while the reeling was done by Franz, who was his sister Clotilda's son. He was unemployed as "ex-first lieutenant". My Aunt Helen also worked there.

I became ill with a very strong flu at the beginning of March. I kept on coughing for quite a long time. Our local doctor made a thorough examination on me and considered my brother Géza's previous bout with tuberculosis. Thank God that nothing could be found on my lungs. Instead they found another problem with my heart. The doctor asked me where I worked. I told him that many nights I had spent doing my job in the factory. Upon learning of my work in the factory he advised me to take a rest from work for a certain time, to eat well and look for another job in an office. I would have to do that if I didn't want my heart to be permanently damaged. According to his diagnosis my heart was enlarged and was quite weak.

When I told the news of my health at home, my Aunt Kate assured me that she would talk to her friend Margaret B about finding me other employment. Margaret worked within the Council of the Capital. She fully supported my position and she agreed to help me. She told me that at that time they were looking for workers in the Music and Physical Education Departments. She knew that I previously had attended a shorthand and typing course after the Collegiate School. She promised that she would make a recommendation for me. Afterwards it was not difficult at all for me to be hired and after interviewing with Emery E., nicknamed uncle Dődi by all, I was chosen to be the office leader. I started working at the Council of the Capital on the 15th of April, 1947.

Another wonderful coincidence of event happened to me again! The Office was on the third floor of the Sugar Street primary school. When I entered there on my first day who was it that I saw to my greatest surprise and joy?! I ran into one of my dear friends from the air-raid shelter Füri B. She had worked there since January of 1947 as a physical education teacher. The Physical Education Department Conservancy was about to be formed at that time. Füri waited eagerly to get a professional chief clerk, as it was a problem for her to type.

She happily explained the details of the work required of me and told me as a friend mentioned the "good and bad habits" of our bosses as well. In the mornings we were alone and had time to discuss everything thoroughly. She explained that my senior boss was uncle Dődi. Under his leadership worked all the physical education supervisors of primary schools in the districts of greater Budapest. There were 4 women and 3 men along with my other bosses. They were all very nice people, who came together in the office after work at around 1 p.m. and usually dictated reports or sometimes held conferences. It was the proceedings that I had to record.

In the mornings I was on my own with the task of supervising the cards of all the primary schools. I had to record all of the newly purchased and distributed sporting goods and also to notify the schools when they could come to collect their items. I was charged with distributing these from the cellar warehouse of the Sugar Street building. I had to receive all the calls and to pass all of the requests of the schools to the appropriate supervisor. Above all Füri told me that in among the supervisors were several interesting people. We had an Olympic judge, the countess Irene B., Mr. Eugene H. and a "wild" communist Franz K. She advised me to be cautious with him!

368. — XXVIII/a FELÜGYELŐIGAZGATÓI HIVATAL
IV., Cukor-utca 6. (Távbeszélő: 189—638)

Sorszám	Az oktató neve	Állása
1.	HALÁPY JENŐ	p. ig. a h. vez.
2.	Lengyel Gyula	ip. ig.
		felügy. ig.
3.	Mezei Béla	p. ig.
		felügy. ig.
4.	Rácz János	n. ig.,
		felügy. ig.
5.	Boros Nándorné	
	Háda Mária	n. r .
6.	Cseresznyés Józsefné	
	Kis Magda	r. isk. kez.
7.	Fákla Jolán	házt. tanf. r.
8.	Haltenberger Alice	r. isk. kez.
9.	Kis István (l.)	n. r.
10.	Dr Kokovay Lajos	p. ig.
11.	Dr Kokovay Lajosné	
	Weörös Sarolta	n. r.
12.	Kiss Ilona	p. r.
13.	Kosch Alfrédné	
	Lápossy Zsuzsa (testnev. felügyelet)	r. isk. kez.
14.	Mezei Mária (testnev. felügyelet)	r. isk. kez.
15.	Rév Sándor	n. ig.
16.	Schaffer Erzsébet	r. isk. kez.
17.	Tóth Béla	n. r.
18.	Ruck István	alt.
19.	özv. Benedikti Istvánné	
	Nyul Mária	alt.-nő
20.	Müller Mária	alt.-nő

Kósa Mária 905., n. r. 925., 927. XIV., Szent Domonkos-u. 19. 217
Kósa Tiborné Kelényi Edit 920., r. óv. 943., 945. XII., Cseresznye-u. 13. 58
Kosaras István 915., kk. r. 941., 945. VIII., Köztársaság-tér 15. 235
Kosári Ilona 891., r. óv. 911., 913. VII., Murányi-u. 2. 16
Kosch Alfrédné Lápossy Zsuzsánna 923., r. isk. kez., 947., XI., Tengernagy-
  utca 3. 368
Kostyalik Ferencné dr, Füzesy Emilia 909., n. r. 930., 940. VIII., Mária-u. 46. 139 140
Koszorú Mária 928., isk. orv. assz. 947., X., Család-u. 35—37. 365

I was listed as office worker

I almost fainted, when uncle Dődi entered and listed the scope of my activities and hoped that we could work together efficiently.

I said farewell to Füri after the first workday and promised to visit her at home soon. She was curious how I managed doing my job and in what measure her advice could have been used. I learned the scope of my activities quickly. None of them were boring at all due to the wide diversity! In May I was given the task of preparing for the regional gymnastic competition in all of the schools. I had to supply the pupils with the necessary clothes, balls, hoops, sporting goods and skipping ropes so that they would all appear uniform. Tickets also had to be given to the students so that they could reach the Stadium on the trams. The physical education teachers and their assistants came to fetch the sporting supplies. I had to organize the distribution of the sporting equipment so that it was done quickly. I did not want any unnecessary crowding in our office as we worked in a big long room.

As I was working I noticed some strange and unknown physical problems. I was suddenly driven to despair thinking that I hardly started working at this excellent job only to get sick right now? When I told this to my mother, she brought me to her gynecologist who examined me. Afterwards the doctor congratulated me for "my would-be baby". She explained that this was the cause of my complaints, but within a short time they would certainly be over. I should not fear as I was not sick at all! The world turned around me at that very moment! I don't know how other expectant women behave, but I was filled with such an indescribable happiness! From that time nothing else interested me except for "my little baby"! At that time doctors did not have ultrasound equipment, but I knew that I would have a beautiful small son! It was with this hope that I lived for 9 months and happily waited for him, together with Alfred! During that time my good humor and energy seemed to double. I was doing so well! I had some favorite meals before, but during that time I ate all kind of foods and still did not put on too much weight.

When I left the textile factory, I had mixed feelings. To my greatest surprise the weaver women told me that I deserved a job more matching to me and they wished me success in all my further works! Andrea, my cousin stayed in the factory as weaver until her husband was allowed to come home after he spent 6 years in the prisoner-of-war camp! My friend Maria visited me regularly. Alfred and I visited her ex-director boyfriend, who managed to at long last find employment in a warehouse. Returning to the tale of my current job while comparing it to the previous one in the factory, the disparity could have not been greater! I had very good time at the Physical Education Department Conservancy with all of my supervisor colleagues. They all cared and helped me out after taking notice that I was pregnant. Because of this "my little baby" was able to develop under the best circumstances!

The regional gymnastic performance was a complete success! At the end of the school year the evaluations for all the physical education workers had to be compiled. At that time the supervisors convened and dictated to me the evaluation of the years work for all the physical education teachers in their region. Somehow I managed to soften the "hard communist" with my compassionate words. I put an end to the vicious words on the records or convinced him to give more leeway with certain teachers so that they could have the possibility to prove their competency. I was the happiest when this supervisor accepted my proposals and this way I was able to save their job and perhaps the life of some teacher.

Uncle Dődi as a bachelor was very versatile man besides his work. He was an educated man who told me about the atom and about the dreadful, horrible effects of the atomic bomb. He had previously studied about it and investigated the topic for quite a long time. One of the supervisors P. Gustavo shared with us that when Uncle Dődi's old flat was damaged by a bomb, they gave him a room to live in. Uncle Dődi then fabricated a small chamber of lamina in the middle of the room. There he could play the violin undisturbed at nights without making any noise. Apparently he played beautifully and no-one was disturbed by his passion.

During the summer I managed to create extra work for myself. With the big typewriter I made new cartons in place of the old and worn out ones for every school. At that time I also visited Füri with Alfred and told about the events in the office. Füri as a young mother also gave me useful advice. Her mother with her little son spent the whole summer in the village of C. at their old family holiday-house. She visited that place with her husband for various times. She couldn't stop praising the clean alpine air, the silence and tranquility that always greeting them there. The families of her sister and brother visited that place in shifts. Around 50 years later I got to know the region, because my son George built a house there on top of a small hill and moved there with his family. When I am at their place it feels just like spending my summer holidays in Verecke.

Later we received another devastating blow from the communist regime! My brother Géza was thrown out of the Veterinary University and could not continue his studies for a second year. The reason given was that our parents had been white collar workers. But my brother could not be disheartened or beat down by the Party leader Rákosi or by his communist regime! Not far from our place there was a construction entrepreneur. Géza visited him and told him of his case and applied for a job. He was given employment as and assistant to the electricians. Because of this, he was also able to provide and extra income. With his strong willpower and diligence for work he quickly learned the trade and was able to master the basic and then later the advanced electrical works. Later he was able to pass a proficiency exam as well.

In 1948-49 the nationalization of private industry began. At that time he has already been employed in the strong demand for electricians but with the nationalization he found work in the state owned factories.

In the meantime he also got to know a beautiful woman, who was very attractive indeed even in the eyes of other women. Géza "fell in love with her at the first sight" and he moved in with her. Ika V. was a divorced woman, who lived with her 3 year old son in her flat on the Round Square. She worked as a draughtsman in one of the large state companies.

My brother Géza had a "prince like" appearance. He was handsome inside as well as outside. Whenever they appeared somewhere, there was no-one, who didn't stare at them!

Ika and Géza

She had older parents as well as an elder and younger sister. Her father was of Serbian origin, so their name was Serb-like, as well. Her hair was black as coal and she had deep brown eyes. She was a tall and slender woman who always wore nice dresses. She was certainly a "Serb beauty". In a short time I was able to make friends with her as she was a very nice woman indeed. Her son Andreas was an animated small child. He spent much of his time at his grandparents' place.

One day I received a notification from the Social Democratic Party to check over at the Communist Party. There was an acquaintance at the Communists Party, a Jewish woman Mrs. Gőbel. Her daughter had been one of my classmates in elementary school. She was the president of the committee. Mostly she was the one who was questioning me and in the end she drew her conclusion. "How do I suppose that the Communist Party would take on the unchecked child of a previous Chief Crown Lawyer?" Because of this I was shut out of the Communist Party! I kept my feelings to myself until I left, so that they didn't notice how happy I was that they did not want me!

At autumn, doctors from Denmark arrived to Hungary and offered to give the whole population an injection against tuberculosis. The injection was called BCG. The medicine was still in the experimental state, but the government allowed it none the less. They had given the whole country over to Denmark for its little experiment. As the laymen we were to be the test subjects.

They started with calling everyone to the doctor's office, where we got a "probe" into our arms and if around it became red and swollen the injection was not given. This test showed the doctors that the person was already "infected". This was the case with my two brothers, Alfred and me, only my mother tested negative. She postponed the injection saying that she would rather pay a penalty than let herself be infected with the Danish experiment. She probably decided correctly, because later we frequently heard about people who had become ill with tuberculosis because of the injection. One of our acquaintances was a young man, who died within a short time after the injection in a fever caused by tuberculosis. (My mother's lungs were completely clean without any calcareous centers till her death at the age of 95.) As a result of the Hungarian experiment the exact quantity of the injection was determined. The worldwide distribution of the BCG was started soon afterwards and from that time every baby now receives it. Because of this tuberculosis slowly started to disappear in our very much infected nation.

By the 1970-80s nearly all convalescent hospitals for lung illnesses were closed. In some years afterwards the national statistics proudly showed that there were no tuberculosis infected people living in Hungary. But this was too early for our joy! (I have to note that after the long waited bloodless triumph and change from socialism to capitalism that happened in 1990, things have become worse. The number of unemployed and homeless immediately rose and because of the suffering, tuberculosis also returned! Poverty, misery, and social insufficiency are the best breeding ground for this ugly illness!)

At the end of November 1947 my uncle Dődi called a physical education teacher into the office. I was instructed to teach her the office work, so that she could do my job during the time of my maternity leave. At that time maternity leave lasted only for three months. I prolonged my first day of maternity leave until the 1st of January 1948, when I was could expect birthing pains at any hour, but thankfully I was still all right. Some days before New Year's Eve, I left and gave the office completely over to my replacement. The supervisors said farewell to me and expressed that they would wait for my return as the mother of a beautiful and healthy small boy.

I made arrangements agreed with my gynecologist that I could visit him any time even at night if I felt it was the time form my child ot be born. My doctor worked in the hospital of the evangelic nuns at Ilka Street not far from the house where the Kosch family had lived after the time their arrival from Transylvania. Could that have been a mere accident?

1948

The 6th of January 1948 arrived, the day of my "Epiphany" and of my first childbirth! This day was very exciting and a significant moment for me, because I have never experienced anything like that before! Half a year before a telephone had been installed in our flat, so at 7 a.m. I called my doctor and told him the frequency of my throes of childbirth. He asked me to call a taxi and to fetch him from his home at the Round Square and we would then drive together to the hospital. We did it and at 8 a.m. we had arrived to the hospital with Alfred.

The hospital was just like a private convalescent hospital. The nuns who acted as nurses glided silently along the corridors. In the patient rooms they were always right on the spot when help was needed.

The winter sunshine illuminated the maternity room and the blue color of the sky looked just like my father's eyes. It was nearly spring-like! Later the eyes of my little Peter turned out to be the same color!

At my head a nun helped me with the pace of breathing and held my hand, while the doctor gave instructions. It was not as dreadful as I had thought to myself, but sometimes I felt a very strong pain. At those times I focused on the coming rest times as I knew they would not last long. At 11.30 a.m. I was given some light sleeping pills and an hour later a small, beautiful and healthy baby was shown to me. My first little son Peter was born. He weighed 3.600 grams wrapped in a towel!

An unbelievable happiness and peace filled my heart, despite the previous pains, because only tears of joy were streaming from my eyes. My mother came into the hospital and she was with Alfred from 11 o'clock. They waited with expectant fever on the corridor. After Peter was born, he was taken to them to be viewed.

Later they went home and made a celebration with my Uncle Charles and my Brother Tom. They had "unforgettable potatoes with eggs" for lunch, as Uncle Charles called it.

Little Peter as the model of the family photo album

As Alfred and my mother viewed Peter I was busy with the after bearing doctoral round of duties. Then they took me into a room of four, where the other three women were already waiting after giving birth. I had my lunch and had a long and relaxing sleep. On the first day it was not allowed to receive visitors. In the afternoon and later two times a day the nun came and put cool pack tightly on my belly so that it would force it back to its original shape.

My little Peter was brought in for the evening nursing. It was so strange to have a close look at his little face and see his small hands and the whole beautiful little boy! He was a good tempered baby, so they left him in the room in a small baby cot! When he was full he fell asleep at once with an adorable smile on his face. The doctors of the other women in the room thought that my son was already a month old or so, because his skin was so beautifully white and he was so large and slept so peacefully. Because of this, my little Peter received his "first excellent mark" from life! My doctor, the nice "Uncle Dr. Raisz" could not stop watching and praising him. Unfortunately he did not have any children.

After eight days I was allowed to leave the hospital. My doctor instructed me that I was supposed to rest an additional four weeks at home, which mother also insisted that I keep. So that I had more milk to give Peter, I drank huge amount of milk, hot chocolate and ate my favorite caraway-seeds soup, fashionable those times. I put on quite a lot of weight and because of this my Peter also developed well.

One thing neither the doctor, nor I could understand was that my son started to weep between 6-8 p.m. every day. It happened for six weeks. Later it suddenly disappeared and he fell asleep and relaxed undisturbed at night. The doctor's opinion was that either he just wanted to speak or he had stomach ache. Thinking back I am sure that it was the latter, possibly because of the caraway-seeds soup.

When he was about two months old we took him to be baptized. Alfred kept his promise indeed, so Peter was registered to follow the Catholic religion as me. The three months of maternity leave passed by very quickly, but our pediatrician kept me on a sickness provision for a time, until July. We started to slowly mixed nutrition, which he liked very much. On the 1st of July I started working again and my old colleagues greeted me with great joy.

Alfred worked diligently in his own mill. He had a purchase order for the brown pure wool robes used by the Franciscan order clerics. It proved to be a good and continuous job.

In the physical education department of the city council there was a possibility to take part in summer physical education courses in July and August. In the morning I was allowed to go to the physical training travelorganized for teachers to move and to do Hungarian folk-dance. This helped me to regain my previous shape after childbirth and made my muscles flexible again. So I did the exercises with happiness and the teacher showed how the exercises should be done, with my help. In the afternoons I did the office work, which matched the course in the morning well. At the end of August I received a "document" about the completion of the course and it continued next year.

Alfred, Peter and me

While working, I eagerly waited every day to go home to my little son. Because I had already been a keen photographer in Verecke, I continued taking photos this time even more diligently! Of course the most important model was my little son Peter! I took photo sequences about his development and enlarged them. His lovely, ever smiling face decorated the walls of our room. Peter's headquarters were along the hall in a big playpen, where the sun shined in so the place was well

Granny and Peter

illuminated in the daytime. I could easily observe him from the kitchen as well. In the hallway there was enough room, so he quickly learned how to turn around, creep and stand up. He was a very peaceful baby and developed well and evenly. Mother told me that sometimes she could not even notice that I had a little baby in the flat!

Later "Aunt Anne" came to our place. She was a wonderful person and a great help for all of us. How she found us I don't know. One day she came up to Budapest from the village Páty, searching for housing in the capital. Mother let our small room to her in exchange for washing Peter's nappies in the evening. On weekdays she went and worked in different houses, to do the washing and the cleaning up. Every week she arrived on Monday mornings and returned home at the weekend. She was of German nationality and spoke Hungarian with an interesting accent. Once a week she did the washing and cleaning up at our place, but for that she was paid by the hour. Once I nearly fainted when seeing what she had done. In the second washtub of the nappies she used the water for washing her face. She claimed that it was very good for her skin. She was around 60 years old perhaps even more, but the skin of her face was always so velvety and unlined as that of a small girl. She told me that the piddle water of babies was her best cosmetics! Aunt Anne had time in the evening for kneading little Peter, because she loved him so very much! At that time my little son started to scream with laughter, apparently she might have been tickling him.

On weekdays Alfred, my busy man only saw his son sleeping. After returning home from work late in the afternoon he was not able to spend time with him. But on the weekends he was always attending to him and pushing his baby buggy on the streets with pride.

During the autumn, in October big changes happened in Uncle Charles's life! First he was able to get a permanent job in the Budatétény district of the capital. The chemist who had worked there died and his wife made an announcement for the job. So he applied for it and they easily agreed on the terms. He received the job, a salary, housing and food. So finally my Uncle Charles was able to start working in a chemist's shop, the thing he liked so very much! He came home to his sister Kate only in the weekends when he was not working.

In the meantime a far relative moved to my mother's friend's house from the town of Szatmárnémeti, Transylvania in Rumania. She was a 46 years old single woman. Her name was Helen (Ilus) and she worked in the county council, just as she had previously done in Rumania.

My mother and her friend started to act in the role of matchmaker. They made arrangements for Helen and Uncle Charles to meet and they liked each other for the first sight. Helen was a kind and cheerful woman. Charles enjoyed her outpouring of happiness and liveliness exceedingly. On the weekends they frequently met and at Christmas of 1948 Uncle Charles proposed marriage to her. Their life was quite similar, because Helen had also left her previous housing and her relatives behind in Szatmárnémeti (actually Satu Mare) and both were single. Charles was a 56 years old bachelor at that time. We held a great engagement party and we were all so happy that his life had suddenly turned for the better.

1949

The "young couple" held their wedding ceremony on May 11th in the district Cistercian Church. Helen moved in with my Uncle Charles' place in Budatétény. The owner of the pharmacy gave them a larger room to live in.

Helen and
Charles

The small room, where my uncle was living in, was remodeled into a kitchen. After that Helen prepared Charles the meals, kept the house clean and became a housewife. After their wedding they visited us quite rarely, because they loved to be in their small home, furnished in good taste by the feminine touch of Helen. It was good for me to take a look at them as they were so happy. Helen pampered him so much, as if they were truly youngsters indeed! They surely wanted to recover the long lost years wasted in their bachelorhood.

My brother Géza took a liking for marriage as well, as he married his "beautiful" girlfriend Ika. Though she was 3 years older than him, their "love" was very great! Géza and his wife moved into a building on Andrew Bajcsy-Zsilinszky Street, opposite the Opera House. They had two rooms of a dual rental flat where a nice old couple lived in the third room. Previously the older couple had been the owners of the entire flat. Unfortunately   Géza's new flat was quite similar to our previous one on Fadrusz Street as it had been also damaged in a bombing attack during the war. When I visited them on the fifth floor, I felt just like I was walking in our own previous flat. Their corner-room had the same kind of balcony as ours once did and there was another room with a hall beside. Seeing their damaged place removed the heart pains at the loss of our old flat. Instead I focused on the time of our honey-moon in a "suite of rooms of a five star luxury hotel" for six weeks.

Peter with me and with his father and on his bike

In the summer of 1949 I continued to take part in the physical education lessons along with my regular work. But at the end of the summer months I had to leave my employment again due to "certain symptoms". Once again I had become pregnant as certified by Dr. Raisz. I was completely sure that I would surely have a son again. When I told Alfred the good news, he was extremely happy! He promised to himself if he would have a son again, then he himself would take up the Catholic Faith. The Catholic clerk Mr. Nyisztor, had attempted to convince him to do so during his ordeals in the prison. In among Alfred's brothers he was the only one who kept the original family name of Kosch. He was very happy that his family name would not die out. I was happy too, because this way my little Peter would have a playmate and a little brother as well!

Little Peter

In August the Educator Union sent me to the Balatonkenese holiday house of the Budapest Trade Union for two weeks. I was in the same room with a woman from the general superiority department. Her name was Yolanda. F. We got a double room and during the first week there we were forced to have a little rest. Lake Balaton was rough and it was quite cold, the rain was sadly splashing against our windows and the fox grapes that were climbing along the wall of the building was tousled and torn. Looking out to the lake from the "Kenese side", it seemed to be unfriendly and the weather made that waves crash furiously along the beach. The waters lumbered with combing waves, just like the enormous volume of the oceans. The air was so cold, that I was forced to call home and ask for some warmer clothes. They were brought down to Kenese by Géza. He spent the night with us at the resort. Of course in the evening, when we walked up to the dance floor, the other assigned guests could not stop watching him. The other women in the room were also jealous of me and my handsome dancing partner!

Yolanda lived in my room, and she was a very comical individual, but she was also a small and quite plump woman. She went for a dance with my brother Géza so as not to offend him. She had the idea to act as he was a flirting friend of mine. She left us dancing all the night and she acted as a chaperone. While we danced she listened to all the hushed words that were whispered about us. Afterwards we all laughed about the opinions of others till dawn. It was a good joke! The next morning Géza traveled home on the train. Yolanda couldn't stop praising Géza's handsome looks and charming manner. It was a case of the Hungarian saying where "the grape is sour". She was quite an aging woman and she was still unmarried. In the end she was the one, who told the other guests that Géza was actually my brother and that they should not misunderstand the case.

In November the Physical Education Supervisors moved into the building of the Archbishop Street primary school in the 4th district. The Sugar Street office was handed over to the other classes to compensate for the increasing number of pupils. The new offices were a bit further from our flat and I had to travel more on the tram than before. With every new day I became more uncomfortable as my pregnancy progressed.

We spent our Christmas time with Helen and Charles, who could hardly express their joy at the wonder of the small child growing within me.

1950

We celebrated Peter's second birthday with a big tart and two candles. He liked blowing out of the candles very much. In February my doctor advised me not to work because of the pregnancy. He didn't want me to be walking with my big belly in the cold weather or on the icy roads. During that time he also prescribed injections of Strofantin to strengthen my heart, so that I would be able to give birth successfully.

Soon my second son was born on the 11th of March 1950! It had happened just like Peter but only much earlier. I woke my doctor at half past five in the morning. Alfred brought a taxi, caught Dr. Raisz from his home and after 7 a.m. I was already in the maternity room in the Ilka-street hospital. I could not believe that only barely an hour after half past seven my son Thomas was born weighing 3500 grams. My happiness and joy was just as big as at it had been for my first childbirth and what's more that the labor went quickly and there were no complications. As people usually say, my Thomas "took exactly after his father". Now, as an adult, he looks just like Alfred did at the same age. Thomas used to have small dark hair, which became later changed to blond. Peter's hair also became blond after a while and his hair became naturally curly like that of small girls. Peter took after my relatives more, but of course he has some Kosch in him. Peter loved his smaller brother and he was eager to help me as a "big boy".

Little Tom

Within two months Thomas was also baptized into the Catholic faith. Alfred himself converted from his evangelistic faith over to the Catholic religion as he had promised. Even the evangelistic preacher helped to convince him. For many hours we tried to persuade him to honor his promise. In the end Alfred won, so that he could set his conscience at ease.

It was a hot Saturday at the beginning of July 1950 when another tragedy struck! I will try to recall the story after Helen recollections. My Uncle Charles was about to close the pharmacy at half past 12. The small delivery van that brought the medicines had arrived at the chemist's shop. The delivery van was late and Uncle Charles was quite angry. He gave the workers a good tongue lashing, asking whether it was right to arrive that late?! Naturally they protested and they told him that they had many other deliveries. Budatétény was quite far away and they had to account for the money as well. Regardless, my poor uncle couldn't do anything else but to accept the invoices, and to start counting and checking the medicines he had received. The July sunshine streamed through the open door of the chemist's shop as it was extremely hot during the non hours. Inside the pharmacy the air was at least 40°C. My uncle was quite nervous and as a "strong tobacconist" he lit his cigarette and stood behind the counter and checked the documents. In the meantime from behind the door leading to their flat the impatiently words of Helen could be heard.

"Charles my dear, please come, otherwise the soup would be cold!"

At that time there was no-one else except for Uncle Charles in the pharmacy. Some time later a courier entered carrying parcels in his hands. He noticed that my uncle was leaning on the counter standing in a odd position. He leaped over to my uncle to catch his unconscious body. The courier began to cry for help at once! People arrived at once as well as Helen. When she saw Charles's condition, she collapsed and fainted. The two women living in the house arrived and dragged Charles and Helen into the room. They went and called the doctor, but he was not at home. Some minutes later Helen revived herself. There must have been so much of a panic that no one considered to call the ambulance! Moments later a man arrived from the doctor, saying that the he had just arrived home and that the doctor would arrive soon.

When the doctor arrived he diagnosed that Uncle Charles had suffered complete brain hemorrhage. Blood started to seep out of his nose, mouth and ears. He never regained consciousness! His heart was still beating until all blood had drained out of him at 4 o'clock p.m. He died at the age of 58, just like my father! The doctor gave us comfort by saying that no ambulance or any kind of hospital could have helped him!

My dear uncle Charles died while doing his job by the counter of the pharmacy. His last glimpse of life could have been the scales on which he had worked all his life with such devotion. The last year of his career was the happiest of all in spite of all that he had gone through! Heaven certainly valued Uncle Charles's good personality and fortunately he did not suffer long but instead endured only a quick death! The funeral was organized a week later in the Farkasrét cemetery. After the funeral Helen stayed with us. We could hardly set her heart at rest, she was constantly crying and tears were always falling down her face. After the funeral Helen stayed in Budatétény until the end of July. She wanted to liquidate her previous little home and irrevocably say farewell to the most beautiful and happiest period of her life!

Peter and me

Fortunately I was on maternity leave and later on illness leave with my little Tom. I could go to Helen's place for entire days with Peter to help her. My little Peter acted as if he had known about the tragedy and he tried to comfort her and stroked her head with gentleness. He spoke to her or recited poems so that he could turn her attention away from her sorrow. At the end of the month she moved to our place, with a few pieces of furniture. She lived there and applied for work at the County Council. In August she was happily received back again. From the 1st of August I started working again.

We all were struck down by the sudden tragedy of Uncle Charles's death and we could not get over our feelings. The mood was always so sad at our place! They also noticed it at my workplace as well. My room-mate in the Kenese holiday resort of the Union, Yolanda, F. managed to get a summer assignment. She got it to the resort of the Educator Union in Balatonfüred for the last two weeks of August. So we traveled there together. The weather was beautiful; the water of Lake Balaton was pleasantly warm. It tried to wash away the dark shades and the thoughts of mourning from my mind.

My friend persisted in having dinner in one of the restaurants in Balatonfüred. There we were able to take part in an interesting meeting. One of my supervisor compeers, Uncle John, K. recognised us by the table and invited us to join their small company. We went to their table and already from afar we recognized the famous sculptor, Zsigmond Kisfaludy Stróbl.

The sculpture

After introducing ourselves we learnt that Uncle John was the brother-in-law of the sculptor. Zsigmond was a very friendly and familiar person. He told us that our compeer John had been a regular model for his sculptures, when he was younger. He told us about a bronze head was fashioned after John that was sold to one of museums in London. It can be seen there till this very day! In addition the sculpture "Shooter" which can be found near the entrance of the Budapest City Park was also modeled from his brother-in-law. Later the Soviet Marshal Voroshilov became keenly interested in the sculpture and in the end Zsigmond 'presented' it to him! Some time later the popular humorist Hofi sang his well known song "Have a rest, try to have a little rest!" concerning this same sculpture. Whenever I looked at the head of this old educational supervisor, it always looked very interesting and commanding. I imagined he must have been a well built young man. The sculpted model, Uncle John, told us he had two daughters with their extended families. He had two grandsons as well from their marriages. He also relayed to us that he also had a son, who had been an aviation lieutenant before the war. Once during practice, his son was flying near the town of Szombathely when his plane crashed. His son perished in the accident. It was so clear that he loved his son very much, because when he told us these things, his eyes became wet. Despite the tales of tragedy, it was an extraordinary evening and we had very nice time. Later, I told Yolanda that it had been the best decision to go out for dinner.

At the beginning of September my office moved once again to the inner city Grammar School at Reáltanoda Street. This time my office was on the first floor and the store-room for supplies was in the cellar. It was a good location as I could easily get to work on the very popular bus Nr. 7.

In the meantime Helen also got a very nice job. She moved to town of Monor to work at the Town Council. She received a flat as a sublet, saying that she "did not want to be a burden for us"! We tried to persuade her to stay, saying that our flat was big enough. Although she had a separate room, she insisted on leaving. Even with our persuasion for here to stay, her departure to Monor proved to be very fortunate for her. Five months after Uncle Charles's death, the district doctor of Monor introduced Helen to his best friend Dr. Louis Reich, the district doctor in Ceglédbercel. Dr Reich had lost his wife in the same time frame as Helen lost her husband. As fate would have it the lots in life were similar and they fit together well.

Louis may have been some years younger than Charles, but he had two teenage sons who were off at school. Louis had an engaging manner and his personality was similar to that of my Uncle Charles. In addition he was a popular and respected doctor in the village. Later he proposed marriage to Helen which she then turned to us for advice. Naturally mother and I urged her not to pass up such an opportunity! It seemed as if my Uncle had sent Louis to be a reliable companion and comfort for her! Hearing this Helen explained to us what she was afraid of. During the war he was only exempted from the regulation of wearing a "yellow star" on his breast and certain deportation because his former wife. She had been a Polish catholic baroness as well as the mother of their sons.

Mother and I blurted out at nearly the same time; "Jewish men are the best husbands and fathers!" We knew this as both of us Jewish acquaintances and friends. From our overwhelming persuasion she then agreed to marry the village doctor. One year after the death of Uncle Charles the two of them were bound in matrimony. We got to know Louis as a square-shooter, sincere, charitable and kind individual. The couple lived together for another 22 years in sweet harmony in Ceg
lédbercel. Helen loved his sons as if they were her own children. One of them later became a doctor, the other one an engineer.

Workers had to hold compulsory discussion group meetings at all workplaces those times. It was organized under the title of the daily newspaper Szabad Nép (Free People) for half an hour every week. We usually did this on Saturday mornings before starting our actual work. At that time uncle Dődi, the "boss" read an article from the daily newspaper to which we were then encouraged to express our opinions. This ritual was done mostly by the men who liked to talk politics anyway. Of course during those times one was required to "closely follow the steps of the official communist line"! Moreover in every office it was compulsory to also form a "red corner". It consisted of a photo of Stalin while in front of it there was a table full of potted plants. It made the appearance of an altar! For the anniversary of the "Great October Socialist Revolution", 7th of November 1950 we all had to make individual offerings.

/On 26th of October 1917 the Russian proletarian revolution won under the direction of Lenin. This way the first worker-

agrarian state of the world was created. This anniversary was celebrated in every communist country-editor./

My personal offering was to teach a "revolutionary song" to my bosses at the Physical Education Supervision. Uncle Dődi and the others also liked this idea. It was decided that my offering would take place during our regular reading time of the "Free People". The aging supervisor women and men diligently learned the text and the tune. Those having good ears could sing it even in two parts. Later Uncle Dődi could "happily" report on this to the communist party, "how an efficient offering" took place at our workplace! To my amusement later on, I could hear my bosses singing this song silently for themselves. Later they asked me to teach the song to them again!

At the beginning of November a retraining course began in the Sugar-Street building for physical education teachers. The course was for those who wished to work as therapeutic physical education specialist. There was great demand for therapeutic exercises, as after the war there were many undernourished children who had chronic orthopedic disorders. The purpose was to start therapeutic physical education lessons in all districts of the capital, but more teachers were needed to that.

In the upper circles the news spread quickly that everyone had to work in his own profession. By the decision of our communist state leader, Rákosi, if anyone had a pedagogical diploma, those individuals could only perform the work of a teacher as of January 1st, 1951. One of the supervisors recommended me to enter the therapeutic physical education retraining course. I had a document that I was a physical education teacher as well.

The "sword of Damocles" was hanging above my head. I checked in and twice a week I took part in the re-training course from 2 to 6 p.m. I was allowed to leave the office for that time. During that time I also made enquiries which district would accept me as a therapeutic physical education specialist. During the 5 months long re-training course we had theoretic and practical education. The medical training was given by Dr. Boldizsár Horváth, a renowned orthopedic doctor of the capital.

At the end of December, I was told to quit as office leader and to begin working in the 4th district at the Elisabeth-Street primary school as therapeutic physical education specialist. I was to organize therapeutic education lessons there. I was quite afraid of teaching, but my supervisors encouraged me that teaching therapeutic physical education is quite different from teaching other subjects in the lower classes. More money was paid for it and the lessons were quite easy as they were held only in the afternoon!

Christmas of that year was very sad without Uncle Charles! But my little sons were growing well. Thomas could already make some side steps in the playpen. Peter's most beloved occupation was when I gave him a pencil and paper to draw on. For Christmas he received lots of color pencils and drawing exercise books. His voice could not be heard for hours, when he "was creating his works"!

1951

After the winter holiday I started teaching. Above all I organized my groups. At that time I realized that my real boss was the district chief doctor. She was a nice and helpful woman. She was transferred to work there from the 11th district, where she lived and worked before the war. I took the children to her and she thoroughly examined all of them. We discussed the backbone distortions one by one and she advised the corresponding exercises. She held the files about every child and every second month she re-examined them. Then she advised me on what to do for each individual child. This was the first time we could fully understand each other. The school gave me free run of the gym and from the director I could lay claim to any of the sporting goods, which I needed for my work. The lessons lasted from 1 to 5 p.m. The boys and girls were separately put into groups of 6-10 years and 10-14 years of age. The children were divided into 4 groups daily and they each took part in the 45 minutes long lessons with clothing breaks.

My mother liked this new job of mine and I did as well. For me it was much easier to stay at home until half past 11. After lunch my sons always went to sleep and I arrived home after 6 p.m. The route to work was always palatable. I took the Nr. 7 bus to the Eastern Railway Station, where I then changed over to Nr. 20 bus that then took me directly to the entrance of the school.

My fears quickly subsided as I learned to do my job well. Aunt Kate agreed with my newfound words of praise concerning teaching. She had always told us that "the teacher is her own lord" in her class!

My Aunt Kate
in 1910 at the
age of 18

185. — 109. XI., Bartók Béla-út 141, általános leányiskola.
Alapítási éve: 1888 — Távbeszélő: 469—190

9 leányosztály, 1 kislétszámú osztály, 2 napközi otthoni csoport

Tanulók létszáma: 6 fiú, 306 leány, összesen: 312

Sor-szám	Az oktató neve	Állás	Sor-szám	Az oktató neve	Állás
1.	KOVACHICH JÓZSEF	n. ig.	13.	Reviczky Ábrahámné	
2.	Albrecht Vilmosné			Szalay Jolán	n. r.
	Szekeres Etel	n. r.	14.	Dr Szigeti Bélané	
3.	Bárdos Józsefné			Torjai Viola	p. h.
	Linhardt Hilda	ny. n. r.	15.	Teleki Irén	e.ö. fővédőnő
4.	Eschenbach Antalné		16.	Vermes Györgyné	
	Zaömböly Franciska	n. r.		Lindner Melinda	p. r.
5.	Faragó Artúrné		17.	Vidosfalvi Tiborné	
	Grün Gizella	n. r.		Kiss Margit	n. r.
6.	Fogarasi László	n.r., isk. gond.	18.	Walkó Györgyi	n. r.
7.	**Lápossy Katalin**	**n. r.**	19.	Dr Zách Lászlóné	
8.	Linczényi Józsefné			Páldi Edit	n. r. ö.
	Munkácsy Matild	n. r.	20.	Zsemlye Margit	n. r.
9.	Lubik Mária Irma	n. r.	21.	Károlyi János	alt.
10.	Dr Makkos Gábor	isk. orv.	22.	Királyfi Vilmosné	
11.	Dr Papp Sándorné			Laibl Anna	alt.-nő
	Szallár Erzsébet	n. r.	23.	Makai Boldizsárné	
12.	Özv. Rattay Bélané			Kovács Mária	alt.-nő
	Szécs Rózsi	n. r.			

Lányi Miklósné dr, Somogyi Irén 920., r. óv. 947., XI., Otthon-u. 1.... 56
Lápossy Ferencné Szlovák Jolán 885., n. r. 925., 934. VIII., Alföldi-u. 18. 29 138
Lápossy Katalin 893., n. r. 928., 940. XI., Bartók Béla-út 86........ 185
László Antal 923., n. r., 946., 947. V., Nádor-u. 20................. 168
László Domokos 912., n. r. 935., 938. IX., Közraktár-u. 12/a 127 155 164
László Gyula 924., ip. h. 947., V., Csáky-u. 33.................... 257 258

Kate listed in the public servant directory

At the end of March I completed my therapeutic physical education exam with the best results. I was able to do this with the assistance of the doctor. Near the end of the exam the chief doctor asked me my opinion. "Apart from the exam" he asked "what could the reason be of the numerous children with right side backbone slanting already in the lower classes?" I replied that due to my previous experiences, taking account of my own right side backbone slanting, the reason could be the writing of characters that tumbled to the right. I showed the position in which we had been writing during the lessons. The writing style was the "left side tumbling exercise book and with right hand and arm direction writing!"

I added that at 10 years of age I had been sent to the Baross-Street hospital to undergo therapeutic physical education exercises. That had been very useful and effective. Those therapeutic exercises had helped a lot for the backbone distortions to be healed! I also went on to explain that such distortions could be prevented in the first place. I recommended that if the exercise book of the pupils would be held in an upstanding position and when writing, both of their hands could be laid on the desk they would be able to write upright characters! "By choice I would give an excellent mark to your reply" said the doctor, "but I can only give you a mark of 5!" (It is the highest grade possible). Interesting that after that time the program of teaching upright writing style was launched all around the country. The beautiful small letter personal writing style suddenly disappeared, but it helped to overcome so much of the child backbone distortion at the time! With great joy I took the certificate of my successful exam to the chief doctor in Újpest and the director of the school. They both congratulated me for my success. Later I started working with even greater pleasure! The children did the exercises diligently and their backbones slowly became healthier which made us all happy.

During the previous year Alfred's production at the mill began to rapidly decline. Forced to get textile yam from a nationalized factory he, as the owner of a small private mill, was slowly denied the base material for his production. By the start of 1951 he was forced to shut down the mill, sell the machines and materials and begin looking for a job. Some months later, in April, he managed to find work in Mezőberény (county Békés) at the Textile Factory as textile engineer. Mezőberény was quite a distance from Budapest and he was only able to come home once a month for a few days. As people usually say, that was when we started to become estranged from each other. The great distance and the infrequent meetings only deepened a growing gap between us. Our difference in age also started to show its presence as well!

At the end of the school-year, in June, my brother Thomas took his final exam for a diploma of merit at the Fazekas High School. How did he get to the Fazekas Grammar School from the Cistercian Order? It was the result of a political failure. The Cistercian Grammar School was nationalized in 1949 and right away the facility was taken away from the priests. In a few exceptions some of the priest teachers were allowed to stay until the end of the year until they were replaced by new civilian teachers. The director of the school was also replaced by a civilian authority. My Brother Tom's favorite teachers were expulsed.

I think he was shocked by all this and that was why he could have "committed" the following inexplicable deed. Near the end of 1950 a boy selling the usual "Pioneer" magazine entered their classroom. He pounced on the boy, tore the whole pack of magazines out of his hand and threw then into the dustbin. Naturally the director and the teacher were informed about the incident. Upon the director's recommendation, my brother Tom was expelled from the school the very same day. His school report was listed as 'bad' although he was right before the final exam.

Poor mother was at a loss for what to do! She ran from one grammar school to the next in search of a school that would accept Tom. In the end the director of the Fazekas Grammar School had pity on her and took into consideration Tom's extraordinary scholastic records. From there he was accepted into the 8th grade where at the end of the year he took the final exam with honors. Due to his permanent exam record of 'bad' he was never allowed to apply for a University! Unfortunately this also occurred due to other factors as well!

To be better understood, I must write the following.
At that time of the "rabid Rákosi era", nearly everywhere one could find "a right-hand man of the house". This was the little title given to those who were faithful to the communist regime. After 1945 the name Admiral-Street was changed to Bucharest-Street. At the same time we received a new member to the building, Rufi, who was the right-hand man of the house. He lived on the ground-floor with his wife and young daughter. Rufi had worked for the Horhty regime before the war and because he was listed as a 'royalist' he could not find regular work. Instead the Interior Ministry welcomed his services as an informant.

Next to our flat, just under us lived a worldly catholic priest with his mother. During the war she had been forced to wear the "yellow star". The priest had taught religion in the Margaret Grammar School to one of my cousins. Now that the priest was unemployed, he too took on the role of an informant and he always looked like a great black spider. He was always watching and monitoring the people from home. Both Rufi and the priest informed about the details of people's lives living in the house to the Inner Ministry and the Communist Party.

I must also note that after the siege an old couple moved into our neighborhood. They were refugees from Transylvania, the husband was a violin virtuoso and his wife was of Armenian origin. They made friends with my mother and once or twice a week they visited us in the afternoon. At that time Uncle Louis V. brought his violin and together with mother they played such beautiful violin-, piano- sonatas, solo and classical works.

Into the other flat next to us was the Balassa family who had moved back home from American captivity, but they only stayed there for a short time. They changed their flat for a bigger one in 1950 due to family reasons. The new resident of their old flat was a writer, Mathias Cs., and his wife with their two daughters (5 and 6 years old). The children became Peter's friends within a short time and therefore the young mother made friends first with my mother and then later with me as well.

The spring of 1951 became known as the "deadly spring". More and more frequently we would learn that someone we knew was taken away by the "black car". Wherever this car appeared it was the omen that some family would be sent away as deportee to some unknown location in the country. At the beginning of June officers came for the ex-lieutenant- general living in the flat above us. They were required to vacate their home within 24 hours. Some weeks later the Horthy party captain and his family living on the third floor was also relocated.

The lightning was striking all around us, but we felt some security as Alfred was away and therefore we didn't really have any officers in our family. It was too unfortunate that we could not see what was to come! On 13th of July 1951, the hottest day of the year, just like the previous year when Uncle Charles died, early at dawn the black car stopped in front of our house. A man from the National Security Service and a policeman rang our doorbell. They carried with them the document that declared our resolution from the Home Office. Each of us received a separate document. The one for mother read "the widow of the public prosecutions director and her son Thomas" the second one read "for Alfred Kosch and his wife". My sons were not written on the document, a fact that I did not even notice when they first handed me the document!

I explained the National Security officer, that my husband had gone to work in the county not long ago and I didn't know his address, because he had not yet written it to me.

"No problem" the security man replied "we would find him anyway! You will have only 24 hours to empty the flat and only the items allowed to take with are the furniture and personal items listed in the document. The next dawn a lorry will come to fetch you!" After saying this they left.

With mother and my brother we just stood there dumbstruck and at a loss. It was as if a huge hammer had struck us down!
I was the first who came to my senses. I had a look at the two orders which listed where our new "home" in Nagyfüged could be found. The document stated that it was in the County of Heves. My mother and Tom had been given the address of one farm and Alfred and I had a separate one. Then we realized that we must have a look at the map! We found where this particular village was situated. It was near the town of Vámosgyörk next to the railway station of Ludas. This was some relief as we certainly were going to the same location with mother but to different farms.

After locating our new home on the map, I read the document again. Embedded in the text was the statement that there could be no appeal! We called my Brother Géza on the phone at once and fortunately they had not yet left for work yet. He said that after arranging to take the day off, Ika and he would come at once. We called other relatives and acquaintances on the phone and asked them to come and help us to pack our belongings and to take some furniture away that we were required to leave behind in Budapest. My Aunts Helen and Kate ran to us in despair. An hour later Géza and Ika also arrived. Géza was soon organizing the packing. He helped to determine which furniture we wanted to take with us and what would remain here or be transferred to the other relatives.

Géza and Helen were ready to accept lots of furniture and personal items. Aunt Kate took the smaller utensils and pots. The piano was given to our neighbor, the old violin teacher. My big combination wall unit and Alfred's bureau was bestowed to one of my cousins. We gave our neighbors many of the other smaller things that could not be taken away by our relatives and friends.

Mother and especially my brother Géza found the silver lining in that a year ago after his wedding, he had checked out of our flat. Otherwise he would have been listed on the order as well! It was also a blessing of God that my poor ill father was spared from such "dishonor". He would have surely died, when the National Security officer arrived!

In the morning one of our friends, Claire Sz. checked in. She lived on the 2nd floor. I must praise her name even to this day! She looked after my two sons for the whole day, so that they should not be obstacles in the great commotion. She also cooked for us as well, so that we could eat our last warm dish in her flat. When it was all done, our flat looked like it had after a bombing attack! I wish it had happened that way, because it would not have goaded other people's jealousy! A bomb ruins everything suddenly, but this slow evacuation was just like slow dying!

According to communist leader Rákosi the middle and upper classes of the previous "Horthy regime" and their descendants should vanish and die. It became the "watchword" during those days!

Claire Sz called us at noon, one by one to spend the lunch there. She told me to pay more attention to little Tom, because he surely had fever. We called the doctor for children at once. He stated that Thomas had inchoate measles. He gave me medicines and asked me to give my son a lot to drink and keep him warm so that all pimples should appear. When the doctor left, I realized the case, what would happen to my children, whether I was allowed to take them with me or not, because their names were not written on the order? Claire advised me to cling to my children till the end! I thought the very same.

At 9 o'clock p.m. our flat was already emptied, we did not leave even a nail in the walls. We sat atop the ruins of the furniture about to be taken away. We were discussing our beyond hope situation with Géza and my aunts Helen and Kate watching our empty flat as the men loaded the future. We would get to kulaks, to the boondocks! /*Kulak- Russian word condemning rich peasants-editor*/ Of course this was not all incidental! It seemed that in Rákosi's diabolic mind, he still had something for us, and obviously it was nothing good!

As it came to the surface later, that Rákosi's real plan was to send the kulaks together with the old middle class as deportees to Siberia. There Stalin would have done his best in destroying them! What was a small number of Hungarians compared to the 60 million Russians killed or disappeared? We certainly would have only raised that number just a little!

Around midnight a lorry came to take mother and my brother with their furniture and the Singer sewing machine, which she insisted on keeping. I sent Helen and Géza home, thinking that in the fight for my children it would be better for me to stay on my own with the state security man. I didn't need my "soldierly" style brother Géza to it all! This is what I decided and it turned out for the better! My dear sweet aunt Kate stayed with me so that she could tell the family whether my fight was successful or not!?

In the empty flat I remembered that earlier in 1945 I had succeeded in persuading another state security officer. Why couldn't the same thing happen again?! At 2 o'clock at night the state security man and the policeman arrived.
"Well, are your ready to go?" - asked me.
At that moment a heavenly strength and firmness possessed me. My eyes were sparkling and I said the following. "I would no way go away from here until I get a permission to take my children with me! I would rather die and I am ready to do it! (My hand was in my pocket in which I held a razor blade!) In this case it would be very inconvenient for you!" I told this turning to the state security man. "I recommend you to call the ministry for home affairs and ask permission to write the names of my two children on the order. When that is done I will be ready to go!"

The state security officer stood there flabbergasted for a minute. After a while he went to the telephone as I proposed and called the Inner Ministry. Later he asked my telephone number, which I told him. He described the problem on the phone, later he hung up saying that we were to wait! The silence was nearly fizzling around us! I experienced indescribable minutes until finally the telephone rang. It seemed to me as a voice coming from eternity. They gave me permission for taking my sons with me. So the security man wrote the names of my sons to the order.
"See how simply the case could have been arranged!" I told.

"But where are the children?" he asked.

"Upstairs on the second floor, they are staying at a kind woman's place. I'll go up, clothe them and then we may go" I replied.

He came with me and when I finished clothing my little Thomas, they learned of his feverish sickness. Then the security man became very doubtful claming that the child needed to go to a hospital instead. I set him at ease saying that his best place was by his mother. I would nurse him, because the doctor who had examined him had given me the medication to treat him as well.

At that very moment the state security man took out a piece of paper and asked me to write on it the following: "If my child died during traveling, I will be the one to go to prison." I had to sign it!

Well, I thought to myself, this case did not go through very easy!

From Claire I was given tea in a thermos and some water in bottles. I had some biscuits for the children and after thanking her for her kindness we said farewell. We were both crying. When leaving I whispered into Aunt Kate's ear: "We have won! Please tell the relatives what happened!"

During that time the movers put my furniture and packages onto the lorry with a dolly and in the end they helped my children and me to get into the truck! The policeman was all the time watching all the events and I could see from his eyes that "he didn't find something in order in this"!

The dawn was about to begin, when the lorry turned out from the Bucharest street with us "for ever"!

We got to the Visegrád-street, where a single woman was taken away with her little furniture. From there we arrived to the Joseph-town railway station. There stood long trains with whitewashed windows which awaited their "victims"! There were lots of policemen with guns about on the platforms and some civilian state security officers as well. I took hold of a man carrying water, who was about to get on the train and asked him to announce that I was looking for the Lápossy family.

Not long after my brother Tom appeared at the door of the compartment and waved to me to get on the train there. He was not allowed to get off. At long last we were together again. Mother was so relieved that I was allowed to bring my children as well. My poor little Peter didn't understand what had happened to us, as he started to tell us how good it was at Aunt Claire's place. He just kept spouting on and on causing our hearts to break.

Later I told my panicky story with the state security officer and described the document I had to sign. My family told me that we were instructed it was not permissible to get off the train. It consisted of only third class compartments and was extremely overcrowded. What's more, it was completely impossible to see through the windows, because all of them had been whitewashed. We were simply standing there in the noon hot weather and it was not even made possible to open the window!

Fortunately the angel Claire had given us much to drink and it was in my handbag! My Poor little Tom sweltered, but thanks to the fever febrifuge he slept long.

It was around 2 o'clock p.m. when the train finally started to move. At both ends of the compartments policemen with guns blocked the way. They did not enter the compartment, where the families were sitting on the benches. In the meantime one man was able to open a small airspace in the window so that we could get some fresh air. Our trip to Hatvan was very slow. When we arrived the policemen told us to get off the train and fetch fresh water. Some of men did it and Tom was among them. We formed a chain in the train and gave down the empty bottles and passed the full ones along. We could have even washed ourselves using that amount! In town of Hatvan, our train had to stop on side rails until 6 p.m. By that time it was fortunately not as hot as it had been. Some time later the train started to move again.

We hadn't had any food the entire day. We were not all hungry at first because of the stressful circumstances and secondly due to the hot weather. But by the evenings our stomachs began to demand food and we knew also realized that for long time we would still not reach our "destination"! Fortunately the railroad workers shouted out the names of towns we passed by as we could not see what was outside.

At the end of our trip we arrived at the Ludas railway station at half past 9 p.m. It was finally a moment where we could stretch our legs. The cool evening air refreshed us as we got off the train. Horsed carriages and trucks were waiting for us. My mother, brother and another family were loaded up into one of the waiting trucks. Our luggage and furniture was also put on the truck and we were at least happy that none of it was missing or destroyed. The driver explained that the first house we stopped at would me my new home. The other couple would get off second and finally my mother would be dropped of at a third home. The truck drove along until we arrived to my destination. All we could see was an illuminated balcony at the end of the service road where a kulak couple was standing and waiting for me. From the distance, the woman looked just like a witch as she was so fat.

Immediately, my little Peter began to cry when he saw her and begged me take him to his grandmother's house. Thinking that it may have been a better idea, I asked the policeman sitting next to the driver whether it would be allowed or not. The policeman simply made a wave of his hand that signaled the consent that Peter could go with his grandmother. Leaving Peter behind, I said farewell to my mother. She told me that either tomorrow or the following day my brother Thomas would visit us and if he needed, would bring Peter back to me. I "fell into" the kulak family's place with little Tom in my hands, whose health was a bit better by that time. I met the elderly couple who lived there with their son who was in his 20s.

At first they received me suspiciously, but as time passed the tensions eased. They showed me a large room that had been emptied for me. It was a nice room as unlike most peasant houses had flooring and two nice windows as well. The husband, who was known as Uncle Stephen F and his son Steve carried in my furniture from the truck. While they worked, the wife, Aunt Maria offered us peppered potatoes to eat. The meal was so delicious as if I had never tasted food before. It was so good that even little Thomas had some to eat! Later on we went to sleep and spent a peaceful night there after our exhausting ordeal. The home was a strange place to be but that soon changed. Unknown to us at the time but that place eventually it turned out to be our home for more than the next two years!

The first morning at Nagyfüged was strange, but not frightening at all. In the morning I left the room with my little Thomas and by that time he only had a low fever. Aunt Maria called us into the kitchen straightaway. She offered me milk or tea to drink. I chose the second one and ate the bread brought from home and the cakes made by Aunt Helen for the journey. Thomas was hungry as well, so began to home that it had been only a light sickness.

After breakfast uncle Stephen showed us their homestead, which consisted of the house, an outbuilding, a big orchard and a vegetable garden with tillage. The two neighbors living next to them were relatives and they owned smaller houses and fields. They didn't count to be "kulaks". Uncle Stephen took me also to them and introduced me as a deportee from Budapest.

In the first house a relatively young couple lived with their son Alexander who appeared to be about 10 years old. The wife of the neighbor, Therese received us very warmly and proposed that we could buy their daily milk, butter and quark. She agreed to this after she found out that I had a 3 year old son. She was the only one in the neighborhood who still personally owned a cow. She also explained that from her vegetable garden she could provide us with vegetables for garden-sauces as well as chicken for eating meat. In talking with her she also told us the story that my hosts had all their livestock and crops officially confiscated, after they were labeled "kulaks". At that time only Stephen's orchard remained under their care and supervision.

I graciously thanked her for her friendly demeanor and her willingness to help! I assured her that I would certainly use this opportunity! It was such a good feeling to find the kindness of the "stranger" Therese during our hour of desperation and uncertainty! I reassured myself that at least we would not die of hunger! When we departed, she left my arms full of milk, green peas, potatoes and some onions.

Aunt Maria became a bit friendlier by that time and allowed me to use her cooker for preparing dinner. In the meantime she told her son to bring the "foal-oven" from the hovel. He set it up in one corner of the veranda right in front of our room. This way we had a separate cooker, which they had previously used for cooking the potatoes for the pigs. At that time there were no pigs, because the authorities had confiscated them all.

These kulaks had suffered the same fate as us, except that they were allowed to partly stay in their own houses, but only as poverty-stricken families. As I got to know Uncle Stephen, I slowly realized that he was a clever, warm hearted, tall and handsome man. It was strange for me to hear all of the blasphemies that flew from his mouth on a regular occasion. It was reassuring when I noticed that he did not do it in anger against us. Subsequently I realized it was better to keep my mouth shut and "get used to it". I simply reasoned that his style of speech was just like that.

Poor Aunt Maria was very obese woman because of an illness. Her body above her legs was filled with water. Because of this illness, she remained in bed frequently and was sometimes reasonably grouchy about her situation. My son Peter took a keen notice to her moods!

After dinner on the second day Uncle Stephen showed me the village from afar. He showed me where my mother had been taken to as the people she was living with were distant relatives of his. Their house stood behind the Bene River. He explained me that after walking straight on foot for about 15 minutes one could reach the river. There was hardly any water in it during such a dry and hot summertime. We could cross the river with dry feet, as we jumped from one cliff to the other one. After climbing the rampart, we would be at B.'s family homestead, where my mother had been taken to. I told Uncle Stephen that was not going to leave and go there at this time, because we had previously agreed that my brother Tom would visit us and probably bring my son Peter.

My mother and my brother had spent that day exploring their new surrounding as well as unpacking the luggage. The very next morning my mother, my brother and my son arrived. They told they lived in a nice big room with very friendly hosts. They lived with a nice couple along with their two adult sons. My mother was not as embittered as I had imagined!

Together we mused with my brother Tom that we had finally gotten to the "utopian Great Plain of our poet Petőfi", where to the north; by distance of Ludas and its railway station, the range of the Mátra Mountains could be seen.

We put first my room into order and furnished it to our liking. From among the collection of furniture I got a studio couch from mother's salon, my sofa, a collapsible iron bed, two baby cots, my cupboard, and a bigger table with four chairs. I had a playpen, two small chairs for the children and their table and a carpet that covered the whole floor.

In the room we had to construct a separate bathroom between the cupboard and the corner by employing two kitchen stools. There was a bigger bathtub for the children, a washing basin, a bucket and a water jar. We even put a mirror on the wall and the whole thing was separated from the room by a curtain. Fortunately there was electricity in the house, so we were able to cook in our room as well. We used the electric oven that we had brought from Budapest so that we could boil water for tea or coffee, warm milk or make even scrambled and boiled eggs. In no time at all we found the right place for everything and it started to feel like at home!

Little Alexander from the house next door visited Peter on a regular basis. It was good for Tom as well as I could put him into the playpen in a shady place of the garden. Peter and Alexander became good friends within a short time. Alexander had already had measles, so he was not afraid of getting the illness. Amazingly Peter neither caught it.

Mother made arrangements with my brother Géza that he would visit on the weekend to get a better understanding of our living circumstances. Instead of returning to their house my mother and my brother Tom stayed at our place for the night. Luckily we managed to fin enough space for us all. That night my little Peter was the happiest of all to see the whole family together again! The real happiness waited for us on Saturday, when the morning train arrived and my brother Géza arrived, burdened with all kinds of delicious food!

The Ludas railway station was about 5 kilometers from the village, but our house was located between Ludas and the village. It could be accessed by the road about 3 kilometers from the railway station. Near the house was a bus-stop as well.

Géza was very impressed by the ease it was to find our house and he reassured us that he would visit us quite frequently and bring everything we wanted or needed! He took a short walk to mother's homestead from the bus-stop. My brother had brought us among others things fresh meat, which we quickly fried and ate as pure meat with potatoes. We also had a cucumber salad, with green pea soup and afterwards the cakes that had been made by Aunt Helen. We certainly enjoyed our meal!

When closing our eyes that night, we could feel as being at home, but when we opened them again it was as if "we spent our holidays from the goodwill of our father Rákosi!" Géza spent the night at our place, because Aunt Maria gave us a pallet that my brother Tom used. He gave his iron bed to his brother. After putting my sons into bed we four adults sat out on the veranda to chat.

There was silence around us; we could hear the chirping of crickets sometimes, the croaking of frogs and two dogs barking amicably. Above us on the dark sky millions of stars twinkled bright in the warm July Hungarian night. Steam engines could be seen in the distant horizon as their smoke twisted up to the sky until they disappeared.

We asked Géza to tell our relatives and acquaintances how we were doing and ask them to write as quickly as possible, because all news from home would only bring us joy. We promised that we would reply, but first we had to find out if it was permitted to do so in letters or only by postcards. People had warned us that we were not allowed to leave the village. We had also been informed that we could neither sit on a bus. Only walking was permitted. We were allowed to enter the village two or three times a week to buy bread, to receive the parcels and post. Large packages could not be received as we had to carry them home on foot.

The following week, my mother and my brother Thomas wanted to see the village. I elected not to as I couldn't leave my children without supervision and little Tom was still recovering from his illness.

We asked Géza to bring bread every time he visited us, as we thought that there would certainly be problems with supplying bread for so many new residents! We also invited him that sometime later Ika and her son would also be happily welcomed for a summer holiday! Géza thanked us for the invitation after seeing that there was enough room for all. This was especially true as Alfred had not arrived. I told Géza, that although I knew Alfred's address, I would not write him because did not want to call the attention of the police on him. I felt that the State Security Service should have to do a little work in order to find him! I had told this to him in a telegram on that dreadful day of 13th of July, so that he would know we had been deported!

Géza told us that on the way to our new home, the bus had been filled with visitors coming to the deported relatives. He decided to return home early on Sunday so that he could tell of our fate to the other relatives more peacefully. My mother asked him not to overburden himself with traveling every weekend to us, because he should spend as much time as possible at home. The reason for this was that on the weekdays he worked in the county and was frequently away from home! So we agreed that in two weeks he would come again. Until that time we would get more information from our other fellow deportees and those living in the village.

Weeping, I said farewell to my dear brother Géza and whispered into his ear that I would take care of mother and the children, and that he should not worry!

Later my mother and Tom left and told us that next day they would go into the village to see how one could buy bread and other things. Two days later they came back to us and told us a great many interesting things about the other deportees.

Mother indignantly told what she heard and could hardly believe. Among the deportees there were three unlucky and previously abject Jewish families, as well. One old couple had been hiding underground during the siege and in this manner had avoided discovery. Another man who was nearly blind was there with his cousin. They had managed to escape execution by a document that had been issued by the Swedish embassy. A third couple and their 18 years old daughter had been forced to come here. Their son was fortunate enough to have immigrated to Israel. During the war the mother, the son and her daughter had been dragged away to Auschwitz in 1944. They survived and managed to migrate to Switzerland and then later back to Hungary. The unfortunate husband had worked as a forced laborer at the Russian front and knew nothing about his family for years. By the time he arrived home, the rest of his family had successfully escaped.

According to Rákosi the "sin" of all three families was to have previously been middle class wholesalers. "Comrade Rákosi" was of course of Jewish descent, but such heritage didn't make any difference to him! It was completely unbelievable!

Among the deportees there was an ex-ministerial councilor at pension age with his wife, their daughter Eva and her retired officer husband. The K. family lived in the village in a great kulak's house, but all four of them shared a single room. Eva's 6 and 8 years old sons' names had not been written on the official order. As such they stayed in Budapest with her brother and attended school from there. Eva waited expectantly for her sons and the summer holiday! Later on we became very good friends with Eva and her parents.

Other deportees were ex-workers of the State Bureau, company directors, officers, judges and public persecutors. To my mother's greatest surprise, when coming out of the bakery she met one of the classmates of her sister Magdalene. It was Helen K., deported with her husband and 8 year old daughter. Her husband worked in the post office and was an active workforce. The only reason why they had been deported was because the 'right-hand man' in their building had wanted to live in their flat. He made a false report as they neither held a title, nor ranking of any kind. After meeting Helen invited mother into their room, which was in the house right next to the bakery. She was very happy to see mother and at once they had a common topic to talk about, Magdalene her previous friend. Helen was a small and very kind woman. Later on I got to know her quite well and she also advised for us to wait in their line when we had to queue for bread three times a week.

How small is the world and there are so many nice people on it! Among them Mrs. Cantor should be mentioned as well. She wasn't at all called Cantor, only her husband worked as the cantor of the local Catholic Church. That was why the whole village called her Mrs. Cantor. My mother met her next Sunday after the mass. According to my mother she was a very kind middle aged woman and was deeply shocked by all of the deportations. She offered her help concerning medicine prescriptions. Twice a week the doctor came from the neighboring village Karácsond to Nagyfüged. We could visit him on Tuesdays and Fridays from 8 to 1 o'clock in the afternoon. She offered to buy the prescribed medicines for all deportees at the chemist's in village Karácsond as the deportees we were not allowed to travel there. She suggested for those regularly taking some kind of medicine to visit the doctor and to have him prescribe more medicines than they normally would take.

Later on she would take the prescriptions and travel to the village to buy the medicine. In this manner, those who needed regular prescriptions would not have to visit the doctor as often. The medicines would then be collected from Mrs. Cantor. Fortunately, the doctor agreed to do that as well. This was a great help for my mother, as well as for the other elderly sick people who constantly needed some kind of medication!

With Kitty and my children in the garden of the farmstead

My brother Thomas had courted a brown haired, brown eyed beautiful girl in Budapest. Kitty lived with her widowed mother in the 11th district. She made arrangements with my Aunt Helen and her mother and they all came to visit us one Saturday at the beginning of August. Shortly after their arrival my brother Géza came and showed them the way to our house. We all were very happy because of the completely unexpected visit, but Tom especially so. He could have even "caught birds" in all of his happiness! We spent two beautiful days together and we nearly forgot where we were! Géza and I took lots of photos, recording the memory of these happy days. On Saturday night mother took her sister Helen, Géza and Thomas to their house. Kitty and her mother stayed at our place as we had comfortable room for all.

It was so good to see the youngsters, so see how full of unlimited joy! Sunday afternoon they all traveled home on the bus and then the train. My Aunt Helen promised to visit us for a longer period, but only by the following year.

With Ika on the Nagyfüged "plain"

Kitty and Thomas

Géza told us that the next Saturday he would bring Ika and her son Andreas. They had planned to stay at my place for a week long holiday. Peter was very excited with the prospects of having a small private guest, only because he was a few years older than Andreas. After some time my mother and my brother Tom came to live at my place and we realized that we could save money if we had common meals. On our road it was easier to walk into the village, as well. This saved mother from the long walks, Tom and I took turns walking into the village for bread and the mail. While we were in the village, mother took care of my children. When Géza, Ika and her son arrived, Thomas then went to their old house for the night to sleep.
At the end of the weekend Géza traveled from our place to his work on Monday morning.

Ika and her son had very good time with us and in the afternoons we usually played bridge, because she had thoughtfully brought cards. The three small boys constantly played with Alexander.

One evening my mother went back to their house with Thomas.

With my brothers Tom and Géza

I talked with Ika on the veranda in the evening for a long time, after we had put the children into bed. She informed me on that day that she had taken a telephone call from one of my supervisor bosses Uncle John who wanted to speak to me on a pay-day in the New Pest School. There had been no news about me as I had not appeared for work. Then Ika told him that we had been relocated and gave him my new address and briefly told him of our awful story. The supervisor was very shocked to hear about our unfortunate circumstances. He added that he wanted to help us by sending a parcel. Firstly he wanted to know what we needed in written letter. It was at about midnight, when we went to bed.

We had to wake from our peaceful deep dreams because of a strong knock on the door. We were terrified when we heard that it was the police. Ika awoke sooner and shouted at them to wait till we get some clothes on. But they continued knocking nonetheless and woke the children up. It could have been no earlier than around two o'clock at night! In the end I opened the door and there stood two bad looking policemen who then pushed themselves into our room.

"Prove your identity!" they shouted. For some minutes we searched for our identity cards and when we gave it to them one of the policemen with the list of names in his hand wanted to check our data. After my name he then searched for my husband. I told him that I had been brought here alone with my children but my husband at that time went to work to the

Group photo with the participants of the two day visit
Standing: Géza, Kitty, Thomas
Sitting: mother, Kitty's mother, Aunt Helen, and little
Peter standing

county. I added that had no idea where he went to, because he had not yet written me. It had been the same story that I had previously told to the State Security Officer! Miraculously, he accepted the story and then turned to Ika asking who she was and how did she dare to stay in such a place as this?

There was no need to egg her on. She reversed the role and roughed them up, certifying that on my inner ministry order, visiting relatives were not forbidden!

With my sister-in-law Ika and my brother Tom in Nagyfüged

"That relative would visit her whoever wants!" she continued angrily "because it was the very thing you made impossible in Budapest." and added "As far as I know we are not in a prison, where one could go for a talk only with permission accompanied by a policeman! Well? And now have a good night!" she continued "leave us sleep!" She managed to say all those things with one breath and in the meantime she managed to make my little Thomas cry.

The policemen, who were young and inexperienced, could not say a word. They couldn't muster their courage to do anything against such a beautiful woman. In retreat, they turned at once out of the room, sneaking past her as if they were asking our apologies. When they left, it was then that I could jokingly say to Ika, "you see the 'peaceful holiday' only lasted until now! We were delivered to such things, so it was good that my mother and my brother Thomas are able to stay here with me!"

My poor children finally quieted down, but only after a long while!

At the end of the week Géza visited us again and he brought food with himself, mostly meat and bread, which is what we had asked for. On Sunday we said farewell with a sad heart. We dearly missed Ika and my sons longed for Andreas.

The following week we received innumerable letters from our relatives and mother's friends. They mediated between the life in Budapest and our dreary conditions!

We received a long letter from my Aunt Kate, as well. She wrote us her interesting discovery as follows. Her custom had long been to put a soft pillow into the window from where she could watch the events as they unfolded along our old section of Ulászló Street. From that window she had full view of our previous house.

She had seen many new faces moving about in our old flat. In the flat opposite to hers on the second floor, she could see Rufi the right-hand man living. A week later she saw Matthias Cs., the writer, in our old flat. Aunt Kate did not understand what had happened and started to search for an answer. She asked Claire Sz., the kind woman who had looked after my children on that dreadful day. Claire explained to her the absurd situation that happened the day after we had been taken away. The writer Mathew Cs. offered his three room flat on the first floor where the Balassa family had previously lived, to Rufi the right-hand-man. The writer told Rufi that he agreed to the exchange to this smaller flat, which certainly proved to be a benefit for the right-hand man of the building. The official transaction was completed the following week!

The main reason for the downgrade in living space was the writer's fear of being deported. He would rather choose to live in a smaller and darker flat on the ground floor than being deported. By appeasing Rufi, the writer successfully escaped relocation! Rufi did not move into our flat, but rather into the one next to ours.

Instead four different families were brought in from the provinces to work in the factories. The government placed one family into each room. This is was why Aunt Kate saw so many different faces there. Clair also told us that from the very first moment the families were constantly arguing with one another! But God sees our souls that we did not wish them to happen so!

Just as in Russia, all the larger flats in Budapest were emptied after the tenants relocation. Additionally, large numbers of associate tenements were formed, which were only abolished in the middle of the 1990s!

Among the letters received I found one from my previous employer. He explained how shocked he was over our unfortunate situation. Realistically he asked whether we had ever thought of wearing high rubber boots. He knew that in the

With my brothers and sons in the Faragó homestead in Nagyfüged

countryside, at autumn and during the winter the mud, snow and slush are usually as high as one's ankles. He asked that we should let him know if boots were needed, because through his good contacts he could acquire some. At those times such things were difficult to obtain in the shops. He said that he wanted to send them in a parcel or bring them himself, but he needed to know the sizes and number of pairs that would be required. Later he asked me to write our other desires as well. He did not want to send us useless things. He wanted to help and asked us to accept these presents with simple appreciation and friendship. He wrote that he was waiting for my quick reply!

At first my mother did not want to hear about rubber boots, but later she accepted that rubber boots would be very much needed. Especially at autumn and winter, when one could not even leave the homestead without a pair. I told her that we were in such a bad position that we had to accept anything from kind people. The generous help of all who had any solidarity towards us, should be welcome! We were not in the position of playing neither the "sensitive plant" nor the self-respecting one!

Granny and grandchildren   **Little Peter swinging**

So I quickly replied to Uncle John's letter and asked for 3 pairs of rubber boots, one for my mother, my Brother Tom and one for me. At that time I also became accustomed to smoking so I asked for cigarettes as well. I liked the Virginia type. My mother smoked one in the evening, when we chatted pensively or played cards. Smoking cigarettes was an easy way to settle our ruffled nerves.

One day towards the end of August, Uncle John my supervisor, appeared bringing a large trunk in his hands. We could hardly drag the case home from the bus stop. After opening it we found three shiny rubber boots that fit our feet perfectly. These boots were such a precious treasure at the time. We could hardly stop thanking him for his numerous practical presents along with a packet full of sweets. Uncle John decided that he would continue to visit us personally. He thought if any boot size hadn't fit then he could return and change them for the right size. He did not trust the post and did not want these valuables to be stolen. Mother made delicious dinner and after that we smoked the "peace pipe" as sign of our "friendship" with the pleasant aromatic smell of the Virginia cigarettes that he had brought us.

The three good friends

With Uncle John we recalled the "good times of peace" that had been spent at the supervisory department! He had given us the solidarity of the other supervisors over to us, especially above all that of uncle Dődi!

Little Thomas During work   **Swinging in the F. homestead**

He said farewell to us and reminded us once again that we could ask for anything we needed and that he would send it to us in a parcel. In the afternoon when he left on the bus, all of our faces were shining with joy. It was such a good feeling after all that had happened that there were still such good and kind people that still lived in this bad world!

Later I told my family that the rest of my supervisor's bosses were similarly kind and nice as well. That was why I so loved working at the Physical Education Supervisory Department.

My mother remarked and I agreed that this supervisor "had been sent" in place of my Uncle Charles. His personality, character and even his physical appearance were all too similar to my Uncle Charles! I thoroughly believe that the characters of those who have passed reappear sometimes as if to take care of ones beloved!

One day I went with my mother into the village to meet Eva K. During that time Thomas took care of my children. I liked Eva's parents very much and so did my mother. It was as if we had known them for a long time. They had been deported from their Villányi-street flat (11th district), where Eva and her husband lived along with Eva's parents. They all received a single order, so when they arrived in Nagyfüged, all four adults had to share a common room. Later my mother spoke to Aunt Ann and found that we had a common acquaintance with Eva K. We were both familiar with the Balassa family.

Before the war Aunt Ann and her family lived in Székesfehérvár, just like the Balassa family. They had been Maria's good friends. Aunt Ann's husband, Nicholas was a small and thin man. He had worked as a State Bureau councilor, when they moved to Budapest. He was the one, who encouraged all of us to endure those times. Endured them we did for more than long two years. He was a very wise and optimistic person who was highly interested in politics. He constantly read the newspapers and explained us the real meaning of the articles. He had a knack for finding the truth between the printed lines.

Eva worked before the deportation as the Travel Agency IBUSZ. She had worked as an interpreter and guide as she spoke both German and French fluently. Her husband had been an officer before the war and as such he was only able to find work in odd jobs. Tragically, their relocation orders had neglected to include the names of their children. Eva's brother took them to and cared for them as he himself also had two children of the same age. So the four small children attended school during the school-year in Budapest.

She wondered how I had been able to persuade the State Security officer to write the names of my children on the document. I told her that to my abject horror there was no one else who could have cared for and educated my children. Otherwise, as the State Security officer told me, they would have been taken to a state orphanage! Miraculously I had managed to persuade him! Eva was a self-assertive and active woman who was 4 or 5 years older than me.

They learned in the village that deported people had to start working from the 15th of September. At least one person from each family had to report for work. The police managed their assignments in the Mátra Forestry Service. Eva had already presented herself for work as well as her husband. We agreed to send my Brother Tom to Eva to discuss the job, because he was the most suited to work for our family. Eva promised to get to know all details of the job in the mean time and she also agreed to organize a place for Thomas as well.

In the village there were more "great kulaks" and each one of them had to provide a room for the deportees. Eva was a friend of old wholesaler couple, whose 18 years old daughter Susan also checked in for work as well. At least Thomas could enjoy the company of a girl the same age as him. Luckily I was not forced to go for work, because I had two small children.
The work was organized in such a way that on Monday morning a bus collected the workers and brought them back Saturday at noon. They worked in the forest of the Mátra Mountain. They planted saplings and slept at a workers' hostel. They received food and a small salary for their labors as well. Money was always needed of course, although mother supplemented the income with a pension. We managed to buy apples, pears and plums from Aunt Maria. Luckily we did not have to bring them home from the market in the village.

Mother managed to make trouble for herself. For quite some time she could not admit to being deported. As such she wrote letters to the Inner Ministry at least once a month protesting the relocation order. For the most part the letters went unanswered until she received an answer. The letter informed her that if she did not stop sending appeals against the order she would be taken away by the police!
Later in January of 1952 her right to a pension was revoked. She was not the only one; all deportees who lived on a pension

suffered in the same way. After loosing her pension she was constantly in correspondence with the Pension Office. They referred to a certain number State Order and wrote her that nothing could be done. Later my mother resigned herself entirely to the inevitable and stopped sending letters.

During the first few weeks Thomas, Eva and all the other workers complained about the exhausting and hard manual work. After some time they managed to build stamina and later in the evenings they even managed to find happier times at the workers' hostel. The weather was favorable for them, as during that particular October the weather was sunny and warm. It was the so called "old women's summer"!

My sons enjoyed the freedom in the garden where we prepared a sand box for them in one corner. Their friend Alexander attended school in the morning, but they managed to come and play with him in the afternoons.

As the end of October was slowly drawing near I held out hope that Alfred had not been found. I hoped that he had simply been forgotten and could go on working undisturbed. But on a sad November day he appeared alone without any police escort. He asked on the bus where our homestead could be found, and they showed him the place to get off.

Peter remembered his father and was happy to see him again, but my Thomas did not know him at all. He drew apart from him as if he was a stranger. It took all of us some days until he got used to Alfred's presence.

My husband told me, that during the previous days the worker in charge of the personnel in the factory had told him that he could no longer stay in Mezőberény. He was a deportee and he was to go and look for the place he had been assigned to. It was useless to say that he didn't possess such order. He was then dismissed from his workplace, paid and then warned to leave the place. After arriving to Nagyfüged he presented himself to the police. At once he was ordered for work in the forests the following Monday together with the other deportees.

Our reunion turned out to be quite rigid and cold!
The very first evening we had a quarrel over the reasons that my mother stayed in the same room with us.

I explained to him that on Saturday my brother Thomas also lived with us for the weekend after work. In also informed him that the police regularly visits us night. Additionally as I spent the whole afternoon queuing for bread, my mother looked after the children. It had also proven to be more economic spending our meals together with my mother and Tom as we had little money. My Brother Tom returned home for the weekend and as such Saturday and Sunday evening it was a hell-hole in our room. After that Alfred went to work on the workers' bus.

Some weeks later we heard that Alfred had made friends with another deportee, the only bachelor counselor-at-law. They were always together during work and at the workers' hostel, whispering into each other's ear. By Christmas our relation was so tense that we decided to divorce "by mutual consent"!

Alfred managed to find every detailed concerning the law of divorce from his friend the barrister. He cited the more recent law by the State Order on divorce, which made the whole procedure run rather quickly. It was not like the older slow system where people had to suffer long. In this manner there was not so much exchanging blows with the "soiled cloth". The new law only required the couple's mutual consent on the divorce and this had to be brought before the law-courts twice a month.

We got to know from the barrister that when our divorce certificate was finalized we could apply for separate housing. The Village Council and the police were required to act.

Alfred told us that he wanted stay in the Faragó homestead and that I should look for another place for myself and the children.

At the beginning of January the barrister launched the divorce procedure. In the meantime we got to know that when we received a warrant to appear before the law-court, the police were required to give us a permit to travel by train. When we did get our warrant from the court, we had to travel to the town of Eger for our day in court.

1952

In the beginning of February we received a warrant to appear in front of the notary in Gyöngyös. The divorce documents had to be signed first in the notary's presence and he was then to forward it to the law court in town of Eger.

I went to the Nagyfüged police and showed them the warrant to appear, as such I then received permit to travel to Gyöngyös. What's more I was allowed to get on the bus as well. Because the date was on a weekday that Alfred worked, I decided that I did not want to be alone so I sent Ika a telegram. I asked her to travel down to town of Vámosgyörk on the train early in the morning. I would arrive there at certain time and we could change over to another train traveling to Gyöngyös. We wanted to visit the notary and later look around in the town for a short time. I simply did not want to be alone! Ika sent me a telegram back saying that she would happily come.

That day I excitedly prepared for the journey. With luck, Ika waited for me in Vámosgyörk. I was supposed to go to the notary at 3 o'clock p.m.

I signed the papers and later we sat into a confectionery, which was a pleasant place to be after the long time of isolation.

The weather was cold and it was snowing slightly. Instead of wandering we decided to stay in the warm confectionery till departure. At 6 p.m. our train was to travel back to Vámosgyörk. The connecting train had already been standing at the station and when we arrived we had to jump on it. The snow had started falling stronger and the wind blew into our faces. In the train the windows were completely covered with steam, so we realized that it was full of passengers even in the corridors. We only had a small place left by the entrance. Once we felt that the train started to accelerate, which was more than suspicious. We could not see the outside because of the steam and snow. So we asked the ticket inspector just coming by, when would we arrive to Ludas? His answer was as follows:

"We have already passed Ludas, because this is a fast train, which stops only in Füzesabony. The slow train comes after us and that is the only one that stops in Ludas."

We felt as if a stroke of lightening had hit us! How could we get home at night? —we asked ourselves.

Some minutes later the train put the brakes on, slowed down and stopped. We got off and stood at the lonely Füzesabony railway station. We were at a loss standing there at 8 p.m. in the "great Hungarian dark night". It was uncomfortable especially for me, who was a deportee, for I did not have any permission to be there as my travel license was not valid at that station.

Ika managed to find the solution! She entered the stationmaster's office and explained him what happened to us and that I was a deportee and we had to get to Ludas before midnight. The stationmaster was a kind and helpful person, and he understood our situation. He looked at the timetable, but could only find trains carrying goods after midnight.
"Is there any other solution?" Ika asked scrupulously and applied her "baiting smile"!

After that the stationmaster speculated for a while and then recalled:
"My ladies, you had luck! On the open rails there is still a railcar not far from the station. It takes two railway workers home to Ludas. Come after me quickly, I will have a look and talk to the driver, perhaps he could take you home!"
We ran after the boss, tumbling in the snow until we saw the misty shape of the railcar from afar. We arrived there at the same time as the railroad workers. The boss explained our situation and they acknowledged their acquiescence with a nod. They said "Ok, we'll take you". But we should only sit in the back. We thanked them for their kindness and jumped into the car. After a while on our way in the mist, the shape of two policemen appeared with a spotlight. They were walking in among the rails slowly towards our car. We were frightened at the sight of the policemen! One of the rail workers told us in the back to hide and stay down.

In the next few minutes the car decelerated, but did not come to a stop. Instead, the rail worker shouted to the policemen convivially through the little opened window: "Comrades Policemen! Are you not yet chilled? —Go to the railway station to get warm!"
After that the railcar accelerated and arrived at Ludas with the stowaways. We were so happy and relieved after that close call. In the village we got off and gratefully thanked the presence of mind and kindness of the railway employees.
"Please don't forget" they told us "that we are with you ladies and will try to help you whenever we can!" then they bid us farewell.

By that time the snowfall had stopped. Ika and I began the 3 and half kilometers path on foot, because there was no other transportation for us.

The northern icy cold wind started to calm down. The landscape looked as if we were at the end of the world, on the edge of the Antarctic. In the complete darkness only the snow coated fields gave some light. Deep tranquility, whiteness and heavenly peace surrounded us. Silence seemed to be even quieter than at other time! There were no other creatures to be seen, only us, two companions hanging on each other's shoulder, easing our nerves in the silence. As we moved along we had to pay attention not to fall into any ditch full of snow. We passed the time by evaluating the past exciting hours. She believed that she drew the attention of the policemen to herself as she was always meeting them. I added that if I would have been noticed in Füzesabony by the police that would have meant direct way to jail or in a "better case" a detention camp.
 But once again I was helped from above! We certainly agreed in that!

Not long after we arrived home. From the light of my window we were able to navigate the last part of our journey. My mother had been waiting for us! It must have been around 11 o'clock but she had not been fretting with herself. She had simply thought that we had missed the bus in Ludas and had simply walked home. Thoughtfully she had turned the lamp on so that we would be able to find our way. She had been simply passing the time by playing cards.

I drew Ika aside and asked her not to tell my mother what happened, so as that it would not excited her. We quickly drank a cup of hot chocolate and went silently to sleep. My sons slept sweetly in their shadowed little beds. I was so glad to see them after the harrowing night! The next morning Ika traveled home to Budapest on the bus and the train. She went directly to her workplace. She wasn't late at all as where she worked they had flexible beginning time. She counted for Géza to arrive home the next day and her little son was at her parents' place.

At the beginning of March I received a warrant to appear for the first hearing at the courthouse in Eger. That time I waited for the slow train in Füzesabony. I had never been to Eger before and I looked forward to at least getting to know the historical town a bit.

After getting off the train I walked through the town and saw lots of beautiful wrought-iron fences in front of the houses. They were covered with white snow and looked like the famous Halas lacework. It was a beautiful scene! In the middle of the town there was a huge catholic church. Its inside was even more imposing than the outside. I prayed to have been so fortunate!

In the courthouse I saw Alfred with his lawyer. We were called in and the only question that was asked by the judge. It was whether or not we had changed our minds. "Do we want to divorce indeed?" We both answered "yes", nearly at the same time and signed the documents on the divorce. That was all and it lasted about for only five minutes! The Judge told that this procedure would be repeated once again at the end of the month. Later we would get our final documents on the divorce.

After that Alfred suddenly disappeared with his barrister and I also departed to the railway station, where the slow train was to take me back home. There was enough time that I was able to catch the afternoon slow train, but this time I made sure that I would not get on the fast train! When I arrived at Ludas, I sat on a horse-carriage because there was no bus at that time. When I arrived home it was still daylight.

Mother wondered how I had managed to arrive home so early.
"Well, this should be repeated again and that will be enough for completing the divorce!" I told her "But it will be good to be over so that I can move to a different place!"
"You are lucky that nowadays it can be done so quickly!" said mother "Your father hated divorce! He said that among all legal cases divorce was the nastiest one. Then the partners always accused one another; saying every kind of obscenities about the other and it all lasted too long till the final verdict." At the end of March everything happened just as the judge promised.
The iron fences in Eger were once again showing their black color, as the snow had melted.

I received my divorce certificate. I assured Alfred that he could see and take away Peter and Thomas every time he wished. I didn't fix any time for that and wouldn't raise my children against him. Concerning financial support we agreed that as long as we were deportees he would pay as much as he could. He needed some money for his own personal needs, as well.

In April the request for lodging had to be given down at the village Council with the document of divorce attached. We asked for the assignment of a new dwelling. We needed one big enough for my mother, my brother Tom and my children. We appealed that my mother's housing was not good for so many people.

When we saw our new flat, we were overjoyed and the police allowed us to move in immediately. We moved in at the beginning of May. This new homestead was on the other side of the stream. It was right next to my mother's homestead, where the owner, our host was a widow. It was our old host's Uncle Stephen's sister-in-law. To the State, she had qualified to be a kulak as well. She lived with her son and daughter-in-law in the old house and had built a new one next to it in 1946 for the young couple. We got a big room in the new building. It had three windows, and in the room to the south there was a closed glassed balcony.

The old woman was the complete opposite of Uncle Stephen. She was a very silent, woman who hardly spoke at all. Her son Béla F. was a real Jász region man; a tall, blond and handsome man with a nice face. He could have even been an actor! His wife Magdalene was some years younger than he, a nice blond, figured woman with good temperament.
The young couple had been educated in a commercial school. Béla liked rearing bees. Later he became first the clerk of the bee rearing association, then its president.

It turned out that the majority of the Nagyfüged inhabitants came mostly from Uncle Stephen's relatives. The neighbors next to our new dwelling were members of the same family. The furniture and all our belongings were transported there from our old dwelling. Alfred got as a doss one of mother's beds, a smaller cupboard, a table with two chairs and some vessels.

Our new room had only one small deficiency. The room didn't have flooring. But the earth underneath had been thoroughly stamped down and was completely covered with the carpets we had received from Magdalene. We were welcomed happily at this new place from the very first minute. It seemed to be that our reputation proved to be good, so there was no reason to be afraid of us!

We furnished our room easily. We had quite a big room and in one corner we had enough place for a bathroom. It consisted of mother's old wall unit and the oven next to it. We had already bought a table and put shelves above it on the wall. The whole thing was separated with a curtain from the rest of the room. My Brother Tom continued sleeping on the collapsible iron bed in the closed veranda, except during the cold winter.

Though the new house was nice, for Thomas it was more difficult to reach the bus, because he had to walk 15 minutes to reach the bus stop in the village. It was more difficult for mother and me, as well. We had to walk into the village by turns for meat and bread or into the market for vegetables and fruits.

Fortunately we could buy milk and other dairy products from one of the neighboring homesteads. Their property was beyond the border of Nagyfüged, so they brought the dairy products to the border line of the village! In this manner my route was shortened and not even the police could quarrel with me.

During the summer Tom didn't have to go for work, because they only worked at the beginning of autumn. Eva and her parents visited us quite frequently. She came once with her sons spending their summer holidays at her place. The children quickly became good friends and the adults loved playing cards, especially bridge. In the meantime I told the story of our divorce and my move from the old place. It turned out that Eva was also thinking of doing the same! The reason was that in the house of the "big kulak" where they lived, there was a room where a deported widow, the wife of a colonel lived with her adult daughter and son. The girl and her brother belonged to a sect and tried at every chance to get more followers from the village. They could have been Jehovah Witnesses. In Eva's opinion, her husband had been the first convert. Not only by the religion of the girl, but her love as well. So she did not want to live in a common room with her husband any more. It had become intolerable for Eva's parents, as well.

So Eva decided to take the necessary steps!
She then visited the Village Council and asked for an empty dwelling for her and her parents. An old Jewish couple had recently moved to be with their daughter living in another deportation place. She reasoned her request that her husband had left her for another woman and that she did not want to live in the same room with him. She wanted to start the divorce procedure. At the council, Eva's request was heard and she was apportioned the "emptied" Jewish homestead to her and her parents. It was the last one in the row after our homestead. During the summer she organized their move to that place. In the end we were only about a 10 minutes walk away from one another.

Finally her parents and Eva were able to set their hearts at ease at the end. Her children were able to find peace and a great liberty in the new homestead. There was a small path all along the Bene stream, which we used when going to visit each other or when we went into the village. The distance at first seemed to be far too long for Eva after the comfortable village room, but later they got used to it on account of the inner peace!
Later our families spent the weekends together and in this manner made our lives bearable.

During the summer my Aunt Helen visited us for a week. After that time Géza, Ika and the small Andreas spent their summer holidays for two weeks at our place. It was beautiful and this time the police left us alone. Géza and his family used to go down to the Bene stream to bathe and took my sons with them. They also went fishing there thought they only caught very small fish. To the fortune of the fish, they decided to throw back into the stream. It was a fantastic experience for the boys!

Alfred took the children for a few days as well. They were not very eager to go, because Alfred could not cook and that was why they had to eat only cold meals for lunch as well.

The summer passed slowly, Thomas and Eve had to start working in the Forestry again, but at a new place. They did not mind it; at least they were not at a common place with Alfred and the barrister.

One day Uncle John, my old colleague, sent me a telegram saying that he would like to have a look at our new home. So I went to the bus station in the village to meet him. Once again he brought a big suitcase and asked a young man with a bicycle just hanging around to help him. Uncle John told him to take his luggage on his bike for money, going in front of us to our homestead. The boy was extremely happy, because he received quite a sum of money from Uncle John. I bet he had something to tell in the pub about the "mysterious man from Budapest", how abundantly he paid for his service. Later we expected the visit from the police, but they did not appear. The boy surely kept this secret for himself!

Many delicious things came out of the luggage, such as tinned ham from abroad, coffee, cocoa- and milk powder, chocolate and more Virginia cigarettes. We set Uncle John's mind at rest that we used the rubber boots diligently and in this homestead we could not even live without it! He was happy to hear that and joyfully stated that thanks to God, our good humor had not disappeared.

"Our hope was strengthened by many benevolent people" said mother. "Such people like you, my son Géza, our hosts and neighbors, the population of Nagyfüged always help us in our distresses and we can count on all of them! If we were not deported" she continued "we could have never experienced how kind and helpful people are who live in this region!"

That night mother returned from the market with the news that Liza, the "religious girl" had been taken away by the police. She was interned because the police didn't believe that the 10-15 people gathered in different houses of the village were talking about religion. They blamed political conspiracy on her! She was taken into the Mosonyi Street jail and as we got to know later, she spent a year there. Later she helped the prisons physician as a professional nurse.

By this manner Eva's husband stayed alone! But Eva did not mind to move away from her husband. Later they divorced and Eva married again. But all that happened much later!

Later my Aunt Kate sent us a thick letter with the first line that read "whoever did you bad, has already suffered horrible death". She continued: The tragedy happened in front of our house, by the house of Béla Bartók Street 86.

"One morning Rufi, the right-hand-man of our house crossed the street, when a big car with four State Security men inside came from the Round Square very quickly and ran him over. They hit Rufi so hard that he was thrown into the air and landed on the street with his skull smashed. The security officers escaped with only light injuries."

"It was a dreadful scene according to those who saw it!" wrote my Aunt Kate, "You see God does not hit to persecute people, but the sin they commit strikes back!

We got up on a misty, cold November morning. I hated the colder autumn months the most. When the colorful autumn leaves of the trees had already fallen and the branches stood naked to the sky. It always seemed as if they asking to be covered with soft white snow. They wanted to be protected against the icy cold and the harsh November winds.

Magdalene our host, behaved remarkably nervous for several days. An unusual sad glimpse pierced her radiant blue eyes. She walked about without saying a word and we did not dare to ask her. We assumed that she was having problems with her husband! One morning she disappeared only to return in the dark hours of the night. She told us she had a headache and went to sleep. We did not see an apprehension in Béla her husband, so mother and I quieted down, saying we could have simply misunderstood something!

We put the children into bed and after that sat down to play cards, as always. We passed the time until about 10 o'clock p.m. and we prepared to go to bed. Then silently, but firmly, someone knocked at our door. "That could not be the police" I said "they were never such tip-toppers!" When my mother opened the door, she could not believe her eyes as she saw the pale and panicked face of Béla. He urged us to come and help Magdalene quickly, because she was bleeding. Fortunately our clothes were still on us, so we ran to her.

When we got to the room, Magdalene was in bed and she pointed between her legs. Mother pulled back to covers and nearly fainted from the image. Red blood was streaming from between her legs and there was a small puddle of it on the sheets.

Mother was as an experienced woman and knew at once what had happened. Fortunately she knew exactly what had to be done. She turned at once to the husband saying: "Béla, quickly call the doctor and the ambulance!" After hearing that Magdalene told us silently. "Please don't do that, because then all of us would surely get into jail. She and the wise woman also, who did the operation!" Béla realized then what had happened, and where his wife had disappeared to.

Hearing that, my mum asked Béla to pray and to bring some buckets full of icy water from the well. He had to supply her with sheets, prepare a light lime-blossom or Camille tee, put honey and salt into it. When lukewarm, he was to give Magdalene drink as much as she could. As Magdalene drank the tea we changed the ice cold fomentation on her stomach. I stood there as useless, only listening to mother's orders and following everything that she told me to do.

As we nursed Magdalene, I remembered what Ika told me about a new law that had been passed. It made it compulsory for all pregnant women to bear their children. If an abortion was performed by a doctor or a midwife, even at the insistence of the mother, everyone taking part in it could be punished with a long prison sentence! This was later known as the "Ratkó plan", which resulted in the birth of numerous "Ratkó children"! *(Ann Ratkó worked as the Minister of Health from 1950 to 1953. At that time abortion was strictly banned and mothers without children were taxed. The ban on abortion was lifted in July 1956 and the tax removed after the 1956 Revolution.-editor)*

I admired my mother's fortitude and prayed to myself that poor Magdalene would not bleed to death. We kept on changing the wet clothes on her stomach. My mother carefully monitored Magdalene's pulse and I noticed that she carried a very worried look on her face.
Béla helped in any capacity that he could and listened carefully to what my mother told him to do.

It was around 4 o'clock in the morning, when bleeding started to lighten. We nursed her with the same procedure until 6 o'clock. We only stopped when her bleeding had stopped for at least half an hour.

My mother called to Béla's attention on changing the wet clothes every half hour. We were happy to see that Magdalene's face confirmed our hopes that the crisis was over. Her pale white face began to show some color and her pulse was stronger. Mother recommended that Magdalene should stay in bed for several days. She would need to drink a lot; such as milk and bouillon, eat poultry meat, so that her body could build up more blood cells and that she would regain her strength.

Béla thanked my mother continually because she had saved his wife's life. He asked us not to tell anyone of what happened and of course we promised to do so. We didn't know how he could have arranged the case with his mother, but the next day we noticed that his mother was diligently taking the meals to her daughter-in-law.

It was nearly unbelievable to see that after a week Magdalene was back to her old self. She thanked my mother for her goodness and know-how. My mother told us at that time that Magdalene's pulse had fallen to 50, but by 6 o'clock a.m. it was back up to 70 again. My mother told us that the only reason she survived was because her body was young and she possessed the will to survive.

Previously we had a good relationship with Magdalene and Béla, but after this event there was such a communion was formed among us. It was just as if we were relatives!

From the time we moved to Magdalene's place, mother had started sewing again. From the textiles received from Ika, she made nice and fashionable summer clothes for herself and me. I found joy in knitting and I managed to do it for money. I bartered with the woman who brought us milk when knitted items for her son. I received a special book on knitting, from that book I was able to get new ideas and she also bought me threads for that as well. I knitted a nice checkered coat and trousers for Peter and Thomas. They looked great in those clothes!

Christmas was drawing near so we wrote in advance to my aunts Helen and Kate. We asked them to give Géza what they wanted to send for my children, because he promised to visit us before the holidays. The "kulak Béla" brought us a nice pine tree, so Peter and Thomas could play and sing happily under it.

We agreed with Eva to go to the Catholic Church in the village and take part in the midnight mass service. We had not yet walked there from our homestead, but this time we went and did not regret it at all.

Previously there was a big snowing that had covered the entire region with a blanket of pure white snow. The air and sky were clear and the stars were so bright, even though their brilliance was overwhelmed by that of the moon. They twinkled as if heaven would have made it so bright for the feast. As the moonlight reached the earth, all the snowflakes seemed to shimmer in a blue hue. Under our steps, the fresh snow crunch with each stride. As we got nearer to the village, this beautiful winter melody could be heard from every direction. It was as if our souls were cleaned by the time we reached the church! It was an unforgettable midnight service! We, the deported people prayed so wholeheartedly that our petition must have surely been heard above. In 1953 our life made a turn for the better, although that event was still half a year away!

We returned to our homestead along our previous path, where Magdalene was taking care of my sons, who slept peacefully and happily smiling!

1953

Towards the end of February, I was woken by mother's loud words. I was frightened and thought that she was not doing well. I went to go and look and I saw her sleeping. She was talking in her sleep and in her dreams she said three times in a very loud voice: "Patrick, Patrick, Patrick!". Then she was startled by her loud voice woke up. When we made clear what she said, we had a look at the calendar as to when the name day of Patrick was on the calendar. It was the 17th of March.

"Well, pay attention!" said mother "on that day something important will happen!"

That weekend, we were eagerly waiting to meet Eva. We told her about this interesting dream and she added that Saint Patrick was the greatest saint of the Irish and probably would help us, as well!

And the wonder happened! On the 17th of March 1953 or around that day (exactly on the 5th of March 1953) Stalin died! The communist party organized a grand funeral and initiated mourning all around the country. Most of the workers were ordered to take part in the funeral activities.

Not being in Budapest we learned of these events only from stories at the capital! Our acquaintances told us that among the mourning crowds there were innumerable secret service workers. They eliminated those poor people at once from the crowd, who dared to laugh or smile during the committal service. The victims were interned at once. This happened to the dearest friend of our acquaintance, as well. She had dared to tell jokes and laugh at them. She was taken at once and interned at the Kalocsa town jail for women for one and a half years!

Eva's father uncle Nicholas, when we spent our time together at the end of March, in April and in May, kept on reciting us articles from the newspaper. He strengthened the hope in us by giving thoughts among the lines. "The tight bow around our necks had now slacked!" – Added the old optimistic man; "See even the population of East Germany is rioting!" Later he called our attention to young university students and Hungarian writers. He said that there was a plot against the communist leader Rákosi and that it would probably end up in beneficial steps concerning the deportees.

Géza brought us good news, as well. He heard that Imre Nagy would put an end to deportation. He wanted to allow us to "move freely" wherever we wanted to, except for Budapest and the big cities. He wanted to allow us to obtain work as well. This news was for the first time just like heavenly manna! But after having a closer look, it seemed to be just like the legendary story of king Matthias. In that tale, a girl gave the king a present, but in the end the king could not keep it. She had given him the gift of a dove, which promptly flew into the air after its presentation!
"Where could we move to except for Budapest?" we wondered aloud with Eva's family.
As I recalled, it was August when we received the written documents that acquitted us of our status as a deportee. The pardon went into effect from the 1st of September, 1953.

Not wanting to wait till then, we decided that Thomas and I would travel up to the capital to see the procession in the cathedral on the 20th of August. We would sleep at my brother Géza place and we wanted to look for a place in the villages surrounding Budapest, where we could move to.

On the fateful day of August 20th, hundreds of people queued in front of the cathedral of Budapest. They all wanted to see the "right hand of King Saint Stephen". *(It is a Catholic relic declared to be the 1000 year old right hand of the first Hungarian king Stephen. They "preserve the hand" in the biggest Budapest Catholic Church and on August 20th parade the hand is taken through the capital.- editor)*

When we reached the relic I was a little surprised to find an acquaintance. Outside the cordon a few meters away from the relic was that certain cleric, Halász standing guard. It was the same Halász, who had lived under our flat. He had the lion's share in our deportation! When our gaze met his and he recognized us, he bowed down his head so quickly as if his bones were deforming! He did not dare to lift his head up more in our presence. For quite a while we kept a firm watch on him from a distance. It was just enough time to impress upon him a bad conscience that he surely deserved!

Thomas and I enjoyed walking freely, traveling on tram, on suburban train and on the bus.

We looked around in Pomáz, Szentendre and that region. Of course, when the local people learned that ex-deportees would be returning to the villages near the capital, the prices jumped up into the sky. We reckoned that it would be far from the 11th district, where our acquaintances and relatives lived. After some days of inefficiently "hiking" Thomas and I went into my Aunt Helen's place.

Uncle Franz was right at home. Anyway he worked in a cooperative not far from Budapest as its leader. When he heard that we were looking for somewhere to live, he offered to take us the next day, on Sunday to Budaörs. There one of his old business partners lived and probably he could help us finding a place. We did it with great pleasure. As we traveled the 40 minutes on the Nr.40. bus from the Round Square we began to feel that this place was very near to the city.

We were so eager to find a place and in fact we succeed! My Uncle Franz made arrangements with Helen P., who lived in a big old house with her son. They were at the end of the Charles Marx street. They had horses and made a living from carrying trade goods. The owner had two big rooms, which she wanted to give out as a rental. We agreed on the terms and reserved one of the rooms for ourselves and the other one for Eva's family. We thought that we should help them with that so that they should not need to travel and organize everything alone. Our theory turned out to be right!

After returning to Nagyfüged we gave a report on our successful trip to mother and Eva. Immediately, we all began to pack up our belongings and said our farewells. Saying farewell proved to be quite difficult and we did it with heartfelt tears! It had been a long time for us, even if it had only been a mere two years! But in the end the deportees were very happy to be free again and that we could go to lay the foundations of a new life!

The kulaks were also pleased and relieved that they were not deported to Siberia and that once again they could stay in their homes alone! We have not thought, not even in our dreams that the move would be done so quickly without problems. Our luggage and furniture were transported by train. The Budaörs house was very near the railway station and from there Helen's son took us to their house.

Eva's family thanked us for the room, but they came only two weeks later. In the meantime we occupied the outer big room and furnished it for ourselves. The smaller one behind was reserved for Eva and her parents, who had enough space there later. There was only one small problem with our room. Namely, they had to walk through our room whenever they came or left. Later, we separated a path with curtains in the room, so then the constant walking in and out was not so disturbing. It was not so difficult as in Nagyfüged we had formed a great relationship with Eva and her parents. It was as if we were a family!

After furnishing the room, I went and immediately began to look for a job. Naturally, I wanted to teach so I first went into the Education Department of the 11th district Council, where I found a dear acquaintance of long ago. Mrs. K. She used to work in the General Supervisor Department right next to my friend Joli F. That had been when I worked as the office leader at the Physical Education Department.

I told her my past and she asked me earnestly not to make it public. I had to avoid entering it into my Worker-book. If it happened, there would be no way for her to help me. During that time they had just finished the construction of a primary school in the Köbölkút Street. They needed a teacher in the day-care and she wanted to find a job for me there. I told her that I would visit my previous workplace in New Pest first to fetch my worker-book and arrange there for a suitable entry. When I arrived only the deputy director was present and she acted very charitably concerning me. We decided to write in my worker-book that I left my job on 15th of July 1951 on my own will because of my two small children. So this harmless entry was written into my worker-book.

I returned to Mrs. K. the next day and we both visited the leader of the Educational Department saying that my children were elder and this time I could attend a day nursery, because I want to start working again. She wrote all this into my worker-book and I wrote it into my CV as well! The leader of the Educational Department happily acknowledged that I would be ready to teach in "only boys" day-care. So she sent me to the Köbölkút street School, where the directress employed me at once. First she employed me only under contract into the day-care of the 5th and 6th class boys from 11 a.m. to 5 o'clock p.m. from the 15th of September 1953.
My fate is just like that I found myself in deep water again!

I didn't want to believe, nor did my mother that I could find a job. It happened so suddenly and above all it was teaching! "I needed good acquaintances and benevolent people to that." I replied. Unfortunately after the time spent in deportation, employers did not want to employ deported people. All of my acquaintances with such background could only later find jobs of physical labor. My brother Thomas worked as a "helper" beside meters. Because of this I doubly appreciated my workplace.

After such long pause it was a bit strange to teach 11 and 12 years old boys. I had to arrange their lunch and later the after lunch relaxation and playing periods. I helped them learn their lessons for the next day and controlled their homework. If someone wanted, I could be asked to help them with the study materials. Later if we still had some time we started playing. There were some animated children in the group, but among them there was a "big rough child". Everyone including some of the women teachers was afraid of this young man. Stephen was an overage, red haired and freckled boy. I realized that he had minority feelings against the others and wanted to and could only excel in doing bad.

On the 25th of November 1953, Wednesday, at 2 p.m. there was the wonderful football match of "the golden football team". That British-Hungarian football match came at the best time for me. I knew that Stephen liked only one thing: football. He didn't like studying very much, but was a big football fan. When the directress was going to allow some of the pupils in day-care to listen to the match on the radio in the teachers' room, I asked the following from Stephen. "Well Stephen, I can't leave these students on their own while they are studying here on the first floor. But please go and report me when the Hungarians kick a goal to the British. Please run up and tell us, because I am very interested in the final result!"

For Stephen, the news was such a surprise to hear that he could only stammer; "Mrs. Teacher you asked me?" "Yes you Stephen" I replied, "because in this subject you are an expert and your legs are very quick, so you can surely run up the stairs quickly! Well, now please go down and listen carefully!" In an instant his face lightened to joy rather than the typical anger. He then straightened himself up proudly and said to me; "Mrs. Teacher I would go and do it!" Then he happily scampered away.

This British-Hungarian match turned to be legendary not only for the country, but also for Stephen and me! The game had hardly begun when "my friend Stephen" appeared for the first time and reported. "Mrs. Teacher, 1:0 in our favor!" Later he ran quickly back. As the goals came so too did Stephen, faithfully until the game was ended 6:3. In the end I could not believe my ears that the Hungarian football players had scored so highly against the British?! Stephen reported the final result, the sixth goal, with radiant beams of joy on his face. I was so happy that I hugged the boy and put a maternal kiss on the top of his head as a sign of thanksgiving. From the moment of the fantastic match, Stephen the "great tough" boy had changed completely! He did anything I asked from him and started to "study" and his marks improved as well!

My colleagues wondered what had happened with Stephen's unusual new behavior. They asked me how I had managed to change him like that?!
"Well" I replied "I trusted him with an important job, he did it and I thanked him and praised him for that." "Well, he surely didn't receive much of that" his chief teacher added.
In the mornings I tried to get somehow near the medicinal physical education. I visited Maria F., the chief orthopedic doctor Mr. Boldizsár Horváth's secretary. She was the interrogator at my exam, whom I knew well. Later she recommended me to go with her to the Heine-Medin Institute. There at Török Street she did therapeutic physical exercises three times a week and asked me to help her with the students. Of course I did it as social work that was free of charge. She later decided that she could use my help on a more regular basis. Happily I agreed to do it on Mondays, Wednesdays and Fridays in the morning from 9 to 11 o'clock.

But I did not know in advance what I had assumed myself to! At that time the horrible child paralysis, polio, still took its numerous victims! This institute was full of these poor sick people, mainly boys, but there was a female department, as well. People came there regularly for taking therapeutic physical exercises. I had come there to help, but the scene that I saw shook me deeply.

There was a boy who was desperately ill, whose limbs and lungs were paralyzed. He had to lie in an oxygen tent with iron lungs. There were some, whose hands and limbs were paralyzed and others, who had one or two limbs or one side paralyzed. I helped all of them in taking therapeutic exercises with their limbs.

Every one of the patients held the common characteristics without exception. They all wanted to be better with the help of their enormous will-power! I still remember one-two young men in particular. One of them was a thin 21 years old young man. He was called Széchenyi, a descendant of the earl, whose all four limbs became paralyzed and became powerless like a cloth. Against all problems he continued his university studies.

There was a book-holder attached to his bed with the university lecture on it and he turned the pages with his nose. The teachers came to him from the university when it was time for taking the exams.

There was a young man, whose both legs were completely paralyzed and he kept on training them doing exercises and massaging them day and night. Due to the help of the doctors his state became slowly better. I admired the man in the oxygen tent with iron lungs. He took a pencil or a paintbrush into his mouth and made drawings or paintings on a white sheet of paper fixed to a board in front of him!

When I looked at the terrible fate of these people I was ashamed of having been "only" a deportee. Because of this, I started to do the exercises with them under the great calling of giving assistance to others, just as I myself had been helped previously. I worked in the Török Street Institution for many long months in the mornings and in the afternoons taught in the Köbölkút Street School.

In our one room flat we still lived just like we had during relocation. The only difference was that except for the furnace we had previously, we now had an iron stove in the room. My mother was allowed to cook in the kitchen, together with Aunt Ann, Eva's mother.

1954

The "first free Christmas and New Years Eve" was celebrated in Budaörs. Géza, Helen with their families and my Aunt Kate visited us for the Christmas feast. We could not stop thanking my Uncle Franz for his brainstorm about our dwelling place. It was only by his help that we had managed to move into neighboring village Budaörs.

At the end of January, my work contract ended. The directress of the school told me with sincere sadness that I could not have a new contract. The second half of the school-year was much smaller and fewer students had applied for day-care especially from the upper 7th and 8th classes. IN that case she put the two class years into one. Because of that she only needed one teacher. Instead of choosing me to stay, she opted for the elderly teacher who would soon collect a pension to stay while I was put out of a job. After our meeting of mutual regret I was actually out and onto the street! But I didn't let myself be torn down by this!

I visited my previous educational supervisor and he agreed to help me. He had learned that the Educational Minister of that time was an academic Dr. Tibor Erdei-Grúz. He was a very humane man and once a week on Wednesdays he held a hearing day for those having problems concerning education. In such cases anyone who registered in advance and wrote his petition down, was called into the Ministry for a hearing, at a given time. Uncle John recommended that I should give it a try!

I was called to the Minister's office at the end of February. I was there well before the given time so I had to wait. Later on the door opened and I remember seeing three happy women from Nógrád county springing from the room. They were clothed in beautiful folk and culturally ethnic skirts, and blouses even with a headscarf on their heads! It was a beautiful scene with the riot of colors that after entering I saw on the minister's face that he had liked the presentation very much as well.

The Minister was a very tall, sparse of build, silent, aging man. He came courteously to me and after the mutual introduction he read my petition and asked me to tell sincerely everything about my life and my past. I told him about the relocation and previously where and how long I worked. I mentioned my divorce and that I have two little sons. I had to fend for them and my mother and as such this was the reason why I would like to go on working and that I was called to teach on a professional level.

The minister listened to me patiently and asked why I had worked in the Goldberger factory? I answered honestly that my husband had been put into jail and I could take him food in the daytime while I worked during the night shift at the factory since brining food was allowed by the jail doctor. Of course he asked the reason why Alfred had been put in prison and what the final verdict had been. I honestly told him everything and added that my husband at that time had saved the lives of 12 people form a forced work brigade and after the hearing he was at once set free.

I spent quite a long time there and after he heard my story he thought it over for some minutes. Then he lifted up the receiver and spoke to someone saying. "I am sending a teacher; give a workplace for her somewhere near to her dwelling place!" After that he stood up smiling and wrote a name on a sheet of paper. He gave it to me and said to descend to the second floor. There I was to find that certain person and he wished me success in my work! I didn't know how to thank him for his kindness. Since that time I often think of him with thankfulness in my heart!

Later I descended to the second floor and found Susanne G. She was the president of the Educators Union and she welcomed me accordingly. I told her my story shortly. She replied that she too knew of those times, because her sister was first dragged away in 1944 and after she had managed to stay alive she was deported upon her return home. She asked me "Where do you live now?" I replied "In Budaörs." "Well in that case you should go over to Budafok", she reasoned and lifted the receiver up. She called the leader of the 22nd district Educational Department. She said that next day she would send a teacher and they were to give me a workplace! I thanked her for her kindness as I happily left the building of the Educational Department.

Later I called Uncle John at once on the phone, because he had been waiting for the results of my request impatiently. When he heard where I was sent to he rejoiced aloud, because the chief Educational leader was one of his dear old friends. They were schoolmates he told me and he would certainly call him. He wanted to refer him to my previous excellent work. He added that when I went to that school and talk to Uncle Colman, I should be sure to mention him! At home I told mother with enormous happiness how I had been granted another chance to work from the mouth of a person in such a high position!

The following day uncle Colman welcomed me very kindly. With his grey hair he looked just like the educational Supervisor. He ordered his deputy to write the papers and he then sent me to the directress of the Budafok Árpád Street Grammar School. They needed a teacher in the 4th grade boys class due to the unexpected arrival of the former teacher's child. This deputy director was none else than the young "comrade Rózsa". Later he worked for a long time as the communist Labor Minister.

As God took my hand and led my steps they all so suddenly turned my life for the better! I took my "assignment documents" to the directress of the school and she then quickly led me into the classroom of the 4th grade boys. She then introduced me to the children as their new teacher. All the 29 children kept on watching me with big eyes as they constantly quizzed me.

My dear Aunt Kate happily helped me in teaching till her death in 1963. In the Budafok primary school I got to know several other teachers. Mrs. Magdalene P. taught in the upper classes and had lived for quite some time in Budaörs with her agronomist husband and their four sons. Luckily she had not been a deportee.

In the mornings we would always met at the station of the suburban rail, which was only about a 5 minutes walk from our home. Magdalene's house was on the Budaörs "hillside" and the station was much more distant for her. I remember we always laughed that she was late every day and it was I who stopped the train to wait for her at six thirty in the morning. The mood was very familiar as it truly was not a joke. The driver of the train knew of Magdalene's tardiness and nearly every time kept the train longer than he should have. At noon we used to return home together. We changed at Kamaraerdő to the Törökbálint train that took us directly home. We had to wait for it sometimes for as much as 20 minutes, so we had plenty of time to chat and to get to know each other better. She had 3 sons, the youngest one 8 years old. She was much older than me. During our travels we became good friends and later we would visit each others home as well. At the end of June we said farewell to each other, because my contract only lasted till that time.

Normally as a contract teacher I did not get a salary for the summer months, but fortunately my luck changed. In September I became a constant employee! Uncle Colman, the leader of the Educational Department called me into his office at the end of June. He wanted to know whether I would undertake a day-care position in a superior class with mixed pupils for the school-year of 1954/55 in Budatétény. I happily agreed to the position as this way my next year's job was a certainty.

There came the providence again!

At the beginning of June my aunt Kate came over to us, because for some time she was taking part in a day-care retraining course in Béla Bartók Street 21. This was my previous elementary school where she usually did duty for other teachers, besides teaching her own classes. She had been at the same place with a beautiful, pretty compeer Gabrielle M. She was desperately searching for a summer helper as a nursery chief in one of the children's camps. (*During that time cheap summer child camps were organized for elementary school pupils and their teachers under the intention of educating them in the spirit of communism / socialism-editor.*)

At that time Aunt Kate thought of me, because she knew that for the summer I would not receive salary. She told Gabi that she could recommend her niece for the job, because she was a teacher as well and she could be called in for the discussion. I agreed with Aunt Kate to go with her the very next day!

Gabrielle and me

When we first met with Gabi, we suddenly had mutual feeling formed between us and she told me the followings:

"The Union of the Transportation Ministry had two vacation houses in the town Balatonlelle. They were built on two building sites beside each other; the bigger one was for parents, the smaller one for the children." The Union could easily arrange the vacation for the families. This way the parents could have a little rest, as they could choose to be with their children or without them. Parents could take away their children from half past 9 to half past twelve in the morning and from half past four to seven o'clock in the afternoon. For the rest of the day, at evenings and nights the children came back to the child- camp.

With Gabi and the children

Gabi had been the leader of the camp the previous year as well. She did it with the help of another compeer and a nurse for the children under 6 years old. This type of summer holiday proved to be a success and the children and their parents had a good time. The Transportation Ministry asked Gabi to do the same job again. It was well paid; she received nearly the double the normal teacher's monthly wage. But quickly a problem arose. The mother of her compeer had broken her leg, so she couldn't take part in the summer camp program in Balatonlelle.

That's why she was quite desperate, because the camp should have been opened on the 1st of July and she needed a helper. So she asked my Aunt Kate. Well, after hearing the new challenge, I took it without deferring any longer in consideration of our financial needs. I could not go the entire summertime without a salary! Gabi happily travel organized my registration at the Ministry and made my job licensed as well.

Her flat was near the Kökörcsin Street, where in the evenings we could discuss the details of the summer holiday camp. It was a good reason for both of us to meet and get to know each other better. She planned to leave her husband and her little son with her mother at home in July and August. My own mother happily offered her help in looking after my children and Alfred wanted to take them to his place for three weeks, as well.

We traveled to the camp with the first group aboard the big bus of the Transportation Ministry. Gabi was a good travel organizer and as she had done the same type of camp the previous year, I was the only one who was new to the rigors of the camp. In the format of the camp, the groups of parents and children changed every two weeks. In the camp boy and girl rooms were fixed up separately for younger and bigger children. The children got up at 8 o'clock in the morning and had breakfast at half past 8. They played from 9 to 10 and later their parents could take their children away. There were unfortunately only 2 or 3 boys, whose parents were divorced and the fathers visited their children only at the weekend. During the weekdays we played the role of the "Mother". It was during these times that we went down to the Lake Balaton to swim.

The children were brought back at half past 12 for lunch. In good weather we ate it outside in the shade of the grassy courtyard. In bad weather we had to stay inside the building or on the veranda. After lunch the children had leisure-time from 2 to 4 o'clock p.m. Some times the children had played so hard that some of them went and took a nap. At half past 4 we had high-tea and later the parents appeared again and took the children for their afternoon programs. The small residents of the camp started returning at around 7 o'clock. At half past 7 we had dinner and then they went and took a shower. At half past 8 the smaller or the tired ones went to sleep. The bigger children would go and play board games until half past 9 and at 10 o'clock they all went to sleep. At that time the whole camp became suddenly silent as the entire day had been filled with the sounds of swimming, playing, and moving around. The children easily fell into a deep sleep. The delicious meals were brought from the kitchen of the parents' holiday house; always fresh and warm.

When a new group was about to arrive, we always had a free day and night. In the daytime the attendants did the cleaning up and changed the bed linens. At that time we did an extra program with Gabi! We went down to the night bar, where a jazz band played with a famous drummer and a woman singer with pleasant voice. Gabi was a well known like a dear old acquaintance so they played our favorite melodies. Our summer holiday had been enormously enjoyable with the children, but we also naturally had great responsibilities as well.

In the middle of August after the children had already left the camp and the attendants started working, we went down to the lake to enjoy swimming and sunbathing without the children. But a very unpleasant northern wind was blowing. Gabi sunbathed on the sand and I lay on the concrete hard shoulder with a blanket under me. I wish I had not done that! After half an hour of sunbathing, my left side started to feel uncomfortably cold from the wind. We entered the lake to swim, which was still pleasant and warm. In the evening I was coming down with a fever. Gabi at once ordered me to go to the separate room for sick people and called the doctor of the holiday home. He diagnosed the beginning of an inflammation of the breast membrane. I was given medicines, but my breathing was very difficult. After six days, when my fever went down, I was sent to the town of Siófok for an x-ray. There they confirmed what the doctor had already suspected.

Poor Gabi had to work all alone during that week, although the nurse stepped in and helped her in my absence. During the second week I started working again, although I was still convalescing. In spite of my discomfort, I eagerly waited for the big bus to come and fetch us with the last holiday group. When I got back to Budapest, I visited my Aunt Helen first. From there I went the following day to the Fehérvár-street surgery. In the meantime it was diagnosed that a developed wet inflammation of my breast membrane had formed! I received a medicine containing salicylic acid that I took in large quantities. The doctor ordered that I had to stay in bed when taking the pills, because otherwise I would be completely drained of all energy! Instead of returning home, Aunt Helen insisted that I stay at her place to heal. She reasoned that from her place it was easier to reach the x-ray machine and the doctor. As I rested for the next three weeks, Aunt Helen fed me abundantly. I can partly thank her for my rapid recovery. At the end of the three weeks the x-rays revealed that there was no longer any water on my breast membrane, only the mark of a previous inflammation.

My Aunt Helen

At the beginning of September I called the leader of the Educational Department and the school in Budatétény on the phone and told them of my unfortunate illness. I was reassured when they informed me that they would hold my workplace. They told me that I should not worry and strive to become healthy again. After that I should return to work. After my health returned in the final days of September, I took my workplace at the Budatétény day-care. I worked in shifts with another younger teacher. She worked during the morning hours and I did the afternoon shift. We were both present when the pupils had lunch from 12 to 1 o'clock p.m.

During the time I had spent at Aunt Helen's place, sick in bed, we had the opportunity to chat. This time make up for the two and half years we had missed because of the relocation.
Interestingly with my Aunt Helen I found it easy to talk about the heart-to-heart topics about which I never could share with my own mother. I told her the details of our "summer holiday"

in Balatonlelle, where the single fathers tried to pay us court. I was always telling a lie saying that it was bad for us!

While I had enjoyed the summer by the lake, Aunt Helen told me of the flooding. In July, the high water along the Danube caused such a panic in their house as the groundwater rose to record heights.

"Well it rose every time higher in the cellar and in the half cellar flat of the caretaker, too. In his flat the water had risen about 60-70 centimeters high. Because of this they had to leave their flats. The rats left the cellars as well and began to climb up. Fortunately they could all be done away with the help of a strong poison. Well! This is how we enjoyed the summer." shared Aunt Helen.

At the beginning of September my Peter started school! For the "school-year opening celebration" and the first day at school I went home to be able to go with him to school on the first day. Peter began school at the Budaörs School. He had been preparing zealously and conscientiously for the first "big test in his little life". Later when I became healthy again, I moved home and experienced how much he learned during September. He got to know the alphabet and wrote in his exercise books and on sheets of paper clean and beautifully.

During that time his favorite subject was drawing!

He attended the same class as the singer Gyula Vikidál. He lived not far from us, so the children used to go to school and return home together and they became good friends.

Interesting that both of them became virtuosi at an adult age!

Mother got to know one of the local reverends after one of the Sunday sermons. She mentioned that he lived nearly like us in times of relocation: all in one room. Hearing that, the reverend introduced mother to an "ex-nun". She lived with two other women on the Budaörs "hill" in her own house that had been inherited from her parents. One of her relatives had recently died, so the house was empty and that's why she was looking for someone to give the house out for rent. We had a look at the small house, my mother, my brother Géza and me. It could be found in the Csata (Battle) Street in a small garden not far from our one room home. We had neighbors to the left and to the right. One of them was a pilot with his wife and two daughters and the other one was a farmer.

I remember that for the first time we had to pay around 2.000 Forint, but after that time only the current expenses of the house that was much less than the rent of our single room.

Géza and Thomas organized our move. Later it was so good to live independently in a small house, where we no longer had to experience members of another family walking through our room. Next to the house of the pilot there was an artesian well on the corner of the street. It was from this well where we brought water for drinking and cooking. There was a well in the garden, too but this water we could only be used for washing and watering plants. In one corner of the garden there was a small workhouse, where we kept the firewood. We furnished our home to be comfortable and had a separate room for my two children. When my Brother Tom came for the weekend, he would sleep there.
We quickly forgot our stormy and stressful past!

In Budatétény I used to work in the afternoons till 5 o'clock. Some times, when entering the teachers' room to put the day-care blotter to its place, I noticed the deputy directress looking out of her room. She was a feared person amongst my other companion teachers. She was considered to be a "hard communist". She was very strict, self-confident woman with a dedicated manner. She was a "sergeant style" person. Her name was Mrs. Maria, M. and we sometimes exchanged ideas. Before the winter holiday she called me into her office. I had no idea what she wanted from me. She offered me to sit down and asked:
"My maiden name had some familiarity to her. Could I possibly have been related to a chemist called Charles Lápossy?"
"Yes, I had a relative by that name. He had been my uncle, the younger brother of my father. He worked here for some years in the local chemist's shop, till his early death."

At that time the deputy directress did not let me say another word, instead she started spouting and praising Uncle Charles for his kindness! She added that when Uncle Charles came to work there they had met. Of course the reason for their acquaintance was her usual headache. She had gone into the pharmacy to buy medicine for that.   My Uncle Charles recommended her a new medicine for headaches, which it turned out worked very well and now she always took that particular medicine when it was needed. When she got to know that Uncle Charles was unmarried and she was a widow, she lingered in the chemist's shop to chat in the evenings. She told so many kind words and praises about my dear dead uncle. I continued praising him, so we once again toasted a last farewell to his dear personality! After that I always questioned Maria's "hard communist" character!

My sons and I eagerly waited for the winter holidays and Christmas to arrive. We spent the holidays in the company of Géza and his family.

1955

On the first day after the winter holidays I was called into the office of the director. He was a beefy and friendly, "bear like" man, who worked as the president of the Educators Union of the district. There he stood and next to him Maria M., the deputy directress. The director started to talk: "Mrs. Compeer, I would like to tell you some good news! As of the New Year I have decided with Mrs Maria M. to petition you for a permanent job as teacher due to your conscientious and punctual work ethics. We have received this resolution on your case from the Educational Department. I would like to hand it over to you and wish you and also your family a successful New Year!(*Decisions in all fields of employment were centralized during the communist / socialist era.-editor*)

Because of this unexpected happy surprise I could only thank him for his kindness with a nearly paralyzed handshake. I then hugged and gave a peck onto Maria's face. It was then that I felt as if Uncle Charles helped my life once again with the help of God from above! At once all of my worries and my periods without money when my contract ended were finally gone. It was at that moment that I became a full member of the educator's society! I arrived home that afternoon with great happiness. Mother thought that I had won the lottery jackpot and I ensured her that this resolution to me was much more valuable! I told her of the things that had previously happened. Mother thought that "you see the members of the Lápossy family help our life, even after their death!" I have rarely seen such a dear present for the New Year than this one in my life!

Later on I frequently talked to Maria, the deputy directress. I mentioned to her my Aunt Kate, who had continually taught first classes and had many corresponding materials. I reasoned that she could help me to be able to teach in first classes, because I wanted to develop and make progress after the day-care classes. To my greatest sorrow there was no such possibility in the Budatétény School. Fortunately, at the end of the school- year Maria had good news for me.

My sons are in the Budaörs garden with their granny

She told me that the director of the Nagytétény School was looking for a teacher in the 1st boy-class from September. This was only a morning job. So later I visited the Nagytétény School and agreed with the director and accepted the new job.

...and with me

Traveling to that place was much easier than to Budatétény. From the Round Square to Nagytétény one could take not only the suburban rail, but the bus as well. I had to get up a bit earlier, but traveling on the bus I could reach Nagytétény very quickly and easy. I worked from 8 o'clock and after 12 I was free again, so I could spend more time with my own children. Maria understood my reasons that I was still young and wanted to test my knowledge. Thankfully she was not at all angry with me. I said farewell to her and to the school with sad heart.

Not long after my little Thomas became fevered and started to cough very strangely, just like barking. We called the doctor. His wife was my mother's good friend through our friends Helen and Louis, the doctor in Ceglédbercel. The doctor diagnosed whooping-cough. He gave him some medicine, but told us that no protective injection existed against it, he had to go through this illness. Although my sons spent the whole time together, luckily my little Peter was not infected.

In the meantime my friend Gabi asked me whether I would take part in a summer camp of children in Balatonlelle. I told her that to my greatest sorrow my son was very sick and I could not leave him only to my mother. It was not as bad as the previous summer as this time I received a salary for the summer as well. Hearing this, Gabi gave her regrets concerning her job as the leader of the summer camp. She reasoned that without the help of someone else the camp would not be such a success as the previous one!

My son Thomas had to stay in bed and suffered due to the strong whooping-cough that's why it was very good that we didn't live at the old place with Eva and her family. It could have been extremely disturbing for especially Eva's father. He worked as a yeoman in a factory at night and in the daytime he slept at home and had rest.

We met Eva and her family frequently. She told us what she was about to do. She had bought part of a bigger Buda flat, where she lived or rather dived into the flats of the house. She went there before the gates were closed in the evening and spent the night somewhere there. It was much closer to her workplace. She needed a "benevolent and helpful" caretaker for that of course. But her parents continued living in Budaörs and Eva was registered living there.

My mother noticed more and more acquaintances of ours after the Sunday mass celebrations. They had previously been relocated and found their new homes in Budaörs. For example Mrs. Elisabeth H., whose far relative was Helen, Uncle Charles' wife, later that of Louis. Elisabeth lamented that at that time they were forced to move to the county of Békés, where they arrived to a very unfriendly place. It was a hell-hole with lots of jealous people living under malevolent circumstances. Her husband was forced to do heavy work and she was driven out to the fields to do agricultural work. Poor Stephen's (her husband) heart could not do the heavy work and not long after they moved to Budaörs he died. After this Elisabeth stayed alone as a widow. Because we regularly exchanged letters with Helen, mother wrote them the sad story of Mrs. Elisabeth H. Helen replied and sent a very kind invitation to mother and Elisabeth for the summer. They both traveled down to Ceglédbercel for two weeks. There they had an extraordinary good time and when returning they praised the couple's appreciation. They noticed their love to each other and the hospitality they received from Helen and Louis.

In the meantime my little Tom recovered. Up to that time so as not to be alone with the two children in Budaörs, we moved temporarily to Aunt Helen's place. Judith and Andreas worked in a construction camp, which at that time was made compulsory for all Grammar School students during the summer. This way I and my sons had a comfortable room at Aunt Helen's place. From there we would regularly go out to the Zoo and the Amusement Park.

In the evenings my aunt Kate visited us, whom my sons took a liking to exceedingly well. They chatted for a long time; she told them stories and gave them books, as well. My Aunt Kate wanted to help them forget the relocation time and the recent times of change.

Later, at the beginning of August Alfred also appeared. By that time he was able to find a job in the Trans-Danube region of the State Farm office not far from Győr. This way he took the boys to county Zala for a three week holiday. From their hosts the husband worked at the State Farm. Peter and Tom regularly mentioned this extraordinary holiday. Firstly they did because of the beautiful Zala region, where their father took them many times for walks. The second reason was that they had so many different kinds of rare and exotic fruits in such a large quantity. At long last this was the first summer after relocation that made the grade for all of us. It was filled with so many experiences!

Well, when my sons left, mother and I decided to stay in the Kökörcsin Street at Aunt Helen's place. My Brother Tom returned there only during the weekends. My mother told her sisters at that time that Helen learned to cook kosher food, because Louis held faithfully to his religiosity. She let them know the recipes of many delicious meals which we also tried. They were very good, in my sight were also healthier and lighter, because everything was prepared with goose fat. The bean sholet became our favorite from that time!

Aunt Kate in 1955 on a class- photo

After bringing the boys back home Alfred said that my little Tom coughed frequently. He asked me to take him for a lung x-ray for children, so as not to leave anything on his lungs after his whooping-cough. Since we still had a week free till the beginning of the school-year, I took them to get a lung x-ray. It was a good suggestion that Alfred had made, because it was discovered on Tom's bronchia that there was a small infiltration. The doctor told me not to panic, as this was not yet tuberculoses, but it could easily become that if neglected. I told the doctor about all the bad circumstances in detail. I told him of the relocation and the previous whooping-cough. He replied that there was no need to continue with my story as his own brother and family had been a deportee, as well. He knew of those difficult times; the lack of proper food and poverty. Later the benevolent doctor continued that these two boys deserved to get into the convalescent hospital's school. For the sake of Tom's lungs, it was a well-founded decision. He drew something onto the photo of Peter's lungs saying; this way the two boys would not feel so lonely. He reasoned that the clean air and convenient circumstances would surely do them good. In Farkasgyepü they would get delicious and abundant food and Peter would have three lessons a day. This way he would not lose a single year from his studies.

He ordered a five months assignment to that hospital. First I had to take them to the Christine-street health centre. There I got the exact date of the assignment and receive the official stamp on the document. Well, we did it and I waited for the document to be mailed to us. While we waited Peter started the 2nd grade in Budaörs.

In Nagytétény new life started for me with teaching boys of 1st grade. The school had a parallel girl class, as well. Its teacher was Mrs. Hilda W., who worked in the classroom next to ours. From the first minute on we became friends and we helped each other. My Aunt Kate helped me a lot by giving me much practical and useful advice. Hilda was a woman of good humor. She lived in Buda in an associate tenement of a villa in one room with her husband. Unfortunately they were without any children.

Her husband worked in the orchestra of the opera house, he played the oboe. Their hosts were also musicians. The wife played the piano, the husband the violin. In the mornings she and their children left for school. After they left the virtuosi staying at home started to do their regular practice. Hilda told me laughingly that I should imagine the cacophony disturbing the silence of the vicinity. Fortunately the thick branches of the high pine trees in the garden of the villa caught some of the escaping noise. They were frustrated at them from mixing the sounds while still being heard from behind the big park.

I did teaching with great enthusiasm. I had around 30 boys in the class, whose parents were mainly factory workers of the neighboring industrial plants. But these boys were so very respectful. They were decent boys in such clean clothes that I had rarely seen in my life. They were very diligent and they eagerly wanted to learn.

At the first meeting with the parents, nearly everyone arrived. Parents asked me to be strict with their sons and to require excellence from them. They wanted their children to be educated so they would formulate "personalities". I ensured them that I would require the proper curriculum of their age and that they would learn it. Furthermore I told them to ask their children in the evening when they had time about their school work. So could the teachers and parents could cooperate in favor of the children!

I received the assignment for my two children to attend the school in Farkasgyepü at the end of September. The information leaflet wrote what they were required to bring. First we had to go to the Eastern Railway Station. From there they took the children in groups and escorted them to the village of Farkasgyepü.

I prepared my sons in both body and soul for the long trip as well as the long separation. In the Eastern Railway Station they started to weep a little, but once they saw the other children they soon quieted down. This was particularly so when I emphasized that Thomas had to go in order to regain his health. Peter as the "big boy" was to take care of Thomas so they would always be together. When the fast train to town Szombathely departed, I was about to cry. The other mothers around me did the same. Five months are a long time indeed! According to the leaflet the children could be visited the last Sunday of each month. The next time I could see my boys was the end of October! Naturally, I waited eagerly for that day!

When I returned to Budaörs mother and I looked at each other and we embraced on each other's shoulder. My sons had certainly left enormous emptiness behind! Though we missed the boys terribly, we also reflected have been blessed with a benevolent doctor, who sent both of the children there. It was a blessing to know that my little Tom did not have to stay there on his own. Knowing my children, Tom was the more delicate child, his little heart would have been broken there if he had been left alone.

Later I was able to keep in touch by corresponding with little Peter. The letters were always signed by Tom with his scratchy writing. He has not quite yet learned to write that time. Peter set my mind at ease in the letters that they did very well, but for him it seemed quite strange to only have three lessons a day. He reassured me that when I would visit them, I would see the beautiful place where they were and I could walk among the pinewoods and smell the good clean air!

Aunt Helen invited me and my mother to spend the winter months at their place. We happily accepted their invitation and we quickly set about packing some clothes and left for their place. Her husband, Uncle Franz returned home every second weekend from his workplace. When he was at home, we would go and sleep at Géza's place or I would simply go and visit one of my cousins, to Mrs. Sz. Pili. Her mother was the first cousin of my mother.

Her husband was a gynecologist. He had been a relative from my father's side. The poor man had recently arrived home from Tbilisi in Russia. During WWII he had suffered there as a prisoner-of-war for 6 long years. After returning, he learned that an air attack in 1944 had nearly completely destroyed their nice third floor flat in the John Arany Street. Pili did not have any children. She lived with her mother and with flat destroyed, they moved to a dark flat on the ground-floor.

When her husband returned he started to work again and they were able to find a bigger flat on Nádor Street. He began working as a doctor again and he was able to find a room for his surgery. Life seemed to start over for them as they started to furnish all three rooms of the new flat just as if they were newlyweds. As a matter of fact they certainly could have been seen as a "newly wedded couple" after that horrible cataclysm!

I liked visiting them very often, because they were nice people with a good sense of humor. The mood was always very good at their place and I also got acquainted with a very diverse company of relatives. Additionally they had also stored some of our furniture from the time of relocation.

At long last the final Sunday of October arrived; the day of my visit to Farkasgyepü. I planned to travel down on Saturday taking the fast train of to Szombathely at 1pm in the afternoon. The train stopped at the town of Városlőd after Herend, where I got off in the company of the other parents. They all had similar intentions as me. There was no bus, so we had to take off along the road on foot to the top of the hillside. We walked some kilometers, when night started to fall quickly. The village of Farkasgyepű could be found atop the hill and it was already dark when we reached it.

One of the couples thought to visit the local wise-woman in search of recommendations for somewhere to sleep. The woman had a big heart and she helped all of us find a place to sleep. A young mother and I were taken to a house in the village. There a couple gave us one of their big beds, where we both slept under a big quilt. In a separate bed our gracious host couple slept. I had never slept in such a huge bed and I thought I was such a big lord! Fortunately the young woman sleeping with me was small and thin, so both of us had enough room in the bed.

It must have been around 9 o'clock p.m., when we finally organized everything. For dinner we had the food brought from our homes. The following morning we asked for breakfast, which we paid for together with the lodgment. They did not want to accept money from us. We were so grateful that their generosity had saved us from spending the night out on the street. Later, the husband escorted me to the convalescent hospital, which was found outside of the village.

The air was so clean, and the compound was in a huge closed park, many small, uniform pavilions among the high old pine trees. There was a bigger room to the left and another one to the right. They both had 10 beds and a small cupboard belonged to each child. In the middle of the pavilion there was a room for the nurses from where they kept watch on the children in both rooms through a window. There were two nurses to every pavilion, one of them worked in the daytime, the other at night. The favorites of both nurses were little Peter and Thomas. Photos were taken about them, as well.

When I arrived Tom had light fever and sore throat. That's why he stayed in bed, but my Peter was already dressed and waiting for me. Later he showed me everything, such as the dining room, the school, and the meeting room. After the tour we returned to Tom's room to chat and play a little. After a short relaxation time we were able to spend an additional hour with our children. Peter and Thomas told me the news one by one and quickly set my mind at ease that they were having a good time there indeed. Later we hurried to the bus stop in the village, from where the bus took us to the fast train heading back to Budapest. By 8 o'clock in the evening we were already back in the capital. I went to sleep at Géza's place and told them everything that had happened.

The following day I went to Nagytétény to teach and then met my mother and Aunt Helen at noon. Then I told them how the boys were doing. I also met Aunt Kate, who appeared in the evening and was in such a flurry to hear about her favorite children. Later, mother decided to go with me in November to visit the children.

In Farkasgyepü I gave lots of pecks on my Thomas's face, so it was no wonder that a few days later I had sore throat. The mucous-membrane of my mouth got inflamed and was red. I could hardly eat. I did not take it light heartedly and I went to an ear-nose-laryngeal examination. The doctor only shook his head and asked me weather I ever had diphtheria? He tested the sample of the mucous-membrane and his suspicions proved to be true. My children had been given the vaccine against diphtheria at young age and it was possible that Tom was going through a light infection. As a result he in turn infected me, because I had not been given the vaccine when I was young.

I could only keep on going for therapeutic treatment, because the doctor was unable to do anything else. I suffered through that period, I could eat only pulped food and in the end my vocal cords also got inflamed. As I did not have fever, I continued to teach, but all the while my throat suffered.

There was a small and clever boy in my class George P., who helped me in a fantastic manner. He came to the pulpit and while I sat at my desk, I would write down on a sheet of paper and also whisper into his ear what kind of exercises the whole class had to do.

It was utterly fantastic! One should have seen, how the whole class worked, without complaint they made math exercises mostly in writing, reading, made drawings, wrote the previously learned characters of the alphabet on sheets of paper or into their exercise books.

My compeer Hilda sometimes had to look into the room believing that there was nobody there. My fellow teachers wondered how I was able to teach in such an orderly and fashionable way! I had to plod away at teaching in this manner for about five days sparing my vocal cords to avoid any further problems!

For the exceptional self-conduct I gave every pupil the best mark; George also received an honorable mention! I thanked them for their contribution to my quick healing and the parents later commented about this as well! I told my class: "See how much could be done in one lesson in your favor if you behaved so collected!" After this the boys settled down and liked coming to school and I also enjoyed teaching them!

The pavilion of the Farkasgyepü convalescent hospital

On the last Sunday of November my mother and I traveled to Farkasgyepü. Quite early in the morning we met at the Eastern Railway Station. Mother came from one of her Aunts, where she slept and I came from Géza's place. We sat into the dining car of the fast train, because neither of us had any breakfast. At that time mother started to complain that the previous evening she had a very delicious stuffed cabbage for dinner. Stuffed cabbage was one of her favorite dishes, but at night she could not sleep well. Apparently the cabbage was bad for her stomach. She took some cooking soda to help with her digestion. But it was of no use, she felt her stomach getting worse on the train. She asked for a mere cup of tea with rum, thinking that it would do her good. It didn't happen; the tea and rum caused even more pain! Later she had a biscuit that I fortunately thought to bring with myself. We spent the time in the dining car until getting off the train. The bus came to the train and took the visitors to the convalescent hospital.

Peter and Thomas were waiting for me in front of the pavilion, dressed in a coat and hat. It was chilly as the end of November had brought a light snow to the Bakony hills.

The boys with me and with their granny

The nurses appeared and I enquired about Tom's illness. It certainly had been diphtheria and some of the other boys also had suffered with the same illness. Luckily, Pete did not get it. I told them how I was doing and how I had recently recovered from the infection. At the same time I asked if they could help with relaxing mother's stomach as she was quite sick. We went and found the physician in attendance, who gave her some medicines to ease her sour stomach.

The school-room was opened for the parents, where we sat on the small school desks. My poor mother disciplined herself as I talked to the boys. She was happy to see them, but I could see it on her face that she was suffering. I took some photos about the children and the nurses. The children were very happy to see their grandmother and they didn't seem to notice anything wrong. Though my mother was happy to see the children, she was eagerly awaiting for the afternoon train home. She ate only biscuits the entire day.

In the evening we went to Géza's place, because they lived the closest to the Eastern Railway Station. There Ika gave my mother the appropriate medicine for heartburn, as she suffered from it sometimes. Because of this mother was able to sleep peacefully. In the morning I left for school from there. Mother went to my Aunt Helen. I encouraged her to visit the doctor with Helen in the morning. The doctor later diagnosed her ailment as the beginning inflammation of the gall bladder. The doctor gave her medicines and ordered a strict diet. Despite all, it took three weeks for her to heal! At that time mother also resigned from eating stuffed cabbage for long time!

That year, the Sunday when I could visit the boys in December was between Christmas and New Year's Eve. I traveled alone on the morning fast train taking packets of toys and cakes for my sons. All parents on the train looked like "Father Christmas". We all wanted to make up for the warmth of home and the happiness of Christmas for our children.

During my visit I asked the doctor about Tom and he set my mind at ease saying that my son was making good progress. He ensured me that by the time they were ready to travel home, the infiltration on his bronchia would surely disappear. About Peter he told that in his case nothing could be seen. I did not say a word, but only praised God and the young doctor, who had previously assigned my both sons here. Peter told me that they would receive a school report in January and his was to be the best mark. They studied only the most important subjects there, because those could be managed into three lessons a day.

The nurses praised my children how well they behaved and how very kind they were. Apparently they did not have such good and nice sick children before! I returned to Budapest happy and proud of my sons. That night I was back at Géza's place.

Because my Brother Tom also had free time from work, we spent Christmas and New Year's Eve in Budaörs. He had lost lots of weight and coughed regularly. Later he was unable to return to work and had an examination done. Needless to say that on his lungs something was found, so he was at once assigned to the Korányi convalescent hospital. After that, my mother visited her son frequently there. Thomas got the same treatment as Géza had before. My mother and I moved to Aunt Helen's place and lived there again.

1956

The beginning of 1956 was quite bad. In January we had an earthquake which we felt in the Kökörcsin-street flat.

After the winter holiday my class and Hilda's, the two second year classes, were moved from the main building to a separate one. It was right next to the bus and the local railway stations. It was nearer for us, because from the station we could almost instantly step into the classrooms. We worked in shifts, once in the morning and other times in the afternoon. Fortunately we were able to go on working together with Hilda.

During that fateful week we had to work only in the afternoon, but in the morning something happened. At around half past six or seven o'clock a.m. we heard an enormous roaring. Everything started to shake. The chandelier and the pictures also moved from their places, the windows started rustling. I remember my Aunt Helen brought the breakfast in for Judith right at that time and placed the tray on the table. Then the cups and spoons started to dance. Judith ran in frightened from the bathroom. Mother and I were still in bed and stared at each other in stunned silence. We held on to the brink of the bed paralyzed, while under us the earth roared and shook. None of us had the idea to flee from the house to the open air!

We waited a little and when it was silence again we turned the radio on. It was announced after a while that the epicenter of the earthquake had been found in Dunaharaszti and its surroundings. There were some old clay and straw mortar houses that had collapsed. Fortunately there were no casualties', only deep cuts in the surface of the roads. We went to work at 1 o'clock in the afternoon and talked about this event with Hilda. We all commented on how good it is that Hungary is not in a zone of great earthquakes. The small one that we had received was frightening and dreadful enough.

In January I went with my Mother to visit my brother Thomas. He was opposite to the Korányi convalescent hospital in a separate place, which was in the big park and consisted of several small pavilions, just like in Farkasgyepü. My Brother Thomas lamented that he was sleeping too much. We set him at ease that it was not at all a problem, because his run-down body was trying to build itself back up. We reminded him that he just needed to eat well, stay in bed, relax and forget the many woes that he had suffered. At that time he was simply to sleep and regenerate!

I traveled to Farkasgyepü on the last Sunday of January and visited my sons. There I happily learned that both of them had put on some weight and Peter received an honorable mention for conduct and diligence. This honorable mention was in addition to his excellent school report. The doctor held a meeting with the parents and told us that there would be no visiting day in February, because at the end of the month the group would return home. We would soon receive a notice with the exact date that our children would arrive at the Eastern Railway Station. A telephone number was also given to us for further enquiries.

At the middle of February we returned with my mother to Budaörs to clean the house left empty for the whole winter and make it warm once again. We also had to buy food so that we could continue our lives with my sons again. I went to fetch them at the railway station, during that same time mother made dinner for us at home.

The fast train arrived around 5 o'clock p.m. at the Eastern Railway Station. The crowd of parents waited for their children. We happily hugged our children and we were so happy to find them well fed and with a healthy appearance. It was a joyful song in our hearts after the five long months of absence! Some of the parents even cried with happiness! At home my mother waited for her grandchildren with a delicious dinner. Later the children started to rediscover their old surroundings and the toys they had left behind were now new to them again. In the evening they went happily to sleep to their own beds and fell into sleep in the longingly absent warm family nest.

In the following days I accompanied little Peter to the school in Budaörs. I took the school report he received in the convalescent hospital. I also asked his teacher to tell me whether any deficiencies could be noticed in the subjects. Nothing like that happened at all and my little son was able to quickly fit back into his old school and with the old friends.

Alfred came at Easter to visit his sons and took them for twice a day with himself to his relatives. He promised to take them for a three week summer holiday. I asked him not to postpone the holiday to the end of August, because Thomas was about to start school in September.

The end of the school-year arrived quickly. The exam of my students was successful and all were content with my class. The students did so well that the director asked Hilda and me whether we wanted a new 1st grade class or take the same children further into the 2nd year. Naturally we chose the second possibility. After that we wished one another good holiday and said farewell to the school for a short while. As the summer passed, my brother Tom returned home relaxed and healthy from the convalescent hospital. My brother Géza visited us more often and in the end he shared with us that he was in a divorce process with Ika, so he moved to Pili's place.

He hoped that the divorce would be announced in September. He did not let us know the details of the circumstances; he simple just told that the mutual understanding was based on disappearance of trust. They didn't want to divorce with anger, but it simply could not be continued on in this manner any longer! So he took mother's furniture to Pili, where he could stay comfortably.

In the meantime Alfred took the children with him near town of Győr for two weeks. But the very much desired Zala county holiday was unfortunately cancelled. Peter started his third year of school in September, while Thomas started his 1st class. I went on to teach the 2nd class.

My Brother Tom has not yet been employed. My brother Géza received the document on the divorce at the end of the month.

At that same time he worked as the lead electrician of the Váci-street Quilt Fabric. Géza asked us to visit the Balassa family frequently, because their daughter Pötyi was already a bride. The lucky and happy bridegroom was Stephen Cz. He was from our father's side, a third degree cousin from the relatives in Munkács. But Pötyi always remained Géza's favorite.

Pötyi

Géza kept on persuading me to come and once I decided to go up to Maria with him, where to my greatest surprise I was welcomed with the old, sincere loving-kindness as if nothing had happened before! At that time I got to know that Louis had married, when his mother died and had a son of three years. Their father lived at Maria's place and they sold their house in Szekszárd. Well, I thought at least Louis found the purpose of his life!

I remember it was 9th of October when we organized a class trip to the Zoo and the Amusement Park with my compeer Hilda with the assistance of some mothers as helpers. In the morning we walked and looked around in the Zoo. In the afternoon after coming out from the Zoo we directed the boys and girls towards the Amusement Park for small children. It was a beautiful beginning to October. The trees of the park started to show the colorful shades of the autumn. We called the children's attention to the colorful leaves and they started to collect autumn leaves for the next drawing lessons.

In the meantime we spent our lunch by taking shifts with Hilda in the neighboring restaurant. I ordered stuffed paprika so that I could finish eating quickly. The lukewarm meal was brought and placed in front of me on the "suspiciously clean" red checked table cloth. I was very hungry, so I ate the two meat balls in no time. Because of the circumstances the place was not at all appetizing. Not long later I felt my stomach to be very heavy, as if I had eaten iron balls! I eagerly waited to start off for home!

Of course we took the classes back to Nagytétény from where I arrived to Budaörs quite late in the evening. I felt quite sick. For some days I kept on a diet. On the 18th of October I became fevered and pain around my gall bladder started to develop. The doctor recommended that I was to take some time off from work. He also prescribed some medicine for my gall. I was not getting better at all, so on the 23rd of October 1956 he sent me to the Budafok surgery for a thorough examination and blood test as we belonged to that surgery.

I took off early in the morning fevered and hungry without eating breakfast because it was required for the blood test. I later received the result of the test around 11 o'clock. In the meantime I ate some food and turned giddy as the pain subsided on the right side of my stomach. Due to the assignment document I visited the gynecologist, where I met my old doctor dr. Raisz, He was the same doctor who had helped me with the birth of my sons. He examined me and said that my problem was not related to his field of medicine. The pain was derived from somewhere else. From there I went to the surgery, where they stated what the results of my blood test backed the finding that I had appendicitis.

The doctor prescribed that I be taken for an operation to the Üllői-street Clinic, saying that I was to go in that very day for surgery at 2 o'clock p.m.! When hearing this, the whole world turned upside down!

With my favorite class in Nagytétény 1956

... and two years later in 1958

I told the doctor that it was impossible for me to go now, because I lived in Budaörs with my old mother and two small sons. "If I didn't arrive home, they could not imagine where I had disappeared to. It was not possible to call them on the phone. This is also with the fact that I have nothing for going to the hospital." Hearing that the doctor asked me malevolently:

"Well, you deny going to hospital?"

"No", I replied "not today, but tomorrow I would surely visit the Clinic."

"Well, as you think", he continued "but sign this sheet of paper that on your own responsibility you decided not to go to hospital today!" He added, "In case of accidental perforation of your appendix, we would not be the responsible ones!" Well, I signed it!

"Anyway, do foment your appendix with ice cold water!" said the doctor. He was quite frustrated at my refusal to go immediately to the Clinic. I anxiously waited to arrive home and tell mother what happened and give her the news of my future perspective! After having something dietetic to eat, I had a little rest. Later in the afternoon my fever went down and I felt better. I decided to visit my hairdresser on the Ferenciek square in the downtown of the Budapest. I was certain that I would spend quite a long time in the hospital!

"But hurry back!" my mother told me "and do not forget that you ought to foment your appendix as well!" Well, I arrived there at 6 o'clock p.m. and my hairdresser started to work on my hair at once. While I was sitting under the hair drier cap I noticed that the hairdresser ran nervously to the door that opened towards Sándor Petőfi Street. The mood was very nervous, just like before an explosion!

By the time I was combed and my hairdo was ready at 7 p.m. I could see from the door that the university students were marching in orderly long lines along the road towards the statue of Sándor Petőfi.

"What could have happened?" I asked, but nobody could answer.

So I entered the church of the Grey Friars from where enthusiastic young people were streaming out. I did not yet understand such a thing! I came out of the church where I prayed for success in the operation, and later I jumped on the Nr. 7 bus and then hurried to my Aunt Helen's place. They were sitting by the table and had already eaten dinner. Franz also was at home and the radio was turned on. They offered me dinner and I quickly told them that the next day my appendix would be operated on.

But they had no time to say even a word, when around 8 o'clock the radio broke its running program and announced that comrade Gerő wished to talk!

(Ernő Gerő was a hard communist politician and economist. He worked as minister of commerce /1945/, of Transport /1945-49/, of Finance /1948-49/, of State/1949-52/, of Interior Affairs /1953-54/ and Prime Minister /1952-56/. Besides Mátyás Rákosi and Mihály Farkas he was one of the three omnipotent State leaders. In his radio speech of 10.23.1956 he roughly attacked the revolution. He is responsible for calling the Russian troops to Hungary to crush the revolution. On 25.10.1956 he was sacked from all his state positions and he fled to the Soviet Union. In 1960 he returned to Hungary and was found guilty by the Communist Party.- editor)

Peter as third, Thomas first class students in 1956

He talked about some kind of counter-revolution. I got so frightened that I quickly said farewell saying that I wished to arrive home at the earliest possible moment!

I traveled on the tram back to the Round Square and then I was going to take the Nr. 40 bus. I saw from Fehérvári and Verpeléti (now Frigyes Karinthy) streets that a crowd was streaming in. They were mostly factory workers holding hand painted signs in their hands and they were shouted something. I jumped on the Nr. 40 bus that was about to leave. I noticed on the side of the bus someone had written in large whitewashed letters: "Down with the communists! Down with the Jews!"- The ticket inspector heard only that a "revolution" had broken out and that the busses would stop running after only one or two more.

In Budaörs I got off the bus and with all my strength I hurried home. In the village it was still silent. I told mother that it was unlikely for me to be operated on tomorrow, because the busses would not be running so I had no way of traveling into the city!

"But where is Thomas?" I asked.

"He went into the capital" my mother replied. We had hardly started guessing where he could have been, when at last Tom arrived with a frightened expression on his face. He told us that in the afternoon he had seen groups of university students gathering and in the evening the crowd had assembled on the street in front of the National Radio. When the sound of gunfire was heard Tom decided to head home and was able to catch the last bus.

"The revolution has broken out against the communists!" he told us.

In the great perturbation we could hardly set our minds at ease. This was especially so with me. I started to foment my appendix with an ice cold cloth, but after some time I felt worse and the pain did not disappear but rather became stronger. Eventually I had to stop fomenting it. In the end I even managed to fall asleep!

Early next morning my brother Tom went up to the bus stop, but a sign was put out that there was a suspension of the bus line. The third day he went back up to the bus stop to make enquiries about the bus. He returned with the news that I should make myself ready, because that day the bus service was going to start again. I had long prepared my luggage for the hospital stay and I said farewell to everybody. I said that I was about to go to the hospital. Thomas kept me company to the bus and I urged him not to leave our mother and the children alone, not even for a minute. Tom made me a promise to stay there, so when I stepped onto the bus my heart was a bit eased.

As we were traveling we were sopped by Russian soldiers near the Osztyapenko statue. The soldiers stopped the bus and called for the passengers to get off. After getting off they searched everyone's luggage thoroughly. They opened my small bag and dug into it and finally understood through an interpreter that I was on my way to the hospital. Once they learned this they let me go. There was a subway stop at the Kelenföld railway station and I quickly disappeared down into it. The tram Nr.49 was just approaching on the other side and I managed to get on it and then traveled further on to Aunt Helen. They nearly fainted when I told that while on the road leading to Budaörs the Russians had gone through my pockets.

"Well, then I give you something to eat" said my Aunt Helen "and later I escort you to the Tétényi-street hospital with your assignment document. A Hospital is a hospital; this operation can be done anywhere, couldn't it? It is impossible to go to the other place, because this very morning the radio announced that there was heavy fighting along the Üllői-street military barracks!"

When we arrived at the nearby hospital we witnessed a huge commotion. The people were coming and going just like an agitated anthill. Injured people were being brought in by the ambulance, but we could see that they were not from the 11th district, as it was still peaceful there.
   It took some time but we eventually found a doctor, whom I showed my assignment to the hospital. He shook his head and told to go down to the basement, where the laboratory had been moved to. This was a precaution that had been planned for times of war. Down in the basement they would take my blood and give me the result at once. He added that in case the number of white blood-cells was less than 12.000, then the operation was not urgency. However he informed me that if the count was higher, I should look for him on the first floor. This hospital could do the operation as well. Until the time that I was to have the operation, I had to foment it with cold cloths and lie down. In case it became worse, I should return. He informed me that there were still some empty beds in this hospital and it was still not overcrowded with injured people. In the laboratory the blood sample was taken and we waited impatiently on the corridor for the result with Aunt Helen. The result was, thanks to God 10.000, so we did not meet the doctor again, but instead went home a bit relieved. At home I went to bed dressed and I only took fever depressants.

   Helen tried her best to cook according to the special diet for me. Poor Aunt Magdalene did all the shopping. She was able to do it, because her workplace was closed. She stood in queue for bread, milk and brought enormous amount of Lipto quark. She always brought what she could. Andreas's school was closed and Judith's workplace was also. Uncle Franz could not travel back to his workplace, because the traffic was completely stopped! We were back into a complete wartime situation. From 5 o'clock p.m. a curfew was initiated!

   My condition improved because of my day long rest and I only had a light fever. I showed Helen, that my stomach was beginning to turn as if I were pregnant. In the end I received a pair of summer trousers from Franz, because he had quite a big belly and his trousers were big enough for me now. My clothes were simply too small for me.

Some days later, when I was doing a little better, Judith and I went to the Gellert square, but dared to walk only in the shade of the houses from Pest. On the Bartók Béla Street, crowds of citizens were walking around but from the Pest side we could see that Gellért square was completely empty. It was under constant gunfire from Pest. Franz was listening to the radio all day long and always told us what he heard about the fights in Pest and the explosions of the petrol filled bottles.

I approached the whole situation as there was nothing that I could do about it. I had my own problems. I constantly had to pay attention to what would happen to my appendix and to relieving the pain.

A week later Aunt Helen and I visited the Tétényi-street hospital again for another blood-test, but fortunately the number of white cells was only 9,000. I kept myself to what the doctor said; I stayed in bed, but I still couldn't foment my appendix anymore. It was just simply quite bad for me. My Aunt Helen's neighbor was a physician and they called him in to examine me. He performed the examination and afterwards set my mind at rest when he revealed that I did not have any problems with my appendix. Rather he diagnosed that I had a strong gall bladder inflammation. He brought me medicines from his flat to fight against the inflammation. He also said that I was not allowed to eat greasy food, especially sheep's quark. It was very greasy and I had to drink tea abundantly instead of milk. Only thin cow's quark was allowed for me. He gave me a leaflet where a diet for bilious patients was written and he asked to keep ourselves strictly to that. Later he told Helen the reason of the great silence in their flat. It was because from the beginning of the revolution he had moved his family to the Orthopedic Clinic not far away. As a physician there he was working day and night, because there were so many patients. Well, after that I cheered up that my appendix would "remain" in its place! I stopped the indiscriminate eating and Helen launched a strict diet for me. Some days later the medicines, the diet and the staying in bed produced the desired results. My fever had completely disappeared and the pain was not so intense.

The 4th of November arrived and late that evening we heard several salvos being fired into the neighborhood. Helen and I ran down to the washing-house of the building, because no air-raid shelter had been built in the house. Uncle Franz stayed upstairs with the two children. They were not afraid, but Helen and I were all the more! We could hear the sound of the volleys down in the cellar as they were closer. We could feel the house shaking as well. We continued sitting there for about four hours in scared panic. The bilious attack appeared at me again on my right side beside the liver and it felt just like a piece of strong iron had been sewn into my stomach. In addition to the fear I suffered terribly from the pain. All of this caused a horrible mood! Helen and I simply held each other's hand and prayed that the whole building would not come down on us. Then all of a sudden there was a silence! We just simply could not imagine what had happened! After going upstairs we saw the others sleeping peacefully. We appreciated their strong nerves. We could only fall asleep against the dawn!

Next day we learned that from the corner of Vincellér and Béla Bartók streets Russian tanks had fired at the Round-square and its houses! The Round square was left in ruins! Some days later around the 10th of November normal everyday life started once again.

In the days that followed Aunt Helen took me to their district doctor F., who examined me and stated an astonishing result! "You neither have inflammation of the bowel, nor that of your gall bladder, but surely do have an inflammation of the right side breast membrane" he said. He prescribed a medicine of salicylic acid and recommended that I take four tablets four times a day.

The following day after taking the ordered first four medicines, pain started to develop around my liver. After taking four more pills in the evening the pain around my liver was so much that I began to cry. The following morning I visited the doctor again and reported on the effects of the medicine and I nearly begged for him to send me for a liver check-up! He replied furiously that the patients always want to be cleverer than the doctor! Despite that he gave me an assignment for a liver-function examination and for a thorough blood test. So I ran to the Heath Centre in the Fehérvári-street and fortunately at that time I had nothing to eat because of the pain. A good amount of blood was taken and they said that the result would be ready the following day at about 11 o'clock a.m. When I received the result the following day, they asked me to hurry back to the doctor, because I had serious liver inflammation.

When Dr. F. saw the test-results, the 13 Tymol and 98 blood counts, he was abashed at it and only stammering he said: "What a good sixth sense the dear patient had!" Mumbling he continued "Taking all medicines must be stopped, except for Vitamins B and C. You have to stay in bed and take an even more strict diet than before!" But as he was not my district doctor, later I had to visit my own doctor.

I bought the vitamins and returned home to Helen with these new medical results, which I thought to be finally accurate!

Fortunately my Brother Tom arrived two days later saying that the regular bus traffic had resumed, so I thanked Helen for her kindness and hurried home with Tom.

At home mother and the children were doing well; except for the constant distress they had suffered after hearing the fearsome news about the fighting near Üllői Street. They had no idea where I could have been operated on and where I had been. I set their fears at rest saying that I had no problems with my appendix, because I only had a liver inflammation! Thomas called the doctor at once, who recommended that I stay at home, because the hospitals were overcrowded with injured people. The buildings had only broken glasses in the windows and I would not get healthier that way, so he decided not to send me there.

He reassured us to keep the previous doctors advice by strictly staying in bed, doing the special diet and taking vitamins. If I followed these rules, I would completely recover at home! The doctor's advice concerning the meals was as follows:

"One could eat chicken or pork soup, completely without grease, but with lots of vegetables. Meat could be eaten with an apple or some other kind of sauce and boiled potatoes. Boiled pasta and rice were also allowed and buns, marmalade, homemade biscuits and thin cow quark in great quantity and lots of sweet fruits as well."

My Brothers Géza and Thomas in Budaörs, November of 1956

The first week I enjoyed staying in bed. At that time I was in bed the whole day long and I slept for long periods of time.

After the turmoil I went through, it was so good to be in our secure sweet home once again. In Budaörs there worked two butchers, from where my mother bought nice meat and cooked the dietary meals for me. At long last my belly became smaller and day after day the pain around my liver gradually reduced.

My Brother Tom was at home and helped mother a lot around the house. One day my brother Géza arrived on a red-cross vehicle, saying that numerous Hungarians were leaving the country. He and Ika had decided to leave, because he was not willing to work for the rest of his life as an electrician. They wanted to cross the border together and take the child also with themselves. Ika wanted to travel to London, because Andreas's father lived there. Géza wanted to go to West-Germany in order to study at the University of Veterinary Sciences. He tried to persuade us also to migrate, saying that there was enough place in the ambulance car. As God has directed my steps again, I told him not to take me, as a seriously ill person would only be a burden on them. What would happen if my condition did not improve? Because of the shaking of the van such circumstances could easily arise. What would happen if we were forced to go on foot as at that time it was impossibility for me!

Later Géza sadly acknowledged that I was right. He called Thomas to accompany them. I saw that Tom did not like the idea and shifted it off saying that in such a state he would not leave his mother and me with the children here alone!

Two days later in the evening Géza arrived with Ika and the small Andreas. They slept at our place and then traveled on a train heading for Győr. They departed from Budaörs towards an unsure future!

The farewell was very-very sad and it lagged especially on mother! Géza promised to write to us from Austria as soon as they arrived there and would send me some medicines for the inflammation of my liver.

Very sad and depressing days followed, but in the end we accepted our portion. We all knew and felt how very much Géza desired to study, which was made impossible for him in this country. So we did not want to hinder his passions in any way!

The doctor visited me every week to check on my condition. Some weeks later he allowed me "to teach my children from bed", especially Tom for making up the first class curriculum that had been left behind. There was no chance to start uninterrupted teaching at school again.

In the afternoons the boys, particularly Peter and his friends had the idea to play combats against the Russians! I always had to calm them down, so as not to sound "the great combat noise" from the Battle-street!

That year we had a sad Christmas, because Thomas learned after visiting Aunt Helen that Judith and Andreas had migrated to the west. They headed for Sweden and left their old parents on their own. This was a similar phenomenon throughout the whole country. There was not a single family that year at Christmastime who was not mourning for somebody who had either died or for those who had escaped to the west!

/The 1956 revolution of the Hungarian nation was against the Stalinist dictatorship and the Soviet occupation. This significant affair began on 23.01.1956 with peaceful demonstrations in Budapest when the crowd was fired at. In the towns people rioted as well, that lead to the fall of the Government, the withdrawal of Russian troops and the establishment of a multiparty system with democratic changes. Hungary withdrew from the Warsaw Pact which was negotiated with the Russians. However, without a firm western backing the Soviets soon changed their mind. On the 4th of November the Russian troops attacked Hungary. The Russians won by force of numbers and the crushing of armed freedom-fighters happened on 10.11.1956. 2652 Hungarians and 720 Russians died in the fighting. 19.226 Hungarians and 1540 Russians were injured. Later a quarter million Hungarians escaped and fled to the West.
From January 1957 the participants of the revolution were jailed and many of them executed later. For the next thirty years there was a complete silence about the things happened and it was labeled by the government as a „counter-revolution". The United Nations along with many nations condemned the brutal revenge of the Russians. In 1989, the 23rd of October became a national holiday.- editor/

The months of January and February proved to be a time of healing for me! During that time the first message arrived from Géza. He wrote that except for a "small incident" they arrived safely to Austria. Shortly thereafter they managed to get into a refugee-camp for a short while! Later he was able to send us a parcel that containing mostly medicines which helped in my recovery! Géza mentioned in his next letter that Ika and her son had arrived to London, and that he had also arrived in Munich. He had immediately applied for a place in the University, where he was then asked to take part in a German language course. After he finished the language program he could begin his studies in September of 1957. He was going to start at the University of Veterinary Sciences!

The three of us were able to sing for joy that Géza's plan had been a complete success! In the meantime Géza informed us that he was diligently studying German and earning money from his profession as electrician. He asked Tom to search for his documents at Pili and send them by air-mail to his address in Munich. Tom managed to find them and they were sent to Géza who then received his documents securely in the post.

Around the middle of February I began to notice that mother was moving with more difficultly. Whenever she did something for a period of time she had to sit down during the work. Her face was pale and she started to loose weight. She complained of the runs as well. We visited the doctor together and he sent us both to get a blood test at Budafok. I also received another examination of the liver. The Tymol value went down to 5 and the lowering to 22. My mother's result however proved to be very bad. Her blood test revealed that she was iron deficient. Seeing her results the doctor said that I was allowed to walk, but I was to continue taking vitamins and was to continue the special diet. He could not declare that I was healed, until the Tymol value was down to 1-2 and the lowering to least down to 10.

The doctor praised her for taking care of me, but unfortunately this time she became the victim! "If it were my choice I would send you into hospital for examination, at least you could take a rest there!" said the doctor. In the meantime mother heard that her old heart specialist, Dr. M. was working at the Széher-street hospital, which had previously belonged to the Grey Friar Order. Mother asked if she could get her assignment there.

My poor Peter, who had not yet had any teaching at school, became fevered and he was assigned to the Saint Stephen hospital because of an inflammation of the kidneys. At Saint Stephen, our old pediatrician was now the director of pediatrics. On the 1st of March I took Peter to the hospital. Then I took my little Tom to Kökörcsin-street and my brother Thomas escorted mother to the Széher-street. Later I met Thomas at Aunt Helen's.

Because the rooms for our children were empty, my Aunt Helen recommended that I stay there at her place as long as the sick members of the family were in the hospitals. At least this way there would be some life in that mournful and silent flat!

The first day I became quite tired after the long four months of staying in bed. Visiting patients was allowed three times a week in hospitals. We divided the visits up with Thomas, because the distance was so big between the two hospitals that in one day I could not have done them both.

Peter's chief doctor recommended that after his inflamed kidneys healed he wanted to take his tonsils out at the same time. He believed that his tonsils were causing the whole problem, because they seemed so inflamed. I agreed that at least we would be over it.

For mother, Dr. M. diagnosed a complete lack of Vitamin B, which caused the constant runs and her weight lost. So mother was ordered to receive a B-12 injection as a cure.

Peter spent four weeks at the hospital while my mother spent six. But thanks to God, they both healed and Peter was able to leave his tonsils behind as well. Aunt Helen was quite happy while Thomas and I lived at their place. In the afternoons Aunt Kate would regularly come over to our flat and help my Tom study. She was such an experienced teacher of first grade.

Well, in the meantime I had a very interesting meeting. I ran into my friend Louise on Béla Bartók-street. I nearly dropped my teeth seeing her approaching me with two little boys. One of them she had been pushing in a baby buggy ad he was only a few months old. The other one walked next to her and he was about two years old. Two nice little brown boys! Louise was a young mother who shined with happiness. We were so happy to meet, because we heard about each other long ago, and life had cast us so far away from each other! We remembered the time, when we had met at the Round Square and she had asked me whether to marry or not. At that time she had attended the university and was studying Russian. One of her fellow students was studying some kind of language and had "pursued" her with a strong and devoted courtship. When my sons were born and I recommended with a sincere heart to say yes to the marriage proposal, because there was no other better thing for us then to become mothers! Then Louise showed me her two little boys as she smiled and said: "As you see I accepted your advice and do not at all regret it at all!"

She invited me to visit their place the following morning. It was still in the building of thee Simplon cinema, but she was now on the third floor in a bigger and more comfortable flat. Later we met and began to unfold the events of the past. Louise told me about the proposal, her wedding and what a nice person her husband was. She told me how well they understood each other! During that time the small little Nicholas slept sweetly in his baby cot while the bigger one, Peter, played quietly in the other room. I congratulated Louise and later we said farewell to each other with the motto "go further than now on this road!"

The 30th of March, Saturday arrived.
In the morning I took Peter out of the hospital. His kidneys had healed and his tonsils had been taken out the previous week. As I was taking Peter out of the hospital Dr. L. told me that Peter would not be susceptible to diseases afterwards as "an ugly purulent centre" had been taken out of his body. Later he would regain strength and develop well.

I took my little son home and Aunt Helen waited for us with loving-kindness and a delicious lunch! But in the afternoon uncle Franz arrived home unexpected from his workplace, so Aunt Helen bewilderedly asked me and Peter to go and sleep at Pili's place. My Brother Thomas and my little Tom had a place to sleep there. From the neighbor I called Pili and told her the case. She was very happy and invited us to go to them and she would prepare a delicious dinner for us. We arrived there in the evening and after dinner Peter fell asleep at once, because it had been simply too much moving around for him in one day!

 The other day I called Aunt Helen and told her that Pili had asked us to stay with them. I had decided that it would not be good to force the convalescing child to travel so much! Later on the 1st of April we returned in the morning to their Kökörcsin-street flat.
 Pili made a delicious lunch with my help and chatted a lot, mostly about Géza. During that time Tibi played with little Peter. He complimented him how well he did with his experiences in the hospital and how he expertly reported on the procedure of removing his tonsils! In the afternoon they showed us a beautiful slide strips about their trips, because they did not have children and spent most of their time driving about in Czechoslovakia.
 We had very good time that Sunday!

I finished writing down the second part of my book in Hungarian on the 27th of June 2000.
/*The American translation Life behind the Iron Curtain I. contains the first two Hungarian parts titled Pre-war peace time and Baptism of fire-editor/*

At that time I decided to take my annual holiday, because two of my sons asked me to spend some time at their places. My son Géza took me down to town Tiszakécske, where they lived and five days later my son Thomas came for me and took me to their place in Nagykőrös.

Both families welcomed me with great love and accommodated me with all the possible earthly goods! I spent beautiful days at their places in and amongst my grandchildren.

I spent the rest of July with rejuvenating and refreshing.

Monday evenings from 11³⁰ at night I always called my dear sister-in-law Martha on the phone and read her my written memoir from the manuscript continuously.

We both eagerly waited for these Mondays, because before reading the story we chatted long about everything that life had brought before us.

We recorded many times those beautiful and peaceful days, weeks and months, namely nine months we had spent together at her home. She accepted me there at once after the death of my mother, when my mother's flat quickly had to be emptied for the new owner.

I could not stress to her enough how grateful I felt, because my house in the county was for sale and I have not yet found a new flat in the capital.

Martha had such a hospitable and lovely personality that when I was at her place it felt as if we were sisters!

But now these are only memories!

On the last Monday of 31st of July 2000 we chatted happily on the phone for two and half hours.

She told me that she could talk to her daughter Susanne only on the phone. She had so much work to do at the end of the each month, but the previous day her son Tibi and the family would visit her to toast her on her name-day. She proudly mentioned her grandchild Tom, who had finished the collegiate school of Music in the clarinet department that year. Her grandchild Tibi had ended up the Ybl Miklós collegiate school for engineers and had already started working. She was the most proud of her great grandchildren, who were twins, a girl and a boy. They were the children of her grandchild Kate.

I could tell from Martha's voice how comforting it was that the life of her grandchildren had turned out to be so good.

After our chat I read my book to her, which ended with the 1952 midnight church service. Martha told me that she shut her eyes and could imagine and see the white snow and could hear it cracking under our feet as well. In her soul she had also taken part in the midnight service. Later she admonished me to start writing the third part, because the letters of the second part "would quickly run out". If I had nothing to I read aloud and at that time what would happen to her? She was always eagerly waiting for Monday evenings, when "Seheresade" told her real stories from the "Thousand and one nights" tales.

I set my sister-in-law's heart at rest that I would continue writing and we said farewell to each other, FOREVER! It had been Tuesday at dawn at one o'clock a.m., when we finished our telephone call.

On the 2nd of August 2000, Wednesday, at 8.15 the phone began ringing and it woke me up.

"Here is Tibi speaking" said the voice, but I was not yet myself, so asked "what kind of Tibi?" He told his name and at that time I felt a tug at my heart-strings! He continued: "My mother died this morning!" I nearly dropped with fear when I noticed that it was the voice of Martha's son.

"It can't be! The day before yesterday we were chatted along and she was so happy!" I replied.

Afterwards Tibi added the following:

"Mother Tuesday morning drank her coffee put the clothes into the washing machine and set it going. After then "she sprayed her petunias with a "strong poison" on the balcony and surely she had breathed the poison in, out on the hot sunshine. She took the clean clothes out of the machine and wanted to take them out to the balcony to hang them, but she had no strength to do that. In the meantime her grandchild Kate called her on the phone so as to congratulate her for her name-day, but hearing Martha's weak voice she asked: "Are you doing well, granny? Then Martha told her that she feels queasy and that her stomach ached." Kate called up her father at once and sent him to her grandmother.

When Tibi arrived, Martha was in bed complaining of weakness and sickish feeling. At that time she began to spit bloody spittle. A doctor was called, who arrived after 6 o'clock p.m. and wanted to send her to the hospital at once, but

Martha disagreed, saying that in the evening nothing could be done for her anyway. So the doctor gave her an injection with a downer and ordered that the next morning she should be taken by force if necessary to the hospital. He added not to leave her alone for the night.

Tibi asked the woman living next door to stay with Martha for the night. She told him that Martha had slept all night, but at dawn she moaned and asked for the bowl to spit into. The woman wanted to help her sit up, but Martha simply reclined back and died within a minute.

My poor Martha always said that she wanted to die quickly without getting to a hospital!

God must have loved my Martha very much, because in the end it turned out to be as quick as she wanted!

The autopsy showed that the hard tissue of the vein in her stomach had ruptured and that she had slowly bled to death!

My dear Martha may the peace of the Lord be with you! I guard your memory forever in my heart!

END OF PART TWO
The story still goes on...

ISBN 142510524-6